LEVEL II PRACTICE EXAMS – VOLUME 1

SCHWESER 2016 LEVEL II CFA® PRACTICE EXAMS VOLUME 1

©2015 Kaplan, Inc. All rights reserved.

Published in 2015 by Kaplan, Inc.

Printed in the United States of America.

ISBN: 978-1-4754-3551-1

PPN: 3200-6863

HOW TO USE THE LEVEL II PRACTICE EXAMS

Thank you for purchasing the Schweser Practice Exams. We hope that you find this volume effective and user-friendly. The following suggestions are designed to help you get the most out of these practice exams and prepare for the actual Level II Exam.

Be ready for a new format. The format of the Level II exam is different from Level I. The exam consists of item sets, which are vignettes or short cases followed by six multiple-choice questions (CFA Institute calls these "mini-cases"). There will be 20 item sets (120 questions) on the exam: 10 item sets (60 questions) in the morning and 10 more item sets (60 more questions) in the afternoon. Each question is worth 3 points (and is allocated 3 minutes), and there are 360 total points available. Each question will have three possible choices (A, B, or C).

Any topic can be tested in the morning and/or the afternoon, so you might have an economics item set in the morning and another one in the afternoon. Don't spend a lot of time contemplating which topics might appear in which session.

Save the practice exams for last. Save the practice exams for the last month before the exam. A good strategy would be to take one exam in each of the three weeks leading up to the test. Do your best to mimic actual exam conditions for at least one of the practice exams (e.g., time yourself, have someone turn the heat down and up so that you go from freezing to boiling, hire a construction crew to do some blasting outside your window).

Remember, no matter how challenging we make our practice exams, the actual exam will be different. Also, mainly due to the stress of the exam day, your perception will be that the actual exam was much more difficult than *any* practice exam or old exam you have ever seen.

After you have completed an exam, use your results as a diagnostic tool to help you identify areas in which you are weak. One good way to accomplish this is to use your online access to Performance Tracker. This is a tool that will provide you with exam diagnostics to target your study and review effort, and allow you to compare your scores on practice exams to those of other candidates.

Make sure you understand the mistake(s) you made on every question you got wrong (or guessed on). Make a flashcard that illustrates that particular concept, carry it around with you, and quiz yourself until you are confident you have mastered the concept. This "feedback" loop (practice exam, diagnosis of results, identification of concepts yet to be mastered, study of those concepts, and then another practice exam) is a very effective study strategy in the last month before exam day.

Topic Area	Guideline Topic Area Weight
Ethical and Professional Standards	10 to 15%
Quantitative Methods	5 to 10%
Economics	5 to 10%
Financial Reporting and Analysis	15 to 20%
Corporate Finance	5 to 15%
Equity	15 to 25%
Alternative Investments	5 to 10%
Fixed Income	10 to 20%
Derivatives	5 to 15%
Portfolio Management	5 to 10%
TOTAL	100%

Expect the unexpected. Be prepared for difficult questions on unexpected topics. Only one thing is certain about the exam: you will be surprised by some of the questions.

Guess if you must. It should take you approximately 18 minutes to read the vignette and answer the six questions that make up each item set. Don't fall behind: successful candidates know when to cut their losses by guessing and moving on. Try to eliminate one of the incorrect answers, and then pick one of the remaining choices. If you successfully eliminate one choice you know is wrong, you have a 50/50 chance of selecting the correct answer. There is no penalty for guessing.

Be ready for more than just number-crunching. Your reading comprehension ability is an important component of success on the Level II exam. The vignettes will be long and full of information. Your job is to focus on finding the important pieces of information and answering the questions correctly.

There are two approaches to these item sets. You can read the vignette first and then tackle the questions, or you can read the first question and then go back to the vignette to find the data needed to answer it. We recommend the second approach because it saves time and helps you to focus on the details you need. When taking the practice exams, experiment with both techniques and do what works best for you!

My thanks to the Schweser team. I would like to thank all of my colleagues at Schweser for their incredible work ethic and commitment to quality. Kaplan Schweser would not be the company it is, nor could it provide the products you see, without the help of these content and editing professionals.

You may expect me to end this introduction with a "good luck on the exam." However, you need not be lucky to pass Level II. With your hard work and our assistance, luck will have nothing to do with it. Instead, I'll simply say, "See you next year at Level III."

Best Regards,

Bijesh Tolia

Dr. Bijesh Tolia, CFA, CA
VP of CFA Education and Level II Professor

Kaplan Schweser

Exam 1
Morning Session

Question	Topic	Minutes (Points)
1 to 6	Quantitative Methods	18
7 to 12	Financial Reporting and Analysis	18
13 to 18	Equity	18
19 to 24	Equity	18
25 to 30	Alternative Investments	18
31 to 36	Fixed Income	18
37 to 42	Fixed Income	18
43 to 48	Derivatives	18
49 to 54	Derivatives	18
55 to 60	Portfolio Management	18

Test Answers

1.	Ⓐ	Ⓑ	Ⓒ		41.	Ⓐ	Ⓑ	Ⓒ
2.	Ⓐ	Ⓑ	Ⓒ		42.	Ⓐ	Ⓑ	Ⓒ
3.	Ⓐ	Ⓑ	Ⓒ		43.	Ⓐ	Ⓑ	Ⓒ
4.	Ⓐ	Ⓑ	Ⓒ		44.	Ⓐ	Ⓑ	Ⓒ
5.	Ⓐ	Ⓑ	Ⓒ		45.	Ⓐ	Ⓑ	Ⓒ
6.	Ⓐ	Ⓑ	Ⓒ		46.	Ⓐ	Ⓑ	Ⓒ
7.	Ⓐ	Ⓑ	Ⓒ		47.	Ⓐ	Ⓑ	Ⓒ
8.	Ⓐ	Ⓑ	Ⓒ		48.	Ⓐ	Ⓑ	Ⓒ
9.	Ⓐ	Ⓑ	Ⓒ		49.	Ⓐ	Ⓑ	Ⓒ
10.	Ⓐ	Ⓑ	Ⓒ		50.	Ⓐ	Ⓑ	Ⓒ
11.	Ⓐ	Ⓑ	Ⓒ		51.	Ⓐ	Ⓑ	Ⓒ
12.	Ⓐ	Ⓑ	Ⓒ		52.	Ⓐ	Ⓑ	Ⓒ
13.	Ⓐ	Ⓑ	Ⓒ		53.	Ⓐ	Ⓑ	Ⓒ
14.	Ⓐ	Ⓑ	Ⓒ		54.	Ⓐ	Ⓑ	Ⓒ
15.	Ⓐ	Ⓑ	Ⓒ		55.	Ⓐ	Ⓑ	Ⓒ
16.	Ⓐ	Ⓑ	Ⓒ		56.	Ⓐ	Ⓑ	Ⓒ
17.	Ⓐ	Ⓑ	Ⓒ		57.	Ⓐ	Ⓑ	Ⓒ
18.	Ⓐ	Ⓑ	Ⓒ		58.	Ⓐ	Ⓑ	Ⓒ
19.	Ⓐ	Ⓑ	Ⓒ		59.	Ⓐ	Ⓑ	Ⓒ
20.	Ⓐ	Ⓑ	Ⓒ		60.	Ⓐ	Ⓑ	Ⓒ
21.	Ⓐ	Ⓑ	Ⓒ					
22.	Ⓐ	Ⓑ	Ⓒ					
23.	Ⓐ	Ⓑ	Ⓒ					
24.	Ⓐ	Ⓑ	Ⓒ					
25.	Ⓐ	Ⓑ	Ⓒ					
26.	Ⓐ	Ⓑ	Ⓒ					
27.	Ⓐ	Ⓑ	Ⓒ					
28.	Ⓐ	Ⓑ	Ⓒ					
29.	Ⓐ	Ⓑ	Ⓒ					
30.	Ⓐ	Ⓑ	Ⓒ					
31.	Ⓐ	Ⓑ	Ⓒ					
32.	Ⓐ	Ⓑ	Ⓒ					
33.	Ⓐ	Ⓑ	Ⓒ					
34.	Ⓐ	Ⓑ	Ⓒ					
35.	Ⓐ	Ⓑ	Ⓒ					
36.	Ⓐ	Ⓑ	Ⓒ					
37.	Ⓐ	Ⓑ	Ⓒ					
38.	Ⓐ	Ⓑ	Ⓒ					
39.	Ⓐ	Ⓑ	Ⓒ					
40.	Ⓐ	Ⓑ	Ⓒ					

Exam 1
Morning Session

Questions 1–6 relate to Goldensand Jewelry, Ltd.

Introduction

Rajesh Singh is the CFO of Goldensand Jewelry, Ltd, a London-based retailer of fine jewelry and watches. Singh has noticed that the price of gold has begun to increase. If economic activity continues to pick up, the price of gold is likely to accelerate its rate of increase as both the level of demand and inflation rates increase.

Implications of Rising Gold Price

Singh has become concerned about the cost implications for Goldensand if gold prices continue to rise. He has requested a meeting with Anita Biscayne, Goldensand's COO. In preparation for the meeting, Singh asked one of his staff, Yasunobu Hara, to prepare a regression analysis comparing the price of gold to the average cost of Goldensand's purchases of finished gold jewelry. Hara provides the regression results as shown in Exhibit 1.

Exhibit 1: 1979–2009 Annual Data (31 Observations)

Variable	Coefficient	Standard Error of the Coefficient
Intercept	11.06	7.29
Cost of gold	2.897	0.615
standard error of the forecast = 117.8		

Exhibit 2: Partial Student's *t*-distribution Table

	Level of Significance for One-Tailed Test					
df	0.100	0.050	0.025	0.010	0.005	0.0005
	Level of Significance for Two-Tailed Test					
df	0.200	0.100	0.050	0.020	0.010	0.001
29	1.311	1.699	2.045	2.462	2.756	3.659
30	1.310	1.697	2.042	2.457	2.750	3.646
31	1.309	1.696	2.040	2.453	2.744	3.636

Reviewing the regression results, Biscayne becomes concerned about the implications for the cost of finished jewelry to Goldensand if the price of gold continues to rise. To remain profitable, the cost of finished jewelry should not exceed $2,000.

Regression Concerns

Overall Concerns

Singh's principal concern about the regression is whether the time period chosen is a good predictor of the current situation. He makes the following statement:

Statement 1: We may have a problem with parameter instability if the relationship between gold prices and jewelry costs has changed over the past 30 years.

Singh also focuses on the value of the slope coefficient. He expected it to be 4.0 based on his experience in the industry. Hara computes the appropriate test statistic and reports the following:

Statement 2: We fail to reject the null hypothesis that the slope coefficient is equal to 4.0 at the 5% level of significance.

Testing for Heteroskedasticity

Biscayne remarks that the dramatic increase in the price level over the past 30 years leads her to suspect heteroskedasticity in the regression results. She suggests to Singh that they should conduct a Breusch-Pagan chi-square test for heteroskedasticity by calculating the following test statistic:

$$n \times R^2 \text{ with k degrees of freedom}$$

where:
n   = number of observations
R^2 = R^2 of the regression of jewelry prices on gold prices
k   = number of independent variables

Model Misspecification

Biscayne and Singh have various views on the potential for model misspecification and the effect of any such misspecification.

- Biscayne worries that the regression model is misspecified because it does not include a variable to measure the cost of the highly specialized labor used by manufacturing jewelers. She points out that the effect of omitting an important variable in a regression analysis is that the regression coefficients will be unbiased and inconsistent.
- Singh adds that another common consequence of misspecifying a regression analysis is creating undesired stationarity.

Multiple Regression

Hara conducts a series of regression analyses using all possible combinations of the suggested independent variables based on their average quarterly values. He returns with the following regression results as shown in Exhibit 3 for the equation which uses all suggested independent variables.

Exhibit 3: 1999–2009 Quarterly Data (44 Observations)

Independent Variables	Coefficient	t-Statistic
Intercept	–3.9	3.7
Gold price	4.7	14.5
Silver price	1.2	7.8
Platinum price	3.5	3.1
Labor costs	0.82	2.4
GDP (EU)	0.000274	5.7
GDP (Middle East)	0.000049	3.6
Personal income (EU)	0.000314	2.1
Personal income (Middle East)	0.009876	2.2

R^2: 0.55

Durbin-Watson: 3.89

Hara is concerned about the equation described in Exhibit 3. He makes the following statement:

Statement 3:   The model appears to suffer from multicollinearity. Dropping one or more independent variables will increase the coefficient of determination.

Biscayne responds with the following statement:

Statement 4:   An autocorrelation problem can be addressed by using the Hansen method to adjust the R^2.

Exhibit 4: Partial Durbin-Watson Table

	Critical Values for the Durbin-Watson Statistic (α = 0.05)					
	K = 3		*K = 4*		*K = 5*	
n	d_l	d_u	d_l	d_u	d_l	d_u
39	1.33	1.66	1.27	1.72	1.22	1.79
40	1.34	1.66	1.29	1.72	1.23	1.79
45	1.38	1.67	1.34	1.72	1.29	1.78

1. The per ounce price of gold that corresponds to the $2,000 cost of finished jewelry is *closest* to:
   A. $687.
   B. $712.
   C. $3,240.

2. Are Singh (Statement 1) and Hara (Statement 2) correct or incorrect regarding the usefulness of regression results described in Exhibit 1 and the value of the slope coefficient?
   A. Both are correct.
   B. One is correct, the other is incorrect.
   C. Both are incorrect.

3. Is Biscayne correct with regard to the specification of the Breusch-Pagan test?
   A. No, because it is an *F*-test.
   B. No, because the wrong R^2 is used.
   C. No, because the degrees of freedom are equal to k and n – k – 1.

4. Regarding the comments on the potential consequences of misspecification in the simple linear regression, is Singh correct or incorrect regarding his comment on his concern over stationarity, and is Biscayne correct or incorrect about the effect of omitting an important variable?
   A. Only Singh is incorrect.
   B. Only Biscayne is incorrect.
   C. Both are incorrect.

5. Is Hara's Statement 3 about multicollinearity accurate?
   A. Yes.
   B. No, because removal of independent variables is a remedy for residual autocorrelation.
   C. No, because the coefficient of determination would not increase.

6. Is Biscayne correct regarding his statement concerning how to correct for autocorrelation?
   A. No, because the White method is used to adjust the R^2.
   B. No, because the Hansen method adjusts the coefficient standard errors.
   C. No, because the Hansen method is used to address the problem of multicollinearity.

Questions 7–12 relate to Karen Rawsfield.

Karen Rawsfield, CFA, works as an equity analyst for a small investment house in the U.S. She is currently reviewing the accounts of Gannymede, Inc. (GNNY), a manufacturing company that supplies games and toys to retailers in the children's market.

GNNY currently focuses on the production of traditional wooden games and puzzles using high-quality materials. These products make up over 80% of its product line. However, growth in this area appears to be slowing, and the latest quarterly earnings announcement was disappointing. During an analyst call following the announcement, the CEO stated that GNNY is planning on moving into the electronic games business, focusing on educational products for the pre-school market. The CEO believes that GNNY can leverage its reputation for making high-quality wooden products to help it enter the electronics market at a premium price point and, hence, capture a significant margin.

Rawsfield also covers Tobby Bang, plc. (TBBB), a European supplier of electronic games. Rawsfield intends to compare TBBB's key ratios to those of GNNY to assess the likely impact of a switch in GNNY's product focus. To assist in the analysis, Rawsfield first wants to make the two sets of financial figures more comparable. The three primary areas she has addressed are as follows:

1.   **Inventory**

     GNNY accounts for inventory under U.S. GAAP using the LIFO basis, which GNNY's management believes best reflects the use of materials in its production process. TBBB uses the FIFO basis for tax reporting purposes as it accounts for income taxes using IFRS.

2.   **Leases**

     One notable aspect of TBBB's business is that it does not lease any assets; all of its operating facilities are owned. GNNY's board believes the company is best served by leasing its major facilities, on the basis that this structure isolates the firm from real estate price movements and provides GNNY the flexibility to adjust its scale of operations along with the business cycle.

3.   **PPE Valuation**

     TBBB accounts for land under the IFRS revaluation method. The current market value is higher than its historic cost.

Rawsfield intends to first adjust for each difference separately and assess the impact. To deal with the inventory issue, she will adjust GNNY's accounts by using the LIFO disclosures to restate the accounts on a FIFO basis. She is assuming a tax rate of 32% in 2015 and 28% in all previous years.

Second, Rawsfield will review the impact on GNNY of capitalizing the firm's operating leases. In order to assess this impact, she will make use of the commitments and contingencies note from the latest accounts to calculate the discount rate GNNY uses to calculate the present value of finance lease commitments. She will then apply this rate to the operating lease commitments to estimate the adjustment required and add the resulting liability to long-term debt.

In order to complete her calculations, Rawsfield intends to assume that capital lease payments after 2020 are $5.8 million per year for five years, and that operating lease payments after 2020 are $12.0m per year for 10 years. Rawsfield has assembled some key extracts from GNNY's latest accounts to assist with the comparison. These values are shown in exhibits 1 and 2.

Exhibit 1: GNNY Financial Statements (extracts)

Income Statement
Year Ended 31 December 2015
(selected excerpts)

	$ million	$ million
Operating income	875	
Interest expense	98	
Income before taxes	777	
Income taxes	251	
Net income		**526**

Balance Sheet as of 31 December 2015

	$ million	$ million
PPE		
Land	450	
Plant and equipment	4,000	
Current assets		
Inventory	400	
Accounts receivable	145	
Cash	75	
Total assets		**5,070**
Liabilities and equity		
Current liabilities	1,200	
Long-term debt	980	
Total liabilities		**2,180**
Shareholder's equity		
Common stock	250	
Additional paid in capital	750	
Retained earnings	1,890	
Total equity		**2,890**
Total liabilities and equity		**5,070**

Exhibit 2: GNNY Accounts (selected notes)

Notes

1. **Accounting Policies**

   Inventory
   In line with industry peers and the nature of raw material usage in the majority of our warehouses, inventory is accounted for on a LIFO basis.

   PPE
   Plant and equipment is depreciated on a straight-line basis over an asset's estimated life, which ranges from 2 to 50 years.

2. **Depreciation expense in 2015 was $350.**

3. **Commitments and Contingencies**
   The company leases several warehouses under both capital and operating leases. Obligations under both capital and operating leases are as below:

	$ million Capital	$ million Operating
2016	5.8	9.8
2017	5.8	9.8
2018	5.8	9.8
2019	5.8	12.0
2020	5.8	12.0
Thereafter	29.0	120.0
Minimum lease payments	58.0	173.4
Less interest	16.3	
Present value of minimum lease payments	41.7	

4. **Inventory**
   The LIFO reserve at the beginning of the year was $35 million; by the end of the year, this had fallen to $28 million.

In order to account for the differing policies for PPE, Rawsfield intends to remove the impact of the IFRS method from TBBB's accounts.

In addition to the three areas already mentioned , Rawsfield is also concerned about the potential impact on the income statement of GNNY decreasing its inventory. In an email to one of her colleagues, Rawsfield noted that:

"If Gannymede ran down its inventory levels over the year during a period of falling raw materials costs, the resulting LIFO liquidation would provide a one-off boost to earnings for the year."

7. If Rawsfield restates GNNY's accounts using the inventory accounting method employed by TBBB, GNNY's total assets at year-end are *most likely* to:
   A. increase as a result of adding the LIFO reserve to current assets.
   B. decrease because the LIFO reserve has decreased over the year.
   C. remain constant as the adjustment will only affect total equity.

8. If Rawsfield restates GNNY's accounts using TBBB's inventory accounting method, GNNY's net profit margin for the year is *most likely* to:
   A. increase.
   B. decrease.
   C. remain constant.

9. Rawsfield's comment in the email to her colleague is *most likely*:
   A. correct.
   B. incorrect because earnings would only be boosted if raw material prices had been rising.
   C. incorrect because earnings would only be boosted if the inventory reduction was coupled with a switch to FIFO accounting.

10. If Rawsfield adjusts GNNY's retained earnings to reflect FIFO accounting, the retained earnings would increase by an amount *closest* to:
    A. $30 million.
    B. $20 million.
    C. $10 million.

11. Using Rawsfield's method to adjust GNNY's accounts by capitalizing operating leases, the adjusted long-term debt-to-equity ratio will be *closest* to:
    A. 0.34.
    B. 0.38.
    C. 0.42.

12. When removing the impact of TBBB's choice of accounting method for PP&E, Rawsfield is *most likely* to adjust:
    A. the income statement only.
    B. the balance sheet only.
    C. both the income statement and balance sheet.

Questions 13–18 relate to O'Connor Textiles, Part 1.

Emily De Jong, CFA, works for Charles & Williams Associates, a medium-sized investment firm operating in the northeastern United States. De Jong is responsible for producing financial reports to use as tools to attract new clients. It is now early in 2009, and De Jong is reviewing information for O'Connor Textiles and finalizing a report that will be used for an important presentation to a potential investor at the end of the week.

Following an acquisition of a major competitor in 1992, O'Connor went public in 1993 and paid its first dividend in 1999. Dividends are paid at the end of the year. After 2008, dividends are expected to grow for three years at 11%: $2.13 in 2009, $2.36 in 2010, and $2.63 in 2011. The average of the arithmetic and compound growth rates are given in Exhibit 1. Dividends are then expected to settle down to a long-term growth rate of 4%. O'Connor's current share price of $70 is expected to rise to $72.92 by the end of the year according to the consensus of analysts' forecasts.

O'Connor's annual dividend history is shown in Exhibit 1.

Exhibit 1: O'Connor Textiles Dividend History

Year	Dividend ($)	% Change		
1999	0.76			
2000	0.76	0.000		
2001	0.76	0.000		
2002	0.82	7.895		
2003	0.91	10.976		
2004	1.03	13.187		
2005	1.16	12.621	Arithmetic mean growth	11.1%
2006	1.34	15.517	Compound growth	10.9%
2007	1.52	13.433		
2008	1.92	26.316		

De Jong is also considering whether or not she should value O'Connor using a free cash flow model instead of the dividend discount model.

In addition, De Jong observes that the current return on 3-month T-bills is 3% and determines that the expected return on the market portfolio is 7%. She has gathered monthly data on company stock returns ($R_{i,t}$) and market returns ($R_{M,t}$) and has decided to run an ordinary least squares regression according to the model $R_{i,t} = \alpha_i + \beta_i R_{M,t} + \varepsilon_t$. De Jong uses the S&P 500 as the proxy for the market portfolio.

The output from the regression appears in Exhibit 2.

Exhibit 2: Summary Output

Dependent Variable = $R_{i,t}$

Regression Statistics	
Multiple R-Squared	0.6275
R-Squared	0.3938
Adjusted R-Squared	0.3891
Standard Error	0.0572
Observations	132

ANOVA

	df	SS	MS	F	Significance F
Regression	1	0.2764	0.2764	8.4437	<0.0001
Residual	130	0.4256	0.0033		
Total	131	0.7020			

	Coefficients	Adjusted Standard Error	t-Stat	P-value	Lower 95%	Upper 95%
Intercept	0.0062	0.0051	1.2067	0.2297	–0.0039	0.0163
$R_{M,t}$	1.0400	0.1136	9.1549	<0.0001	0.8190	1.2685

Charles Wang, De Jong's colleague, is of the opinion that O'Connor's growth rate will be 11% but will decline linearly to a long-term growth rate of 4% over the next six years. Wang also feels that the required rate of return for O'Connor should be 9.50%.

13. Based on information in Exhibit 2, the required return on equity (according to the CAPM) for O'Connor is *closest* to:
    A. 4.2%.
    B. 7.2%.
    C. 9.2%.

14. For this question only, assume that O'Connor's cost of equity is 10%. The value of one share of O'Connor stock in early 2009 using the two-stage dividend discount model (DDM) is *closest* to:
    A. $38.50.
    B. $40.00.
    C. $47.50.

15. For this question only, assume that De Jong's estimate of the value of O'Connor stock using a two-stage DDM is $75. Assuming the market has also applied a two-stage DDM, and the market's consensus estimate of dividend growth and required return are the same as De Jong's, the market's consensus estimate of the duration of the high-growth period is *most likely*:
   A. less than three years.
   B. equal to three years.
   C. greater than three years.

16. In what situation is it *most appropriate* for De Jong to employ a:

Dividend discount model?	FCFE model?
A. Non-control perspective	FCFE aligned with profitability
B. Control perspective	FCFE aligned with profitability
C. Non-control perspective	FCFE aligned with dividend policy

17. The value of O'Connor stock using Wang's assumptions is *closest* to:
   A. $43.65
   B. $48.75
   C. $52.35

18. For this question only, assume that the market price of O'Connor stock is $48.00 and the linearly declining high growth period is 5 years. The required rate of return implicit in the market price is *closest* to:
   A. 8.86%
   B. 9.22%
   C. 10.81%

Questions 19–24 relate to O'Connor Textiles, Part 2.

De Jong continues her analysis of O'Connor. She is concerned that along with a dividend discount model approach she would also like to get a measure of the contribution that the key managers, Melanie and Arthur O'Connor, have made to the company's apparent ongoing success.

She considers using NOPAT and EVA to assess management performance. She believes that increasing invested capital to take advantage of projects with positive net present values increases both NOPAT and EVA.

However, De Jong decides to use residual income analysis instead. She provides the following justification for using the residual income model:

- The calculation of residual income depends primarily on readily available accounting data.
- The residual income model can be used even when cash flow is difficult to forecast.
- The residual income model does not depend on dividend payments or on positive free cash flows in the near future.
- The residual income model depends on the validity of the clean surplus relation.

She also considers the following assumptions about continuing residual income:

Assumption 1:   Residual income is positive and continues at the same level year after year.

Assumption 2:   ROE declines over time to the cost of equity.

Assumption 3:   Residual income declines to zero immediately.

De Jong gathers recent financial information data on O'Connor, as shown in Exhibit 1.

Exhibit 1: O'Connor Textiles, Inc. Summary Income Statement (U.S. $ thousands, except per share data)

	2008	2009
	Actual	*Projection*
Sales	$509,447	$529,429
Cost of sales	398,100	405,068
Selling and administrative expenses	49,608	59,378
Depreciation and amortization	18,562	22,979
Total operating expenses	466,270	487,425
Earnings from operations	43,177	42,004
Interest expense	28,004	28,906
Earnings before income taxes	15,173	13,098
Provision for income taxes	5,138	4,453
Net earnings for the year	10,035	8,645
Earnings per share: basic	$0.59	$0.51
Fully diluted	$0.56	*

*Non-dilutive

De Jong has also determined that at the beginning of 2008, O'Connor had total capital of $324,000,000, of which $251,000,000 was debt and $73,000,000 was equity. The company's cost of debt before taxes is 7%, and the cost of equity capital is 8%. The company has a tax rate of approximately 34%. Weighted average cost of capital is 5.4%. Net operating profit after tax (before any adjustments) is $28,517,640.

De Jong is interested in obtaining the market's assessment of the implied growth rate in residual income and notes that the book value per share for O'Connor at the beginning of 2009 was $4.29, and the current market price is $70. She forecasts the return on equity (ROE) for 2009 to be 11.84%.

De Jong discusses her analyses with a colleague, who makes the following general statements:

Statement 1:   It is usually the case that value is recognized later in the residual income model than in the dividend discount model.

Statement 2:   When the present value of expected future residual income is negative, the justified P/B based on fundamentals is less than one.

19.   Is De Jong correct about the *likely* effects on NOPAT and EVA from increasing invested capital to take advantage of projects with positive net present values?
A. Yes in both cases.
B. Yes in one case, and no in the other.
C. No in both cases.

20.   Are De Jong's justifications for using the residual income model correct?
A. Yes.
B. No, because the residual income model should be not be used when cash flows are difficult to forecast.
C. No, because the residual income model depends on positive free cash flows in the near future.

21.   Which of De Jong's assumptions about continuing residual income will lead to the highest persistence factor?
A. Assumption 1.
B. Assumption 2.
C. Assumption 3.

22.   O'Connor's residual income and economic value added (EVA) for 2008 are *closest* to:

Residual income	EVA
A. $6.1 million	$11.0 million
B. $4.2 million	$11.0 million
C. $4.2 million	$2.6 million

23.   The implied residual income growth rate for 2009, based on the residual income model, is *closest* to:
A. 7.75%.
B. 8.16%.
C. 8.82%.

24.   Are the statements made by De Jong's colleague correct?
A. Both statements are correct.
B. Only Statement 1 is correct.
C. Only Statement 2 is correct.

Questions 25–30 relate to Jeff Markgraf, CFA.

Jeff Markgraf, CFA, is the managing director at Alpha Alternatives LLP. Markgraf has a successful track record of investing in real estate for his institutional clients. Markgraf is seeking to diversify his scope and is looking into investing in commodities and in private equity.

Markgraf reaches out to his college friend, Bill Small, who manages a private equity fund specializing in leveraged buyouts. Markgraf asks Small about ways in which private equity funds add value to their portfolio investments.

Markgraf concludes that futures contracts offer the best mechanism for him to gain exposure to the commodities market. He seeks to develop further understanding of the components of total return of a portfolio invested in commodity futures.

Markgraf observes that cattle futures prices are greater than the expected future spot prices while the corn futures prices are less than the expected future spot prices. Markgraf also read that futures prices may be influenced by weather.

Markgraf wants some exposure to precious metals and expects to use silver futures contracts to accomplish this. Markgraf will roll over maturing contracts to the next shortest available contract. Markgraf believes that silver will help diversify his overall portfolio, especially since silver futures prices are less than silver spot prices.

25. Which of the following would be *least* appropriate as a part of Small's response to Markgraf's question?
    A. Optimizing financial leverage.
    B. Creating operational improvement.
    C. Incentivizing the general partner.

26. Which of the following factors is *most likely* to influence the price of a corn futures contract?
    A. Interest rates.
    B. Cattle futures prices.
    C. Global demand and supply conditions.

27. Early frost in some parts of the country has resulted in damage to corn crops and a temporary shortage in the supply of corn. Under the theory of storage, relative to the spot prices, futures prices are *most likely* to:
    A. remain the same.
    B. increase.
    C. decrease.

28.   When considering total return of commodities futures portfolios, the rebalancing effect is *most likely* to be positive and significant under which of the following conditions?
A. Commodity spot prices are flat over the long term but volatile over the short term.
B. Convenience yield is low.
C. Storage costs are high.

29.   Which theory is *least likely* to explain the pricing relationship in the cattle futures market?
A. The insurance perspective.
B. The hedging pressure hypothesis.
C. The theory of storage.

30.   Markgraf's position in silver futures contracts is *most likely* to produce a roll return that is:
A. zero.
B. negative.
C. positive.

Questions 31-36 relate to Susan Evermore.

The Wyroman International Pension Fund includes a $65 million fixed-income portfolio managed by Susan Evermore, CFA, of Brighton Investors. Evermore is in the process of constructing a binomial interest-rate tree that generates arbitrage-free values for on-the-run Treasury securities. She plans to use the tree to value more complex bonds with embedded options. She starts out by observing that the yield on a one-year Treasury security is 3.50%. She determines in her initial attempt to price the two-year Treasury security that the value derived from the model is higher than the Treasury security's current market price.

After several iterations Evermore determines that the interest rate tree that correctly values the one and two-year Treasury securities has a rate of 4.50% in the lower node at the end of the first year and a rate of 7.0% in the upper node at the end of the first year. She uses this tree to value a two-year, 6% annual coupon bond with a par value of $100 that is callable in one year at $99.50. She determines that an OAS of 50bps is appropriate for this bond.

Evermore also uses the same interest rate tree to price a 2-year 6% coupon bond that is putable in one year, and value the embedded put option. She concludes that if the yield volatility decreases unexpectedly, the value of the putable bond will increase and the value of the embedded put option will also increase, assuming all other inputs are unchanged. She also concludes that the computed OAS for the bond would decrease as the estimated level of yield volatility decreases.

Evermore also uses the interest rate tree to estimate the option-adjusted spreads of two additional callable corporate bonds, as shown in the following figure.

Issuer	Option-Adjusted Spread
AA-rated issuer	53 basis points
BB-rated issuer	−18 basis points

Evermore concludes, based on this information, that the AA-rated issue is undervalued, and the BB-rated issue is overvalued.

At a subsequent meeting with the trustees of the fund, Evermore is asked to explain what a binomial interest rate model is and how it was used to estimate effective duration and effective convexity. Evermore is uncertain of the exact methodology because the actual calculations were done by a junior analyst, but she tries to provide the trustees with a reasonably accurate step-by-step description of the process:

Step 1: Given the bond's current market price, the on-the-run Treasury yield curve, and an assumption about rate volatility, create a binomial interest rate tree.

©2015 Kaplan, Inc.

Step 2: Add 100 basis points to each of the 1-year rates in the interest rate tree to derive a "modified" tree.

Step 3: Compute the price of the bond if yield increases by 100 basis points using this new tree.

Step 4: Repeat Steps 1 through 3 to determine the bond price that results from a 100 basis point decrease in rates.

Step 5: Use these two price estimates, along with the original market price, to calculate effective duration and effective convexity.

Lucas Davenport, a trustee and university finance professor, immediately speaks up to disagree with Evermore. He claims that a more accurate description of the process is as follows:

Step 1: Given the bond's current market price, the Treasury yield curve, and an assumption about rate volatility, create a binomial interest rate tree and calculate the bond's option-adjusted spread (OAS) using the model.

Step 2: Impose a parallel upward shift in the on-the-run Treasury yield curve of 100 basis points.

Step 3: Build a new binomial interest rate tree using the new Treasury yield curve and the original rate volatility assumption.

Step 4: Add the OAS from Step 1 to each of the 1-year rates on the tree to derive a "modified" tree.

Step 5: Compute the price of the bond using this new tree.

Step 6: Repeat Steps 1 through 5 to determine the bond price that results from a 100 basis point decrease in rates.

Step 7: Use these two price estimates, along with the original market price, to calculate effective duration and effective convexity.

At the meeting with the trustees, Evermore also presents the results of her analysis of the effect of changing market volatilities on a 1-year convertible bond issued by Highfour Corporation. Each bond is convertible into 25 shares of Highfour common stock. The bond is also callable at 110 at any time prior to maturity. She concludes that the value of the bond will decrease if either (1) the volatility of returns on Highfour common stock decreases or (2) yield volatility decreases.

Davenport immediately disagrees with her by saying "changes in the volatility of common stock returns will have no effect on the value of the convertible bond, and a decrease in yield volatility will result in an increase in the value of the bond."

31. The value of the 2-year 6% callable bond today using the interest rate tree is *closest* to:
    A. $95.24.
    B. $101.01.
    C. $102.21.

32. Is Evermore correct in her analysis of the effect of a change in yield volatility?
    A. Incorrect on the puttable bond only.
    B. Incorrect on the put option only.
    C. Incorrect on both the bond and the option.

33. Is Evermore correct about the effect of a decrease in estimated level of yield volatility on the computed OAS?
    A. Yes.
    B. No, OAS depends only on credit and liquidity risk and hence would be unchanged.
    C. No, the computed OAS would increase.

34. Is Evermore correct in her analysis of the relative valuation of the bonds?
    A. Correct on both issues.
    B. Correct on the AA issue only.
    C. Correct on the BB issue only.

35. Which of the following statements regarding the methodologies for estimating effective duration and convexity is *most accurate*?
    A. Davenport's description is a more accurate depiction of the appropriate methodology than Evermore's.
    B. The two methodologies will result in the same effective duration and convexity estimates only if the same rate volatility assumption is used in each.
    C. The two methodologies will result in the same effective duration and convexity estimates only if the same rate volatility assumption is used in each and the bond's OAS is equal to zero.

36. For this question, analyze each effect separately. Is Davenport correct in disagreeing with Evermore's conclusions regarding the effect on the value of the convertible bond resulting from a change in volatility?
    A. Davenport is correct on both conclusions.
    B. Davenport is correct on stock return volatility only.
    C. Davenport is correct on yield volatility only.

Questions 37–42 relate to Natalia Berg.

Natalia Berg, CFA, has estimated the key rate durations for several maturities in three of her equally-weighted bond portfolios, as shown in Exhibit 1.

Exhibit 1: Key Rate Durations for Three Fixed-Income Portfolios

Key Rate Maturity	Portfolio 1	Portfolio 2	Portfolio 3
2-year	2.45	0.35	1.26
5-year	0.20	0.40	1.27
10-year	0.15	4.00	1.23
20-year	2.20	0.25	1.24
Total	5.00	5.00	5.00

At a fixed-income conference in London, Berg hears a presentation by a university professor on the increasing use of the swap rate curve as a benchmark instead of the government bond yield curve. When Berg returns from the conference, she realizes she has left her notes from the presentation on the airplane. However, she is very interested in learning more about whether she should consider using the swap rate curve in her work.

As she tries to reconstruct what was said at the conference, she writes down two statements about the swap rate curve:

Statement 1:   The swap rate curve typically has yield quotes at more maturities than government bond markets have.

Statement 2:   Retail banks are more likely to use the government spot curve as a benchmark as they have minimal exposure to swap markets.

Berg also obtains information on several bonds issued by Salant Enterprises as shown in Exhibit 2.

Exhibit 2: Selected Information on Salant Enterprises Bonds

Label	A	B	C
Bond type	Callable	Putable	Extendible
Option type	European	European	
Exercise date	2 years	3 years	
Maturity	3 years	4 years	3 years
Extension period	-	-	1 year
Coupon Rate	5%	5%	5%
Value	$99.50	$100.69	

Berg determines that to obtain an accurate estimate of the effective duration and effective convexity of a callable bond using a binomial model, the specified change in yield (i.e., Δy) must be equal to the OAS.

Berg also observes that the current Treasury bond yield curve is upward sloping. Based on this observation, Berg forecasts that short-term interest rates will increase.

37. If the spot-rate curve experiences a parallel downward shift of 50 basis points:
    A. all three portfolios will experience the same price performance.
    B. Portfolio 1 will experience the best price performance.
    C. Portfolio 3 will experience the best price performance.

38. If the 5- and 10-year key rates increase by 20 basis points, but the 2- and 20-year key rates remain unchanged:
    A. all three portfolios will experience the same price performance.
    B. Portfolio 1 will experience the best price performance.
    C. Portfolio 2 will experience the best price performance.

39. Are the two observations Berg records after the fixed income conference accurate?
    A. Both statements are accurate.
    B. Only Statement 1 is accurate.
    C. Only Statement 2 is accurate.

40.   Based on the information in Exhibit 2, the value of Bond C is *most likely:*
        A. $99.50.
        B. between $99.50 and $100.69.
        C. $100.69.

41.   Is Berg correct about the specified change in yield needed to obtain an
        accurate estimate of the effective duration and effective convexity of a
        callable bond using a binomial model?
        A. No, because the specified change in yield must be larger than the
            option-adjusted spread (OAS).
        B. No, because the specified change in yield must be smaller than the
            OAS.
        C. No, because the specified change in yield can be larger than, smaller
            than, or equal to the OAS.

42.   Is Berg's short-term interest rate forecast consistent with the pure
        expectations theory and the liquidity premium theory?
        A. Consistent with both theories.
        B. Consistent with the pure expectations theory only.
        C. Consistent with the liquidity premium theory only.

Questions 43–48 relate to Jonathan Adams.

Jonathan Adams, CFA, is doing some scenario analysis on forward contracts. The process involves pricing the forward contracts and then estimating their values based on likely scenarios provided by the firm's forecasting and strategy departments. The forward contracts with which Adams is most concerned are those on fixed income securities, interest rates, and currencies.

The first contract he needs to price is a 270-day forward on a $1 million Treasury bond with ten years remaining to maturity. The bond has a 5% coupon rate, has just made a coupon payment, and will make its next two coupon payments in 182 days and in 365 days. It is currently selling for 98.25. The effective annual risk-free rate is 4%. Adams is also analyzing forward rate agreements (FRAs).

The LIBOR spot curve is as follows:

30-day: 3.12%	60-day: 3.32%	90-day: 3.52%
120-day: 3.72%	150-day: 3.92%	180-day: 4.12%

Adams determines the price of a 2×5 FRA from the spot yield curve using the following calculation:

$$\left[\frac{1+0.0352\left(\dfrac{90}{360}\right)}{1+0.0332\left(\dfrac{60}{360}\right)}-1\right]\left(\frac{360}{90}\right)$$

Finally, Adams wants to price and value a currency forward on euros. The euro spot rate is $1.1854. The dollar risk-free rate is 3%, and the euro risk-free rate is 4%.

43. The no-arbitrage price for the forward contract on the Treasury bond is *closest* to:
   A. 98.54.
   B. 98.57.
   C. 98.62.

44. If the Treasury bond price decreases to 98.11 (including accrued interest) over the next 60 days, the value of a short position in the 270-day forward contract on a $10 million bond is *closest* to:
   A. $76,500.
   B. $76,800.
   C. $78,000.

45. How many of the following terms are correct in the calculation of the FRA price: 0.0352, 0.0332, 60/360, 90/360?
    A. Two.
    B. Three.
    C. Four.

46. After 30 days, Adams wants to value a $10 million short position in the 2×5 FRA. The 90-day forward rate in 30 days is now 4.14%, and the original price of the FRA was 4.30%. 120-day LIBOR has changed to 3.92%. The current value of the $10 million FRA to the short position under this scenario is *closest* to:
    A. $15,794.
    B. $3,948.
    C. −$15,794.

47. The no-arbitrage price for a 1-year forward contract on euros is *closest* to:
    A. $1.1401.
    B. $1.1740.
    C. $1.1969.

48. Suppose that at maturity of the forward contract on euros the spot rate is greater than the forward rate at the initiation of the contract. Which party is exposed to credit risk, and why?

	Exposed to credit risk	Reason
A.	Long position	Long position value < 0
B.	Long position	Short position value < 0
C.	Short position	Long position value < 0

Questions 49–54 relate to GD Barton, Inc.

GD Barton, Inc., (GD) is a large multinational company headquartered in the U.S. Through a series of subsidiaries around the world, GD operates in multiple sectors including retail, engineering, health care, and reinsurance. The company has a large treasury and risk management arm based in the U.K., and all responsibility for cash and risk management is centered in this London office.

Recently, a major breach of controls was discovered in the office; a junior employee had bypassed internal controls and opened large positions in several derivative contracts. The employee in question was only authorized to use such contracts for hedging purposes, but the company fears that it may have exposure in excess of $100 million on unhedged positions opened by the employee.

Following an internal investigation, Miguel Hernandez, CFA, has been assigned to review and value several contracts that were flagged during the audit.

Details of three of the contracts, confirmed as being unauthorized (i.e., not used for hedging), have been summarized in an email to Hernandez. Extracts of this email are shown in Exhibit 1.

Exhibit 1: Unauthorized Contracts

Contract 1 – Interest Rate Swap

Term:	2 years
Fixed rate:	3.50%
Settlement:	semi-annual (30/360)
Opened:	180 days ago
Notional:	$150 million
Position:	Fixed-rate payer
Current term structure:	$LIBOR_{180}$ 2.90%, $LIBOR_{360}$ 3.00%, $LIBOR_{540}$ 3.20%

Contract 2 – Equity Swap

Term:	1 year
Fixed rate:	3.70%
Equity index at last settlement:	1926.64
Settlement:	quarterly (30/360)
Opened:	120 days ago
Notional:	$250 million
Position:	Fixed-rate payer
Current term structure:	$LIBOR_{60}$ 2.70%, $LIBOR_{150}$ 2.85%, $LIBOR_{240}$ 2.95%
Current equity index:	1892.23

Contract 3 – Forward Rate Agreement

Contract:	90-day forward rate on 180-day LIBOR (i.e., 3 × 9 FRA)
Price:	3.8%
Opened:	50 days ago
Notional:	$125 million
Current term structure:	**NOTE:** Which LIBOR rates do you require here?

In addition to the confirmed breaches in Exhibit 1, the investigation also discovered a number of transactions related to credit default swaps (CDS). Hernandez has received an email from a member of the investigative team asking for his advice on GD's exposure as a result of these transactions. An extract from that email is shown in Exhibit 2.

Exhibit 2: Credit Default Swaps

"…without authorization, the employee sold $350 million notional of protection on the iTraxx Main[1] index, a position that remains open. GD has no exposure to debt instruments issued by any of the constituents of the index, and there appear to be no other transactions in any index CDS. There were, however, two other transactions in single-name CDS. On behalf of GD, the employee purchased $2.5 million of notional exposure on a single-name CDS protection on POPRT corporation debt and $3.5 million of notional exposure on TRTRS corporation debt.

POPRT is a constituent of the iTraxx Main index, but TRTRS is not. Since the single-name positions were opened, the credit spread on both POPRT and TRTRS has increased by over 250 basis points."

[1] The iTraxx Main is an equally weighted CDS index consisting of 125 investment-grade entities.

Hernandez thinks the TRTRS transaction may actually be a legitimate contract undertaken by another employee of the firm, Dan Eagen. Hernandez recently spoke informally with Eagen, who stated that he believes that "TRTRS is currently preparing to undergo a leveraged buy-out at a significant premium to current market value." Eagen's intention was to make a gain by taking a position in the CDS and TRTRS stock.

49. The value to GD of contract 1, as described in Exhibit 1, is *closest* to:
    A. −$8,400,000.
    B. −$2,990,000.
    C. −$765,000.

50. The value to GD of contract 2, as described in Exhibit 1, is *closest* to:
    A. $2,510,000.
    B. −$2,510,000.
    C. −$6,500,000.

51. Which of the following current LIBOR rates would Hernandez *most likely* require in order to value contract 3?
    A. 90-day LIBOR and 180-day LIBOR.
    B. 40-day LIBOR and 130-day LIBOR.
    C. 40-day LIBOR and 220-day LIBOR.

52. As a result of the transactions described in Exhibit 2, GD's current net notional exposure to POPRT debt is *closest* to:
    A. $3.5 million.
    B. $0.3 million.
    C. zero.

53.   If GD were to enter into an offsetting contract to hedge its exposure to TRTRS under the CDS described in Exhibit 2, this would *most likely* result in:
        A. a loss on the CDS position.
        B. a gain on the CDS position.
        C. no gain or loss on the CDS position.

54.   Eagen is *most likely* to take advantage of his prediction for TRTRS by:
        A. purchasing CDS protection and selling the underlying stock.
        B. selling CDS protection and buying the underlying stock.
        C. buying CDS protection and buying the underlying stock.

Questions 55–60 relate to Terry Holt and Bill McGuire.

Terry Holt, CFA, is an investment consultant that advises several institutional clients, including pension funds and endowments. Holt is evaluating the performance of Magna Alpha fund. He obtains the fund's active weights and expected returns relative to the benchmark as shown in Exhibit 1.

Exhibit 1: Magna Alpha Fund

Asset Class (i)	Portfolio Return $E(R_{Pi})$	Benchmark Return $E(R_{Bi})$	Active Weight
Equities	13%	12%	10%
Bonds	7%	5%	−11%
Cash	3%	3%	1%

Bill McGuire, Holt's supervisor, makes the following statements:

1. The optimal risky portfolio for any investor is the one with the highest Sharpe ratio irrespective of the risk tolerance of the client.

2. The Sharpe ratio would be the same as the information ratio for a market-neutral long-short equity fund that has the risk-free asset as the portfolio's benchmark.

Holt then obtains data on three active funds specializing in commodities investing. Exhibit 2 presents data on these funds.

Exhibit 2: Fund Data

Fund	Prime	Redux	Optimus
Expected active return	2.40%	1.25%	1.28%
Active risk	6%	5%	4%

McGuire recommends that Holt investigate two other funds, run by active managers A and B, as well. Exhibit 3 shows the relevant information.

Exhibit 3: Active Managers A and B

Manager A: Invests in stocks and makes bets annually. Has an information coefficient of 0.20 and transfer coefficient of 0.4.

Manager B: Unconstrained optimization involving monthly bets on market timing (rotation between equity and cash). Manager B is correct 55% of the time.

©2015 Kaplan, Inc.

Holt mentions to McGuire that one has to be careful about actively managed funds that are actually closet index funds. These funds tend to be characterized by very low active risk, low information ratio, and a Sharpe ratio that is almost the same as the Sharpe ratio for the fund's benchmark.

55. Using the information in Exhibit 1, the expected active return from asset allocation for Magna Alpha fund is *closest* to:
   A. 0.68%.
   B. 1.25%.
   C. 1.93%.

56. Regarding McGuire's statements:
   A. both statements are correct.
   B. only one statement is correct.
   C. neither statement is correct.

57. Which component of the fundamental law of active management captures the relationship between risk-adjusted active weights and risk-adjusted forecasted returns?
   A. Transfer coefficient.
   B. Information coefficient.
   C. Information ratio.

58. Using the information in Exhibit 2, which fund would be *most* suitable for an investor with a constraint of maximum active risk of 5%?
   A. Prime.
   B. Redux.
   C. Optimus.

59. To achieve the same information ratio as Manager B, the number of stocks that Manager A must make independent bets on is *closest* to:
   A. 14.
   B. 19.
   C. 22.

60. Holt is *least likely* to be correct about which factor as an indicator of a closet index fund?
   A. Low active risk.
   B. Low information ratio.
   C. Same Sharpe ratio as the benchmark.

End of Morning Session

EXAM 1
AFTERNOON SESSION

Question	Topic	Minutes (Points)
61 to 66	Ethics	18
67 to 72	Ethics	18
73 to 78	Economics	18
79 to 84	Financial Reporting and Analysis	18
85 to 90	Financial Reporting and Analysis	18
91 to 96	Financial Reporting and Analysis	18
97 to 102	Corporate Finance	18
103 to 108	Corporate Finance	18
109 to 114	Equity	18
115 to 120	Equity	18

61.	(A)	(B)	(C)		101.	(A)	(B)	(C)
62.	(A)	(B)	(C)		102.	(A)	(B)	(C)
63.	(A)	(B)	(C)		103.	(A)	(B)	(C)
64.	(A)	(B)	(C)		104.	(A)	(B)	(C)
65.	(A)	(B)	(C)		105.	(A)	(B)	(C)
66.	(A)	(B)	(C)		106.	(A)	(B)	(C)
67.	(A)	(B)	(C)		107.	(A)	(B)	(C)
68.	(A)	(B)	(C)		108.	(A)	(B)	(C)
69.	(A)	(B)	(C)		109.	(A)	(B)	(C)
70.	(A)	(B)	(C)		110.	(A)	(B)	(C)
71.	(A)	(B)	(C)		111.	(A)	(B)	(C)
72.	(A)	(B)	(C)		112.	(A)	(B)	(C)
73.	(A)	(B)	(C)		113.	(A)	(B)	(C)
74.	(A)	(B)	(C)		114.	(A)	(B)	(C)
75.	(A)	(B)	(C)		115.	(A)	(B)	(C)
76.	(A)	(B)	(C)		116.	(A)	(B)	(C)
77.	(A)	(B)	(C)		117.	(A)	(B)	(C)
78.	(A)	(B)	(C)		118.	(A)	(B)	(C)
79.	(A)	(B)	(C)		119.	(A)	(B)	(C)
80.	(A)	(B)	(C)		120.	(A)	(B)	(C)
81.	(A)	(B)	(C)					
82.	(A)	(B)	(C)					
83.	(A)	(B)	(C)					
84.	(A)	(B)	(C)					
85.	(A)	(B)	(C)					
86.	(A)	(B)	(C)					
87.	(A)	(B)	(C)					
88.	(A)	(B)	(C)					
89.	(A)	(B)	(C)					
90.	(A)	(B)	(C)					
91.	(A)	(B)	(C)					
92.	(A)	(B)	(C)					
93.	(A)	(B)	(C)					
94.	(A)	(B)	(C)					
95.	(A)	(B)	(C)					
96.	(A)	(B)	(C)					
97.	(A)	(B)	(C)					
98.	(A)	(B)	(C)					
99.	(A)	(B)	(C)					
100.	(A)	(B)	(C)					

Exam 1
Afternoon Session

Questions 61–66 relate to Mike Zonding.

Mike Zonding, CFA, is conducting a background check on CFA candidate Annie Cooken, a freshly minted MBA who applied for a stock-analysis job at his firm, Khasko Financial. Zonding does not like to hire anyone who does not adhere to the Code and Standards' professional conduct requirements.

The background check reveals the following:

(i)   While doing a full-time, unpaid internship at Kale Investments, Cooken was reprimanded for working a 30-hour-a-week night job as a waitress.

(ii) As an intern at Lammar Corp., Cooken was fired after revealing to the FBI that one of the principals was embezzling from the firm's clients.

(iii) Cooken performed 40 hours of community service in relation to a conviction on a misdemeanor drug possession charge when she was 16 years old.

(iv) On her resume, Cooken writes, "Recently passed Level II of the CFA exam, a test that measures candidates' knowledge of finance and investing."

During the interview, Zonding asks Cooken several questions on ethics-related issues, including questions about the role of a fiduciary and Standard III(E) Preservation of Confidentiality. He asks her about her internship at Kale Investments, specifically about the working hours. Cooken replies that the internship turned out to require more time than she originally planned, up to 65 hours per week.

Zonding subsequently hires Cooken and functions as her supervisor. On her third day at the money management boutique firm, portfolio manager Steven Clarrison hands her a report on Mocline Tobacco and tells her to revise the report to reflect a buy rating. Cooken is uncomfortable about revising the report.

To supplement the meager income from her entry-level stock-analysis job, Cooken looks for part-time work. She is offered a position working three hours each Friday and Saturday night tending bar at a sports bar and grill downtown. Cooken does not tell her employer about the job.

During her first week, Cooken has lunch with former MBA classmates, including Taira Basch, CFA, who works for the compliance officer at a large investment bank in town. Basch arrives late, explaining, "What a day, it's only noon and already I have worked on the following requests:

1. A federal regulator called and wanted information on potentially illegal activities related to one of the firm's key clients.

2. A rival company's employee wanted information regarding employment opportunities at the firm.

3. A potential client contacted an employee and wanted detailed performance records of client accounts so he can decide whether to invest with the firm."

Zonding appeared on a financial news network program to discuss Orlando Stores, a discount clothing chain. Khasko's investment banking department has completed transactions for Orlando in the past 12 months and currently is working with Orlando to conduct a secondary offering; Khasko has a policy in place that separates the activities of investment banking and research.

At the beginning of the interview, Zonding disclosed that Khasko has an investment banking relationship with Orlando Stores and that his wife holds Orlando shares. He also stated that his research is available on Khasko's website, although he forgot to comment on the risk profile and suitability of investing in Orlando shares.

The host asked Zonding to comment on Khasko's outlook for the stock, given Orlando's recently announced expansion plans. Zonding stated that he officially had a 12-month buy rating on the stock, though he is concerned about potential oversaturation in some of Orlando's markets. When asked about his conviction level in his buy rating, Zonding replied that if there is a sharp share price increase next week when earnings are released, viewers should take the opportunity to sell shares since there are always long-term risks inherent in expansion. Zonding also mentioned that he did not want to be negative about Orlando shares since Orlando is a valuable client of Khasko.

61. In the context of the Code and Standards, which of the items from the background check would *most likely* indicate that Zonding should not have hired Cooken?
     A. Item i.
     B. Item ii.
     C. Item iii.

62. Which of the following statements provides the *least appropriate* justification for Cooken's caution about revising the report on Mocline Tobacco?
     A. Cooken knows next to nothing about Mocline stock.
     B. Cooken's uncle, George Whates, is the CFO of Mocline.
     C. In college, Cooken worked for Mocline but never declared the income on her taxes.

63. By not telling Zonding about the bartending position, Cooken has *most likely* violated:
    A. no Standards.
    B. Standard IV(B) Additional Compensation Arrangements.
    C. Standard IV(A) Loyalty (to employer) and Standard IV(B) Additional Compensation Arrangements.

64. Which of the requests, if fulfilled, is *most likely* to place Basch in violation of Standard III(E) Preservation of Confidentiality?
    A. Request 1.
    B. Request 2.
    C. Request 3.

65. Was Zonding in compliance with regard to CFA Institute Research Objectivity Standards (ROS) recommendations on public appearances?
    A. No, because Zonding neglected to discuss Orlando's suitability as an investment.
    B. No, because Zonding failed to disclose Orlando's plans to announce a secondary offering in the near future.
    C. Yes, because Zonding disclosed his firm's relationship with Orlando, his wife's ownership of the shares, and the availability of his Orlando report.

66. Did Zonding follow the recommended procedures of the CFA Institute Research Objectivity Standards (ROS) with regard to Khasko's rating of Orlando Stores?
    A. No.
    B. Yes, because Zonding stated his rating recommendation and his time horizon on his rating.
    C. Yes, because Zonding discussed his concerns about Orlando's expansion plans, so it was appropriate to recommend selling the shares to capitalize on near-term price increases.

Questions 67–72 relate to Andrea Vrbenic.

Andrea Vrbenic, CFA, was recently promoted to supervisory analyst at a boutique investment bank that specializes in managing initial public offerings for firms in the biotech industry. The firm also manages assets for high net worth clients. Vrbenic will report to Tom Sheffield, a senior manager and director in the investment banking department at the firm.

Wilhelmina Scott, CFA, who also reports to Sheffield, will be Vrbenic's supervisory analyst counterpart on the investment management side. Vrbenic will assume responsibility for all research prepared on subject companies that engage in investment banking business with the firm, while Scott will continue to supervise research covering a small group of companies that constitutes the firm's approved list.

Sheffield assigns Vrbenic the task of ensuring compliance with CFA Institute Research Objectivity Standards that cover herself, Scott, and other analysts at the firm. Sheffield recognizes that this policy is comprehensive and must apply not only to analysts on the investment banking side, but also to research analysts on the investment management side.

Vrbenic soon realizes that investment bankers at the firm use her research reports to help attract new investment banking clients. Vrbenic also learns that coverage of subject companies on the investment banking side will move over to the investment management side if these companies decline to continue an investment banking relationship. Sheffield tells Vrbenic that "the companies are golden while they have an investment banking relationship with us, but may lose their luster after they move to the investment management research side."

Vrbenic and Scott each receive a salary and two bonuses—one based on the investment banking division performance and one based on investment management division performance during a quarter. Sheffield attests annually that the firm has followed CFA Institute Research Objectivity Standards (ROS).

Sheffield attends a meeting with Vrbenic and her analysts. During the meeting, Jamie Verhallen, a research analyst reporting to Vrbenic, presents an overview of a biotech firm that will soon issue additional equity through their investment bank. While Verhallen recommends a favorable rating for the stock, Vrbenic recommends a higher rating due to the investment banking relationship with the firm. Verhallen refuses to sign the report with the changes that Vrbenic recommended during the meeting. Vrbenic transfers responsibility for research on the company to herself and issues the report with a higher rating.

Later that week, Verhallen tells Vrbenic of her father's impending kidney transplant. Verhallen's father has limited income, and Verhallen has agreed to assist with the medical expenses. Verhallen has decided to sell her holdings of the biotech company to raise cash for the operation.

Vrbenic appears on a financial news TV channel that same week describing the positive attributes of the biotech company. To protect her privacy, Vrbenic does not disclose her position in the securities. Vrbenic suggests that members of the audience must become clients prior to receiving any research from her firm.

67. Under the Research Objectivity Standards, Vrbenic's firm:
    A. may permit Sheffield to supervise investment management research.
    B. must segregate analysts reporting to Scott from the investment banking department.
    C. must prevent research analysts from covering companies that have an investment banking relationship with the firm.

68. According to the Research Objectivity Standards, Verhallen may sell her stock in the biotech company only if she:
    A. disagrees with a recommendation.
    B. has encountered a financial hardship.
    C. has encountered a financial hardship and disagrees with the recommendation.

69. Vrbenic's recommendation to raise the biotech company's rating solely based on investment banking relationship violates the Research Objectivity Standards:
    A. only because the analyst reports to her.
    B. because the standards require a reasonable basis for research recommendations.
    C. because the standards require that firms refuse to provide research recommendations when there is any conflict of interest.

70. Under the Research Objectivity Standards, an acceptable compensation system for research analysts is *most likely* to:
    A. have an incentive component.
    B. align analyst compensation with the accuracy of research at the end of every quarter.
    C. be based on measurable criteria for quality of research.

71. Vrbenic has violated the Research Objectivity Standards through her public appearance by failing to:
   A. disclose her position in the securities but not by failing to provide a copy of the research that she discussed.
   B. provide a copy of the research that she discussed but not by failing to disclose her position in the securities.
   C. disclose her position in the securities as well as by failing to provide a copy of the research that she discussed.

72. To be consistent with the Research Objectivity Standards, Vrbenic's firm is required to issue research reports:
   A. at least annually.
   B. at least quarterly.
   C. on a regular and timely basis.

Questions 73–78 relate to Robert Williams.

Robert Williams is a junior analyst at Anderson Brothers, a large Wall Street brokerage firm. He reports to Will McDonald, the chief economist for Anderson Brothers. McDonald provides economic research, forecasts, and interpretation of economic data to all of Anderson's investment departments, as well as to the firm's clients. McDonald has asked Williams to analyze economic trends in the country of Bundovia. Bundovia has strict capital controls limiting the flow of capital into and out of the country. The currency of Bundovia is the bunco (BUN).

One of Bundovia's major exports is high quality carpets. However, human rights activists have recently begun to complain about child labor practices among Bundovian carpet manufacturers, and this has resulted in negative publicity for the industry. Concerned about the impact on Bundovian exports, the Bundovian government banned child labor and provided oversight authority to the Bundovian carpet manufacturer's association. The Bundovian carpet manufacturer's association is an independent, membership-based organization. Most large carpet manufacturers in Bundovia are members.

McDonald believes that the Bundovian economy is experiencing a hyper-inflationary environment and that the Bundovian government is poised to follow a restrictive monetary and fiscal policy to combat high inflation.

In analyzing Bundovian economic performance, Williams notices that Bundovia has been able to grow rapidly in the past few years and has reached a steady state of growth. Compared to its trading partners, Bundovia has low capital-to-labor ratios; this situation is expected to continue.

Williams is also permitted to trade in the forex markets when he sees an opportunity to make a profit. Williams' bank quotes the following exchange rates to him:

- USD/GBP = 2.0010 – 20
- USD/SFr = 0.8550 – 60

Williams asks the bank for a GBP/SFr cross rate.

Williams receives the following forward rate quotes from the same bank:

- 30-day forward rate: USD/GBP = 2.0045 – 55
- 60-day forward rate: USD/GBP = 2.0075 – 85

Williams decides to go long 1 million GBP (and short USD) in the 60-day forward contract.

30 days after the initiation of the USD/GBP forward contract, the exchange rate and interest rates are as follows:

Quotes	USD/GBP
Spot	2.0086/2.0089
30-day forward	+7.6/+8
60-day forward	+8.7/+9.1
90-day forward	+9.2/+9.8

Interest Rates	USD	GBP
30 day	4.00%	3.00%
60 day	4.25%	3.00%
90 day	4.29%	3.00%

Williams spots another potential arbitrage opportunity in the foreign exchange markets. The current spot rate is $2.00 per BUN. The Bundovian risk-free interest rate is 3%, the one-year forward rate is $2.10 per BUN, and the U.S. risk-free rate is 5%.

73. To carry out the objectives of the Bundovian child labor regulations, the *most important* requirement is that the Bundovian carpet manufacturer's association should:
    A. have the ability to effectively supervise the industry practices.
    B. be properly supervised by the government.
    C. be able to impose sanctions.

74. Based on McDonald's beliefs about Bundovian government monetary and fiscal policies, under the Mundell-Fleming model the Bunco is *most likely* expected to:
    A. depreciate.
    B. appreciate.
    C. remain unchanged in value.

75. Under neoclassical growth theory, the Bundovian growth rate is *most likely* to increase due to:
    A. capital deepening.
    B. technological growth.
    C. either capital deepening or technological growth.

76. Based on the bank's USD/GBP and USD/SFr quotes, Williams's bank is *most likely* to quote a cross rate of:
    A. GBP/SFr = 0.4271 – 78.
    B. GBP/SFr = 2.3375 – 14.
    C. GBP/SFr = 0.4273 – 76.

77.   30 days after initiation of the USD/GBP forward contract, the mark-to-market value of the contract is *closest* to:
   A. USD 860.
   B. USD 1,195.
   C. USD 2,190.

78.   The maximum profit available from covered interest arbitrage in the USD/BUN market by borrowing $1,000 or the BUN equivalent is *closest* to:
   A. $19.05.
   B. $31.50.
   C. $72.50.

Questions 79–84 relate to High Plains Tubular.

High Plains Tubular Company is a leading manufacturer and distributor of quality steel products used in energy, industrial, and automotive applications worldwide.

The U.S. steel industry has been challenged in recent years by competition from foreign producers located primarily in Asia. U.S. producers are experiencing declining margins as labor costs continue to increase. In addition, most U.S. steel mills are technologically inferior to those of foreign competitors and U.S. producers have significant unresolved issues related to complying with environmental protection laws.

High Plains is not immune from the problems of the industry and is currently in technical default under its bond covenants. The default is a result of the firm's failure to meet certain coverage and turnover ratios. High Plains has argued that this is largely due to the favorable credit terms it has given to its customers (major customers are given 90 days to settle) in order to gain market share.

Earlier this year, High Plains and its bondholders entered into an agreement that will give High Plains time to come into compliance with the covenants. If High Plains is not in compliance by year-end, the bondholders can immediately accelerate the maturity date of the bonds. In that case, High Plains would have no choice but to file for bankruptcy.

High Plains follows U.S. GAAP. For the year ended 2014, High Plains received an unqualified opinion from its independent auditor. However, the auditor's opinion included an explanatory paragraph about High Plains' inability to continue as a going concern in the event its bonds remain in technical default.

At the end of 2014, High Plains' Chief Executive Officer (CEO) and Chief Financial Officer (CFO) filed the certifications required by the Securities and Exchange Commission (SEC).

Jon Farnsworth, CFA, is reviewing High Plains' financial accounts to gain a better understanding of credit risk of the company. The first element that causes Farnsworth some concern is the cash flow statement. This is shown in Exhibit 1.

Exhibit 1: Cash Flow Statement

High Plains Tubular Cash Flow Statement		
	Year ended December 31,	
in thousands	2014	2013
Net income	$158,177	$121,164
Depreciation expense	$34,078	$31,295
Deferred taxes	$7,697	$11,407
Receivables	($144,087)	($24,852)
Inventory	($79,710)	($72,777)
Payables	$36,107	$22,455
Cash flow from operations (CFO)	$12,262	$88,692
Cash flow from investing (CFI)	($39,884)	($63,953)
Cash flow from financing	$82,676	$6,056
Change in cash	$55,054	$30,795
Cash flow from financing	$82,676	$6,056
Change in cash	$55,054	$30,795

Exhibit 2: Selected Financial Footnotes

1. During 2014, High Plains' sales increased 27% over 2013. Its sales growth continues to significantly exceed the industry average. Sales are recognized when a firm order is received from the customer, the sales price is fixed and determinable, and collectability is reasonably assured. In limited cases, some product is sold on a bill-and-hold basis provided that the goods are completed, packaged and ready for shipment; such goods are segregated and the risks of ownership and legal title have passed to the customer. Total revenue from such sales amounted to $907.95 million in 2014. (2013: zero.)

2. The cost of inventories is determined using the last-in, first-out (LIFO) method. Had the first-in, first-out (FIFO) method been used, inventories would have been $152 million and $143 million higher as of December 31, 2014 and 2013, respectively.

3. Effective January 1, 2014, High Plains changed its depreciation method from the double-declining balance method to the straight-line method in order to be more comparable with the accounting practices of other firms within its industry. The change was not retroactively applied and only affects assets that were acquired on or after January 1, 2014.

4. High Plains made the following discretionary expenditures for maintenance and repair of plant and equipment, and for advertising and marketing:

in millions	2014	2013	2012
Maintenance and repairs	$180	$184	$218
Advertising and marketing	$94	$108	$150

5. During the fiscal year ended December 31, 2014, High Plains sold $50 million of its accounts receivable to a third party.

6. High Plains conducts some of its operations in facilities leased under noncancelable finance (capital) leases. Certain leases include renewal options with provisions for increased lease payments during the renewal term.

7. High Plains reclassified $2.9 million of inventory as other assets in 2014. This material had been reported within inventory as work-in-progress in 2013.

After reviewing the cash flow statement and footnotes, Farnsworth analyzes the impact of the bill and hold sales outlined in Exhibit 1 using the assumptions shown in Exhibit 3.

Exhibit 3: Bill-and-Hold Analysis

High Plains EBT margin	5.1%
Average tax rate	28%

79. Which of the following statements regarding High Plains' cash flow quality is *least* accurate?
     A. The transaction described in footnote 5 of Exhibit 2 would have increased cash flow from operations (CFO) in 2014 but decreased the quality of cash flow in 2014.
     B. The decrease in accounts payable in 2013 increased the quality of cash flow as High Plains is paying off suppliers more rapidly.
     C. The divergence between net income and cash flow from operations (CFO) may be an indication of earnings manipulation.

80. What is the *most likely* effect of High Plains' revenue recognition policy on net income and inventory turnover?
     A. Both net income and inventory turnover are overstated.
     B. Only net income is overstated.
     C. Only inventory turnover is overstated.

81. Applying the assumptions in Exhibit 3 to the relevant disclosures given in Exhibits 1 and 2, Farnsworth is *most likely* to conclude that bill-and-hold sales contributed:
    A. more than 20% of net income in 2014.
    B. approximately 10% of net income in 2014.
    C. less than 10% of net income in 2014.

82. Using only the information found in Exhibit 1 and Exhibit 2, which of the following is *most* indicative of lower earnings quality?
    A. High Plains' discretionary expenses.
    B. The change in High Plains' depreciation method.
    C. High Plains' inventory cost flow assumption.

83. Which of the accounting treatments described in footnotes 6 and 7 of Exhibit 2 is *likely* to lower High Plains' financial reporting quality?
    A. Both treatments lower financial reporting quality.
    B. Only the treatment in footnote 6 lowers financial reporting quality.
    C. Only the treatment in footnote 7 lowers financial reporting quality.

84. Which of the following statements about High Plains' financial reporting quality is *least* accurate?
    A. High Plains may have manipulated earnings due to the risk of default.
    B. High Plains' extreme revenue growth will likely revert back to normal levels over time.
    C. Due to High Plains' lengthy credit terms for customers, analysts should place a higher weighting on the accruals-based element of earnings rather than the cash-based element.

Questions 85–90 relate to Stanley Bostwick.

Stanley Bostwick, CFA, is a business services industry analyst with Mortonworld Financial. Currently, his attention is focused on the 20X8 financial statements of Global Oilfield Supply, particularly the footnote disclosures related to the company's employee benefit plans. Bostwick would like to analyze the effect on the reported results of changes in assumptions the company used to estimate the projected benefit obligation (PBO) and net pension cost. But first, Bostwick must familiarize himself with the differences in the accounting for defined contribution and defined benefit pension plans.

Global Oilfield's financial statements are prepared in accordance with International Financial Reporting Standards (IFRS). Excerpts from the company's annual report are shown in the following exhibits.

Exhibit 1: Reconciliation of Projected Benefit Obligation

(in thousands)	20X8	20X7	20X6
Change in projected benefit obligation:			
Benefit obligation at beginning of year	€64,230	€50,534	€39,132
Service cost	8,091	8,038	6,607
Interest cost	4,335	3,158	2,641
Actuarial loss (gain)	(1,932)	5,034	4,590
Benefits paid	(3,824)	(2,534)	(2,436)
Projected benefit obligation at end of year	€70,900	€64,230	€50,534

Exhibit 2: Reconciliation of Fair Value of Plan Assets

(in thousands)	20X8	20X7	20X6
Change in plan assets:			
Fair value of plan assets at beginning of year	€65,164	€44,296	€35,796
Actual return on plan assets	7,084	9,916	(1,868)
Employer contributions	5,000	13,486	12,804
Benefits paid	(3,824)	(2,534)	(2,436)
Fair value of plan assets at end of year	€73,424	€65,164	€44,296

Exhibit 3: Reported Pension Expense

(in thousands)	20X8	20X7	20X6
Service cost	€8,091	€8,038	€6,607
Net interest cost (income)	(63)	390	225
Pension expense	€8,028	€8,428	€6,832

Exhibit 4: Weighted Average Pension Assumptions

	20X8	20X7	20X6
Discount rate	6.75%	6.25%	6.75%
Rate of compensation growth	5.00%	5.00%	5.00%

85. If Global Oilfield's retirement plan is a defined contribution arrangement, which of the following statements would be the *most* correct?
    A. Pension expense and the cash funding amount would be the same.
    B. The potential gains or losses from the assets contributed to the plan are borne by the firm.
    C. The firm would report the difference in the benefit obligation and the plan assets on the balance sheet.

86. If Global Oilfield were to adopt U.S. pension accounting standards, what adjustment, if any, is necessary to its balance sheet at the end of 20X8 assuming no taxes?
    A. Decrease assets by €7,222, decrease liabilities €2,524, and decrease equity by $4,698.
    B Decrease assets by €4,698 and decrease equity by €4,698.
    C. No adjustment is necessary.

87. What was the *most likely* cause of the actuarial gain reported in the reconciliation of the projected benefit obligation for the year ended 20X8?
    A. Increase in the average life expectancy of the participating employees.
    B. Decrease in the expected rate of return.
    C. Increase in the discount rate.

88. Which of the following *best* describes the effects of a decrease in the rate of compensation growth during 20X9 all else equal? Global Oilfield's:
    A. service cost is lower and the projected benefit obligation is higher.
    B. pension expense is lower and the plan assets are higher.
    C. net income is higher and the funded status is higher.

89. As compared to Global Oilfield's reported pension expense, total periodic pension cost expense for the year ended 20X8 is:
    A. higher.
    B. lower.
    C. the same.

90. Assume for this question only that Global reports under U.S. GAAP and that the total periodic pension cost for the year ended 20X8 was €4,250. Ignoring income taxes, which of the following statements *best* describes the adjustment necessary for analyzing Global Oilfield's cash flow statement?
    A. Increase operating cash flow €750 and decrease financing cash flow €750.
    B. Decrease operating cash flow €2,084 and increase investing cash flow €2,084.
    C. Increase operating cash flow €5,000 and decrease financing cash flow €5,000.

Questions 91–96 relate to Valley Airlines.

Jason Bennett is an analyst for Valley Airlines (Valley), a U.S. firm. Valley owns a stake in Southwest Air Cargo (Southwest), also a U.S. firm. The two firms have had a long-standing relationship. The relationship has become even closer because several of Valley's top executives hold seats on Southwest's Board of Directors.

Valley acquired a 45% ownership stake in Southwest on December 31, 2007. Acquisition of the ownership stake cost $9 million and was paid in cash. Valley's stake in Southwest is such that management can account for the investment using either the equity method or the acquisition method. While Valley's management desires to fairly represent the firm's operating results, they have assigned Bennett to assess the impact of each method on reported financial statements.

Immediately prior to the acquisition, Valley's current asset balance and total equity were $96 million and $80 million, respectively. Southwest's current assets and total equity were $32 million and $16 million, respectively.

While analyzing the use of the equity method versus the acquisition method, Bennett calculates the return on assets (ROA) ratio. He arrives at two conclusions:

Conclusion 1:   Compared to the acquisition method, the equity method results in a higher ROA because of the higher net income under the equity method.

Conclusion 2:   Compared to the acquisition method, the equity method results in a higher ROA because of the smaller level of total assets under the equity method.

He also makes the following statements regarding the acquisition method and equity method:

Statement 1:   The applicability of both methods is identical under U.S. GAAP and IFRS.

Statement 2:   Both methods report the same net income on the parent's consolidated income statement.

Statement 3:   Both methods report the same equity on the parent's consolidated balance sheet.

In addition, Valley has always wanted to pursue its goal of vertical integration by expanding its scope of operations to include the manufacturing of airline parts for its own airplanes. Therefore, it established a subsidiary, Mountain Air Parts (Mountain), in Switzerland on January 1, 2008. Switzerland was chosen as the location for economic and geographical diversification reasons. Mountain will operate as a self-contained, independent subsidiary. Local management in Switzerland will make the majority of operating, financing, and investing decisions.

The Swiss franc (CHF) is the official currency in Switzerland. On January 1, 2008, the USD/CHF exchange rate was 0.77. At December 31, 2008, the exchange rate had changed to 0.85 USD/CHF. The average exchange rate in 2008 was 0.80 USD/CHF. In its first year of operations, Mountain paid no dividends and no taxes. Mountain uses the FIFO assumption for its flow of inventory.

Mountain Air Parts
Balance Sheet

(in CHF thousands)	12/31/2008	1/1/2008
Assets		
Cash and accounts receivable	600	400
Inventory	500	500
Property, plant, and equipment	600	700
Total assets	1,700	1,600
Liabilities and equity		
Accounts payable	200	100
Long-term debt	100	200
Common stock	1,300	1,300
Retained earnings	100	0
Total liabilities and owner's equity	1,700	1,600

Mountain Air Parts
Income Statement for 2008
(in CHF thousands)

Sales	7,000
COGS	(6,800)
Depreciation	(100)
Net income	100

91. The balance of Valley's current assets as of December 31, 2007, using the acquisition method, is *closest* to:
    A. $87 million.
    B. $119 million.
    C. $128 million.

92. Are Bennett's Conclusions 1 and 2 regarding ROA correct?

	Conclusion 1	Conclusion 2
A.	Yes	Yes
B.	Yes	No
C.	No	Yes

93. How many of statements 1–3 made by Bennet are correct?
    A. None.
    B. One.
    C. Two.

94. Using the appropriate method of translation, the amount of total assets reported on Mountain's balance sheet at the end of 2008 is *closest* to:
    A. $1,325.
    B. $1,375.
    C. $1,445.

95. Using the appropriate method of translation, the translation gain (loss) for the year ended 2008 is *closest* to:
    A. $99.
    B. $104.
    C. $109.

96. For this question only, assume that Mountain is operating in a highly inflationary environment. Which of the following statements is *least* correct? Mountain's:
    A. nonmonetary assets and nonmonetary liabilities are adjusted for inflation in accordance with U.S. GAAP.
    B. functional currency is the U.S. dollar.
    C. financial statements are adjusted for inflation, and the net purchasing power gain or loss is recognized in the income statement in accordance with IFRS.

Questions 97–102 relate to Alertron.

Alertron is a pharmaceutical company with approximately $3.5 billion in annual sales that specializes in the development, manufacturing, and marketing of neurology and oncology drug therapies. The firm is seeking to achieve more rapid growth, and Alertron's executive management team feels that the company can grow faster by making acquisitions than it can by trying to grow organically. As a result, management asks the firm's Director of Strategic Planning, Kanna Ozer, CFA, to analyze potential alternatives. At Alertron's next executive management team meeting, Ozer presents the report shown in Exhibit 1 concerning four potential acquisition targets:

Exhibit 1: Report 1—Description of Potential Acquisition Targets

Potential Target	Potential Acquisition Description
BriscoePharm	Firm develops, manufactures, and markets prescription drugs for humans and animals. BriscoePharm has annual sales of $1.2 million, but only certain BriscoePharm drugs are attractive cash flow generators.
Carideo	Firm develops and manufactures oncology and neurology drugs in the United States and abroad. Carideo has annual sales of $1.2 million, and all assets and liabilities would likely be absorbed by Alertron in a potential merger.
Dillon Biotech	Firm designs and manufactures analytical instruments used in drug development. Dillon has $3.5 billion in annual sales. A successful acquisition by Alertron would involve combining operations and forming a new company.
Escarigen	Firm is a pharmaceutical company specializing in cardiology medications. Escarigen is well known among heart surgeons and has a blockbuster cholesterol drug called Karlynivus that is well known in the medical community. In an acquisition, Alertron would want to maintain the successful Escarigen brand and operational structure.

Alertron's executive team agrees that the report is helpful for initiating discussion but decides they need more information concerning the form of each potential acquisition and the most appropriate method of payment. Alertron's management is also concerned whether each potential target would view a takeover attempt as friendly or hostile. Paul Mussara, Alertron's CEO, asks Ozer to prepare a second report that specifically describes the transaction characteristics corresponding to each deal. Ozer's second report is shown in Exhibit 2.

Exhibit 2: Report 2—Merger Transaction Characteristics

Potential Target	Optimal Form of Acquisition	Method of Payment	Likely Attitude of Target Management
BriscoePharm	Asset purchase involving 30% of BriscoePharm's assets	Cash offering	View offer as friendly
Carideo	Stock purchase	Securities offering	View offer as friendly
Dillon Biotech	Stock purchase	Mixed cash and securities offering	View offer as hostile
Escarigen	Stock purchase	Cash offering	View offer as friendly

As Alertron was conducting its analysis, Bhavik Kumar, CEO of Dillon Biotech, hears rumors that Alertron may attempt a hostile takeover of his firm. Kumar calls an emergency meeting with Dillon's four executive vice presidents and expresses his concern that Alertron may attempt a bear hug by submitting a merger proposal directly to the board without informing Dillon's management. Kumar concludes the emergency meeting by asking each executive vice president to brainstorm defense mechanisms that Dillon could employ before a takeover attempt is made and also defenses that could be employed after a hostile takeover offer.

After intense discussions, Alertron decides that a takeover offer for Carideo would be most beneficial due to the net present value of cost reduction synergies of $600 million that Ozer estimates would result from the merger. Mussara asks Ozer to evaluate the deal based on a stock offer in which Alertron would exchange 0.75 shares of Alertron stock for each outstanding share of Carideo stock. Ozer compiles the information shown in Exhibit 3 for her analysis.

Exhibit 3: Merger Evaluation Inputs

	Alertron	Carideo
Pre-merger stock price	$60	$39
Number of shares outstanding (millions)	150	80
Pre-merger market value (millions)	$9,000	$3,120
Estimated NPV of Cost Reduction Synergies	$600 million	

Ozer, and the rest of the executive management team at Alertron, is extremely confident in the $600 million dollar estimate of cost reduction synergies that are likely to result from the merger and feel that the estimate may actually be conservative. However, when analysts at Carideo review the figures, they have a much different opinion and are less certain that $600 million worth of synergies could be realized. While Carideo believes the net present value of synergies from the deal would still be positive, its estimates are much lower than Alertron's.

Carideo's management is also concerned that a merger between Alertron and Carideo could face scrutiny from regulators. Although neither firm is the largest in the pharmaceutical industry, their combined market power could raise antitrust concerns. Phillip Wu, an analyst with Carideo, compiles the following table showing the market share of each of the 12 firms in the pharmaceutical industry to determine whether the concerns were valid. Both Alertron's and Carideo's management teams decide that if regulators are unlikely to challenge the deal, they will proceed with the necessary steps to complete the merger.

Exhibit 4: Market Share of Firms in the Pharmaceutical Industry

Firm Name	Market Share in Pharmaceutical Industry
Munnzer Pharmaceuticals	20%
Spencer Corp.	18%
Alertron	15%
Escarigen	12%
Carideo	10%
Faltysgen	7%
Six other firms	Each have 3% market share

97. Based on Ozer's description of potential acquisition targets, which form of integration and type of merger would *best* describe the transaction if Alertron tried to acquire Escarigen?

Form of integration	Type of merger
A. Statutory	Horizontal
B. Subsidiary	Horizontal
C. Subsidiary	Vertical

98. Based on the information in Exhibit 2, which of the following statements concerning the transaction characteristics of the potential mergers with Alertron is *most accurate*?
    A. Purchasing Escarigen is likely to reduce Alertron's financial leverage.
    B. Carideo would likely avoid paying corporate taxes in the potential deal with Alertron.
    C. BriscoePharm's shareholders would likely be required to approve the deal with Alertron before any proposed deal is completed.

99. Which of the following *best* satisfies Kumar's request to identify a pair of defense mechanisms that consist of a pre-offer and a post-offer defense?

	Pre-offer defense mechanism	Post-offer defense mechanism
A.	Poison put	Fair price amendment
B.	Greenmail	Restricted voting rights
C.	Supermajority voting provision	Leveraged recapitalization

100. Using Ozer's estimates of the cost reduction synergies, the gain that would accrue to Carideo's shareholders as a result of the merger with Alertron is *closest* to:
    A. $108.5 million.
    B. $455.6 million.
    C. $514.2 million.

101. Based on each firm's forecasts of the estimated NPV of synergies from a merger between Alertron and Carideo, what payment method is each firm *likely* to prefer in the deal?
    A. Both firms prefer a cash deal.
    B. Only Alertron prefers a cash deal.
    C. Only Carideo prefers a cash deal.

102. What would be the increase in the Herfindahl-Hirschman Index (HHI) as a result of a merger between Alertron and Carideo, and the *most likely* reaction by regulators to the merger?

	Increase in the HHI	Probable response by regulators
A.	75	No antitrust challenge
B.	300	No antitrust challenge
C.	300	Potential antitrust challenge

Questions 103–108 relate to Jacob Marlinton.

Jacob Marlinton, CFA, works for Bantanaya Modros, Inc. (BATNM), a small, independent brewery in the United States. The company was originally privately owned and all profits were distributed to the ownership group at the end of every year. Last year, however, the company wished to expand its operations and used the proceeds of an IPO to fund a bottling plant and expand its distribution network.

At this year's annual general meeting, the board faced several questions about its intended dividend policy in the future. The CEO is currently in favor of a residual policy, which closely matches the policy before the IPO. He believes that a residual dividend policy will have the following two benefits:

1.   The policy should boost the company's share price as it will provide a stable long-term dividend.

2.   The policy prioritizes investing in positive NPV projects ahead of considering a reduction in dividends.

Marlinton has been asked to calculate the dividend for 2016 if a residual dividend policy is adopted, given capital expenditure levels in the two scenarios in Exhibit 1.

Exhibit 1: Capital Expenditure Levels

Scenario I
The company further expands operations with the opening of a restaurant/brewery. The estimated total required capital expenditure for this plan is $28 million. The project would be financed with a mix of debt and equity in line with the BATNM's target debt and equity weightings. If earnings are not available, the shortfall would be financed with debt, leading to what is expected to be a temporary deviation from the target capital structure.

Scenario II
No significant expansion undertaken. The only capital expenditure would be the replacement of existing equipment. Existing brewing equipment would be sold for $2.2 million and replaced with new equipment costing $3.8 million. The old equipment is three years old and is being depreciated over five years with no salvage value in the financial statements. BATNM received 100% of the cost of the old machine as a tax deduction when it was purchased three years ago because the company is located in a designated tax enterprise zone. The new equipment would similarly qualify for a 100% deduction allowance in the year of purchase. Note that as a result of the replacement of equipment, inventory levels would increase by $200,000.

To help with the calculation, Marlinton has obtained a current summary balance sheet for the firm and a forecasted summary income statement for the year ahead, as shown in Exhibit 2. Marlinton assumes that the current balance sheet levels of debt and equity reflect BATNM's target capital structure. The tax rate for the company is 35%.

Exhibit 2: Summarized Financial Statements (current/forecasted)

Current Balance Sheet as of 1 January 2016

Assets	($ Thousands)	
Current assets		
Inventory	51,307	
Accounts receivable	36,860	
Cash	76,402	
Other	42,893	
Total		**207,462**
Long-lived assets		
PPE		381,569
Goodwill		3,683
Other		12,447
Total		**605,161**
Liabilities and equity		
Current liabilities		
Accounts payable	22,576	
Short-term debt	120	
Other	74,539	
Total		**97,235**
Long-term liabilities		
Long-term debt		74,953
Other		7,606
Total		**179,794**
Equity		
Common stock		200,458
Additional paid in capital		224,909
Total liabilities and equity		**605,161**

**Forecasted Income Statement
Year Ended 31 December 2016**

	($ Thousands)
Revenue	248,303
Operating income	40,502
Net income	26,034

Marlinton is concerned that any dividend policy adopted should allow BATNM to stay closely aligned with its target capital structure. He is concerned that any significant increase in debt would lead to a sharp increase in the cost of equity. He has prepared an analysis to test this effect using Modigliani and Miller's theory of capital structure in a world with taxes.

In his analysis, Marlinton assumes that the cost of equity if BATNM was all equity financed would be 15%. He intends to work out the increase in the current cost of equity if $40 million of debt at a cost of 8% was added to the current balance sheet. In his analysis, he intends to also assume that the amount of equity remains constant. Marlinton recognizes that most of the assets of the company (e.g., brewing equipment) are tangible, and, hence, the cost of financial distress will be lower for BATNM relative to companies with mostly intangible assets.

Marlinton believes that maintaining the target capital structure is much more important than dividend policy. He thinks that the company should finance its projects by giving the highest preference to the method with the least potential information content and the lowest preference to the form with the greatest.

103. Regarding the CEO's comments regarding the benefits of a residual dividend policy, Marlinton will *most likely* conclude that:
    A. both are correct.
    B. only benefit 1 is accurate.
    C. only benefit 2 is accurate.

104. The expected 2016 dividend under a residual dividend policy and scenario I is *closest* to:
    A. $3,000,000.
    B. $2,230,000.
    C. zero.

105. The initial outlay to be included in Marlinton's NPV calculation for the project in scenario II is *closest* to:
    A. $3,250,000
    B. $2,900,000
    C. $2,570,000

106. Using Marlinton's assumptions in his capital structure analysis, after the additional debt of $40 million, the cost of equity would *most likely* be:
    A. 16.2%
    B. 17.7%
    C. 18.1%

107. Marlinton's assumptions regarding BATNM's costs of financial distress are *most likely*:
    A. Correct.
    B. incorrect as the costs of financial distress are related to debt levels and not related to assets.
    C. incorrect as the costs of financial distress are higher if the company's balance sheet is made up of mostly tangible assets.

108. Marlinton's suggested method of financing projects is *most likely* to be referred to as:
    A. the pecking order theory.
    B. the static trade-off theory.
    C. Modigliani and Miller proposition II.

Questions 109–114 relate to Trailblazer, Inc.

Louise Valentine, CFA, is analyzing the financial information of Trailblazer, Inc., a company in the retail sector. She is preparing to write a report on her findings. Valentine is considering various valuation approaches and is convinced that a dividend discount model (DDM) would be among the best choices in this case. She notes that Trailblazer does not vary its dividend payments significantly from year to year.

In preparing to estimate a suitable required rate of return on equity for Trailblazer, Valentine notes that the current T-bill rate is 3.5% and that the yield on the company's 10-year bonds is 7.25% while the yield on a 10-year Treasury bond is 4.4%. Additionally, Valentine estimates that the appropriate equity risk premium in excess of the company's cost of debt is 3%. Valentine estimates that average dividend yield for the S&P 500 (the market proxy) is 2.1% and a consensus long-term EPS growth rate of 3.5% is forecast for S&P 500 index.

Valentine also gathers the information shown in Exhibit 1.

Exhibit 1: Trailblazer, Inc. Multifactor Sensitivities (APT)

Factor	Factor Risk Premium	Trailblazer, Inc. Factor Sensitivities
1	1.91%	0.81
2	1.22%	−0.45
3	3.47%	0.24
4	4.15%	0.74

In her report, Valentine makes the following statements about Trailblazer dividends:

Statement 1:   Trailblazer is expected to pay a dividend next year and will continue to do so for the foreseeable future.

Statement 2:   The required rate of return for Trailblazer stock will likely exceed the growth rate of its dividends.

Statement 3:   Trailblazer is in a mature sector of its industry, and accordingly, I expect dividends to decline at a constant rate of 4% indefinitely.

In speaking to a colleague at her firm, Valentine makes the following additional statements after her report is released:

Statement 4:   Trailblazer has a 10-year history of paying regular quarterly dividends.

Statement 5:   Over a recent 10-year period, Trailblazer has experienced one 3-year period of consecutive losses and another period of two annual losses in a row but has been extremely profitable in the remaining five years.

Valentine is concerned with some of the inputs for estimating the cost of equity for other companies that she follows. Based on her research, she makes the following statements:

Statement 6:   We have used historical equity risk premium as input into the CAPM. However, we should adjust the said equity risk premium because it includes some unfavorable surprises in productivity declines and higher inflation due to oil price shocks.

Statement 7:   When estimating beta of a private company using a public company peer, the private company beta should be adjusted for the difference in leverage between the public company and the private company, as well as the difference in their respective sizes.

Valentine is also analyzing the stock of Farwell, Inc. Farwell shares are currently trading at $48 based on current earnings of $4 and a current dividend of $2.60. Dividends are expected to grow at 5% per year indefinitely. The risk-free rate is 3.5%, the market risk premium is 4.5%, and Farwell's beta is estimated to be 1.2.

109.   Based on the APT model and the bond yield plus risk-premium (BYPRP) method, the discount rate Valentine should use in valuing the equity of Trailblazer is *closest* to:

Rate based on APT	Rate based on BYPRP
A. 8.40%	10.25%
B. 4.90%	10.25%
C. 4.90%	7.25%

110.   The forward-looking estimate of average equity risk premium (based on the S&P 500 index as market proxy) is *closest* to:
   A. 1.2%.
   B. 2.1%.
   C. 5.6%.

111. How many of the first three statements Valentine made concerning Trailblazer's dividends are consistent with assumptions of the Gordon growth model (GGM)?
    A. None.
    B. Two.
    C. Three.

112. Do statements 4 and 5 support the decision by Valentine to use a dividend discount model?
    A. Both statements support the use of DDM.
    B. Only Statement 4 supports the use of DDM.
    C. Only Statement 5 supports the use of DDM.

113. Are statements 6 and 7 correct?
    A. Both statements are incorrect.
    B. Only Statement 6 is incorrect.
    C. Only Statement 7 is incorrect.

114. The justified leading and justified trailing P/E ratios of Farwell are *closest* to:

	Justified leading P/E	Justified trailing P/E
A.	16.67	9.42
B.	8.97	17.50
C.	16.67	17.50

Questions 115–120 relate to Tom Vadney.

Tom Vadney, CFA, is president and CEO of Vadney Research and Advisors (VRA), a large equity research firm that specializes in providing international investment and advisory services to global portfolio managers. He has a staff of five junior analysts and three senior analysts covering industries and firms across the Americas, Europe, and Asia-Pacific regions.

In a recent meeting with an institutional portfolio manager, Vadney is asked to review the differences between U.S. GAAP and International Financial Reporting Standards (IFRS) as well as provide a comprehensive industry analysis for the telecommunications sector in Europe and the Asia-Pacific region. Vadney asks Maria Mnoyan, a senior analyst covering the sector, to research the requested information for the client meeting.

Prior to the meeting, Vadney and Mnoyan meet to prepare for the client presentation. They first discuss differences between U.S. GAAP and IFRS. Mnoyan states that although there will be increasing convergence between the two accounting standards, one major difference currently is that IFRS permits either the "partial goodwill" or "full goodwill" method to value goodwill and a noncontrolling interest under the acquisition method, U.S. GAAP requires the full goodwill method. Vadney adds that U.S. GAAP requires equity method accounting for joint ventures, while under IFRS proportionate consolidation is preferred, but the equity method is permitted.

Vadney then asks Mnoyan to share her findings on the telecommunications sector. Mnoyan first presents an overview of the competitive forces that characterize the sector in the two regions. In particular, she notes that the sector is characterized by high switching costs in both regions. Vadney asks how high switching costs would affect the bargaining power of buyers and suppliers.

Mnoyan firmly believes that investing in companies located in developing countries provides strong return prospects as the growth rate in labor productivity increases through technological change and increases in capital.

For example, Mnoyan considers Dien Thoai Corporation, a rapidly growing telecommunication firm in an emerging market country. Dien Thoai is likely to be an acquisition target given the global ambitions of larger firms in developed markets. Mnoyan is interested in calculating the present value of growth opportunities (PVGO) for Dien Thoai. She proposes dividing the last dividend paid by Dien Thoai by the required rate of return to find the value of Dien Thoai's assets in place, and then subtracting this from fundamental value to find PVGO.

Dien Thoai's dividend yield based on the most recent dividend paid is 5%. Dividends and earnings are expected to grow 12% next year, but that rate is expected to decrease linearly over the next six years to a long-term rate of 3% per year.

115. Are Mnoyan and Vadney correct about differences between U.S. GAAP and IFRS?
    A. Both are correct.
    B. Only Mnoyan is correct.
    C. Only Vadney is correct.

116. Mnoyan's *best* response to Vadney on how high switching costs affect the bargaining power of buyers and suppliers, respectively, should be:
    A. only the bargaining power of buyers will decrease.
    B. only the bargaining power of suppliers will decrease.
    C. the bargaining power of buyers and suppliers will decrease.

117. Mnoyan's description of the growth potential of developing countries is *best* described as the:
    A. classical growth theory.
    B. neoclassical growth theory.
    C. endogenous growth theory.

118. What adjustment to her calculation method does Mnoyan need to make to correctly calculate PVGO? The value of assets in place is given by:
    A. the previous dividend multiplied by one plus the sustainable growth rate, divided by the required rate of return.
    B. earnings divided by the required rate of return.
    C. earnings, divided by the required rate of return minus the sustainable growth rate.

119. For this question only, suppose that the current market price of Dien Thoai Corporation is $78.50. The required rate of return on Dien Thoai stock is *closest* to:
    A. 9.5%.
    B. 10.8%.
    C. 11.3%.

120. Which of the following is NOT a strength of multistage Dividend Discount Models?
    A. Models can be used either in forward or reverse to identify values given assumptions of growth and required return or to derive required returns and projected growth rates implied by market prices.
    B. Models are straightforward in the relationship between assumptions and resulting estimates of value, allowing the analyst to review all the assumptions built into the models and to consider the impact of different assumptions.
    C. Models are sensitive to assumptions of growth, allowing variability in potential values.

End of Afternoon Session

Exam 2
Morning Session

Question	Topic	Minutes (Points)
1 to 6	Ethics	18
7 to 12	Corporate Finance	18
13 to 18	Equity	18
19 to 24	Equity	18
25 to 30	Equity	18
31 to 36	Equity	18
37 to 42	Fixed Income	18
43 to 48	Derivatives	18
49 to 54	Derivatives	18
55 to 60	Portfolio Management	18

Test Answers

1.	Ⓐ	Ⓑ	Ⓒ		41.	Ⓐ	Ⓑ	Ⓒ
2.	Ⓐ	Ⓑ	Ⓒ		42.	Ⓐ	Ⓑ	Ⓒ
3.	Ⓐ	Ⓑ	Ⓒ		43.	Ⓐ	Ⓑ	Ⓒ
4.	Ⓐ	Ⓑ	Ⓒ		44.	Ⓐ	Ⓑ	Ⓒ
5.	Ⓐ	Ⓑ	Ⓒ		45.	Ⓐ	Ⓑ	Ⓒ
6.	Ⓐ	Ⓑ	Ⓒ		46.	Ⓐ	Ⓑ	Ⓒ
7.	Ⓐ	Ⓑ	Ⓒ		47.	Ⓐ	Ⓑ	Ⓒ
8.	Ⓐ	Ⓑ	Ⓒ		48.	Ⓐ	Ⓑ	Ⓒ
9.	Ⓐ	Ⓑ	Ⓒ		49.	Ⓐ	Ⓑ	Ⓒ
10.	Ⓐ	Ⓑ	Ⓒ		50.	Ⓐ	Ⓑ	Ⓒ
11.	Ⓐ	Ⓑ	Ⓒ		51.	Ⓐ	Ⓑ	Ⓒ
12.	Ⓐ	Ⓑ	Ⓒ		52.	Ⓐ	Ⓑ	Ⓒ
13.	Ⓐ	Ⓑ	Ⓒ		53.	Ⓐ	Ⓑ	Ⓒ
14.	Ⓐ	Ⓑ	Ⓒ		54.	Ⓐ	Ⓑ	Ⓒ
15.	Ⓐ	Ⓑ	Ⓒ		55.	Ⓐ	Ⓑ	Ⓒ
16.	Ⓐ	Ⓑ	Ⓒ		56.	Ⓐ	Ⓑ	Ⓒ
17.	Ⓐ	Ⓑ	Ⓒ		57.	Ⓐ	Ⓑ	Ⓒ
18.	Ⓐ	Ⓑ	Ⓒ		58.	Ⓐ	Ⓑ	Ⓒ
19.	Ⓐ	Ⓑ	Ⓒ		59.	Ⓐ	Ⓑ	Ⓒ
20.	Ⓐ	Ⓑ	Ⓒ		60.	Ⓐ	Ⓑ	Ⓒ
21.	Ⓐ	Ⓑ	Ⓒ					
22.	Ⓐ	Ⓑ	Ⓒ					
23.	Ⓐ	Ⓑ	Ⓒ					
24.	Ⓐ	Ⓑ	Ⓒ					
25.	Ⓐ	Ⓑ	Ⓒ					
26.	Ⓐ	Ⓑ	Ⓒ					
27.	Ⓐ	Ⓑ	Ⓒ					
28.	Ⓐ	Ⓑ	Ⓒ					
29.	Ⓐ	Ⓑ	Ⓒ					
30.	Ⓐ	Ⓑ	Ⓒ					
31.	Ⓐ	Ⓑ	Ⓒ					
32.	Ⓐ	Ⓑ	Ⓒ					
33.	Ⓐ	Ⓑ	Ⓒ					
34.	Ⓐ	Ⓑ	Ⓒ					
35.	Ⓐ	Ⓑ	Ⓒ					
36.	Ⓐ	Ⓑ	Ⓒ					
37.	Ⓐ	Ⓑ	Ⓒ					
38.	Ⓐ	Ⓑ	Ⓒ					
39.	Ⓐ	Ⓑ	Ⓒ					
40.	Ⓐ	Ⓑ	Ⓒ					

Exam 2
Morning Session

Questions 1–6 relate to Carol Blackwell.

Carol Blackwell, CFA, has been hired into the research department of Blanchard Investments. Blanchard's manager, Thaddeus Baldwin, CFA, has worked in the securities business for more than 50 years. On Blackwell's first day at the office, Baldwin gives her an incomplete research report on Tops Groceries, Inc., to finish up.

Upon researching Tops, information about the financial instability of Tops Groceries' largest customer surfaces. Blackwell revises the research report by lowering the earnings projections. The day the report is to be released, Blackwell learns that Baldwin has replaced the lower, revised earnings projections with his earlier estimates.

Baldwin realizes that many of the firm's practices and policies would benefit from a compliance check. Because Blanchard recently adopted CFA Institute's Research Objectivity Standards, Baldwin wants Blackwell to ensure that the policies and procedures at the firm are in compliance.

During one of his many television interviews, Baldwin was asked about Patel, Inc. Baldwin replied that he had dropped coverage of Patel, but he hadn't had the time to publish a drop coverage note in light of his extensive travel schedule. Since Patel's auditors had announced uncertainty about the firm's ability to remain a going concern five months ago, Baldwin decided to focus on other stocks in the industry instead.

Blanchard's investment banking department recently announced that they were successful in obtaining the account of Teos Toys, Inc. In light of this announcement, Baldwin wants to know whether he can continue to rate Teos' stock favorably.

During a local society luncheon, Blackwell is seated next to CFA candidate Lucas Walters, who has been assigned the task of creating a compliance manual for Borchard & Sons, a small brokerage firm. Walters asks for her advice.

When Walters returns to work, he is apprised of the following situation: Borchard & Sons purchased 25,000 shares of CBX Corp. for equity manager Quintux Quantitative just minutes before the money manager called back and said it meant to buy 25,000 shares of CDX Corp. Borchard then purchased CDX shares for Quintux, but not before shares of CBX Corp. declined by 1.5%. The broker is holding the CBX shares in its own inventory.

Borchard proposes three methods for dealing with the trading error.

Method 1: Quintux directs additional trades to Borchard worth a dollar value equal to the amount of the trading loss.

Method 2: Borchard receives investment research from Quintux in exchange for Borchard covering the costs of the trading error.

Method 3: Borchard transfers the ordered CBX shares in its inventory to Quintux, which allocates them to all of its clients on a pro-rata basis.

1. Blackwell's *most appropriate* course of action to remain in compliance with the Research Objectivity Standards (ROS) is to:
    A. include a disclosure indicating that lower earnings estimates are available.
    B. follow up the first report with a second report emphasizing lower earnings projections.
    C. remove his name from the report if they release the report with higher earnings estimates.

2. When updating the proxy-voting policy to conform to CFA Institute recommendations, which of the following recommendations is *least appropriate* for Blanchard to adopt?
    A. Determine the economic impact of non-routine proxy votes.
    B. Follow the same proxy-voting procedures regardless of the nature of the proposal.
    C. If the proxy voter's preference differs from the preference of a client who has delegated his voting powers, go with the client's preference.

3. According to the Standards of Professional Conduct, Baldwin's *most appropriate* action regarding Teos Toys would be to:
    A. refuse to have any involvement with Teos because of a conflict of interest arising from the firm's other relationships with the company.
    B. complete an independent and objective analysis of Teos and issue a report accordingly.
    C. provide a copy of the research report to analysts at reputable research outfits and ask for some input.

4. Was Baldwin in compliance with the recommended procedures of the CFA Institute Research Objectivity Standards (ROS) with regard to the timeliness of research reports on Patel, Inc.?
    A. Yes, because he announced that he had dropped coverage in a public appearance on television.
    B. Yes, a negative report from an auditor is sufficient justification for dropping coverage of a stock.
    C. No.

5.   If Walters wants the manual to satisfy the requirements and recommendations of the Code and Standards, which of the following instructions is *least appropriate* to include in the section on fair dealing?
      A. Whenever possible, disseminate investment recommendations to all clients at the same time.
      B. Execute all clients' requested trades promptly and without comment, regardless of the company's opinion on the stock being traded.
      C. Members of the investment-policy committee should not discuss possible changes in investment recommendations with anyone else in the firm until after an official decision has been made.

6.   Which method for dealing with the trading error is *most* consistent with the Code and Standards?
      A. Method 1.
      B. Method 2.
      C. Method 3.

Questions 7–12 relate to Dan Andrews.

Dan Andrews, CFA is the equity analyst for a large pension fund. One of the fund's holdings is Debian Corporation. After a period of rapid growth, Debian has underperformed its peers over the past two years. Debian's management has announced a change in ownership structure for part of its business, or possibly a disposal of part of the business. Several options are under consideration: a spin-off, a carve-out, or an asset sale. Andrews decides to research each of these options to understand the impact on Debian's business and their shareholders. He has read the following comments regarding the various methods:

Statement 1: Involves shares being issued to the general public.

Statement 2: Shareholders have a choice of holding onto the new shares automatically issued to them or disposing of the shares on the open market.

Statement 3: Shareholders will be more easily able to link executive compensation to the performance of the business involved.

Statement 4: The firm separates a portion of its operations from the parent company.

Statement 5: A new independent entity will be created that is completely distinct from the parent; the parent will lose all control of the business.

Debian's management announced in the last conference call that a potential buyer, Fedora, Inc., is interested in buying Ubuntu, one of Debian's divisions. Fedora has offered to pay $90 million cash to buy Ubuntu. Relevant information is provided in Exhibit 1.

Exhibit 1

Value of Ubuntu as a stand-alone business	$78 million
Value of Ubuntu to Debian	$85 million
Value of Fedora (5 million shares, $10 par)	$132 million
Value of Fedora and Ubuntu as a combined entity (post cash acquisition of Ubuntu)	$135 million

Alternatively, Fedora is prepared to offer to buy Ubuntu by directly issuing to the shareholders of Debian a total of 3 million $10 par value shares that will rank equally with its existing shares.

Andrews frequents continuing education seminars offered by his local CFA society. During one of these seminars, Andrews meets Jason Arnold, a corporate governance specialist. Andrews agrees with Arnold that a comprehensive equity analysis should include an analysis of corporate governance. Andrews, however, is unsure of the core attributes of an effective corporate governance system. Arnold states that he could recall two specific attributes:

Attribute 1: Description of rights and responsibilities of shareholders and other stakeholders.

Attribute 2: Fairness and equitable treatment in all dealings between managers, directors, and shareholders.

Among other companies that Andrews is researching, he has identified a potential acquisition target, Mandriva, Inc. Mandriva has enjoyed good growth over the past few years and is expected to continue to do so in the near future. Andrews wants to value Mandriva using both the comparable company method and the comparable transaction approach. Andrews obtains data on recent acquisitions of similar companies. Exhibit 2 summarizes this data:

Exhibit 2

- The mean price-to-book ratio of comparable firms is estimated to be 2 times, and the mean price-to-earnings ratio of the same comparable firms is 25 times.
- The mean acquisition price-to-book ratio of recent targets is estimated to be 2.80 times, and the mean price-to-earnings ratio of the same firms is 30 times.
- Mandriva's book value per share is $18, and EPS is $1.50.
- The mean takeover premium of recent acquisitions in the same industry as Mandriva is estimated to be 30%.

---

7. Which of the statements correctly reflect aspects of a carve-out?
    A. Statements 1, 4, and 5 only.
    B. Statements 1, 3, and 4 only.
    C. Statements 2, 3, and 4 only.

8. If Fedora pays $90 million cash for the purchase of Ubuntu from Debian, what will be the gain to Debian's and Fedora's shareholders?

	Debian's S/H	Fedora's S/H
A.	$5 million	$3 million
B.	$12 million	$5 million
C.	$12 million	$7 million

9. If Debian shareholders accept the stock offer by Fedora, the economic impact on them would be *closest* to:
   A. a gain of $630,000.
   B. a loss of $630,000.
   C. a loss of $1,612,500.

10. Under Fedora's stock offer, the economic impact on the current shareholders of Fedora is *closest* to:
    A. a loss of $7.5 million.
    B. a gain of $8.6 million.
    C. a gain of $1.6 million.

11. Are Arnold's attributes 1 and 2 of an effective corporate governance system correct?
    A. Both of these attributes are incorrect.
    B. Only one of these attributes is correct.
    C. Both of these attributes are correct.

12. Using the data collected by Andrews, the target takeover price per share of Mandriva under the comparable company analysis and under the comparable transaction analysis is *closest* to:

Comparable company	Comparable transaction
A. $24	$48
B. $24	$50
C. $48	$48

Questions 13–18 relate to Pacific Computer Components (PCC).

General Investments is considering the purchase of a significant stake in Pacific Computer Components (PCC). Although PCC has stable production output, the company is located in a developing country with an uncertain economic environment. Since the monetary environment is particularly worrisome, General has decided to approach the valuation of PCC from a free cash flow model using real growth rates. In real rate analysis, General uses a modified build-up method for calculating the required real return, specifically:

required real return = country real rate + industry adjustment + company adjustment

Elias Sando, CFA, an analyst with General, estimates the following information for PCC:

Domestic inflation rate = 8.738%
Nominal growth rate = 12.000%
Real country return = 3.000%
Industry adjustment = 3.000%
Company adjustment = 2.000%

Additionally, Exhibit 1 reports information from PCC's financial statements for the year just ended (stated in LC).

Exhibit 1: Selected Financial Statement Information for PCC

Investment in fixed capital	LC3,200,000
Investment in working capital	LC400,000
New borrowing	LC2,400,000
Debt repayment	LC2,000,000
Depreciation	LC3,500,000
Interest expense	LC5,000,000
Net income	LC7,000,000
Tax rate	34%
Dividends	LC0

PCC generally maintains relatively constant proportions of equity and debt financing and is expected to do so going forward.

Sando has gathered information on earnings before interest, taxes, depreciation, and amortization (EBITDA) and is contemplating its direct use in another cash flow approach aimed at valuing PCC. Consider the following two statements regarding EBITDA:

Statement 1:   EBITDA is not a good proxy for free cash flow to the firm (FCFF) because it does not incorporate the importance of the depreciation tax shield, nor does it reflect the investment in working capital or in fixed capital.

Statement 2:   EBITDA is also a poor proxy for FCFE.

13.   Free cash flow to equity (FCFE) is *closest* to:
    A. LC7,300,000.
    B. LC8,400,000.
    C. LC10,200,000.

14.   Free cash flow to the firm (FCFF) for PCC is *closest* to:
    A. LC7,300,000.
    B. LC8,100,000.
    C. LC10,200,000.

15.   The current value of PCC equity using a FCFE model is *closest* to:
    A. LC150,380,000.
    B. LC173,420,000.
    C. LC215,150,000.

16.   Suppose that PCC initiates a cash dividend, with a target payout ratio of 25% of net income. What is the *likely* magnitude of the effect of the new cash dividend and the net change in the outstanding debt on future FCFE, all else equal?
    A. The dividend has a large effect, and the debt change has a small effect.
    B. The dividend has a large effect, and the debt change has no effect.
    C. The dividend has no effect, and the debt change has a small effect.

17.   Under the assumption that PCC maintains relatively constant proportions of equity and debt financing, the *most appropriate* valuation model is the:
    A. FCFF approach.
    B. FCFE approach.
    C. residual income approach.

18.   Are the statements concerning EBITDA correct or incorrect?
    A. Only Statement 1 is correct.
    B. Only Statement 2 is correct.
    C. Both statements are correct.

Questions 19–24 relate to Global Drug World.

Carl Warner, CFA, has been asked to review the financial information of Global Drug World (GDW) in preparation for a possible takeover bid by rival competitor Consolidated Drugstores International (Consolidated). GDW has produced impressive results since going public via an initial public offering in 1998. Through a program of aggressive growth by acquisition, GDW is currently seen as a major player and a threat to Consolidated's own plans for growth and profitability. In preparation for his analysis, Warner has gathered the following financial data from GDW's year-end statements:

GDW Statement of Income for Year ended May 31, 2008

Sales	4,052,173
Expenses	
Cost of goods sold, general and operating expenses	3,735,397
Noncash charges	56,293
Interest on long-term debt	20,265
Other interest	5,223
	3,817,178
Income before income taxes	234,995
Income taxes	70,499
Net income	164,497
Earnings per share	0.72

Partial GDW Balance Sheet on May 31, 2008

Assets	
Current assets (excluding cash)	
Accounts receivable	284,762
Inventories	490,755
Prepaid expenses	23,743
Total current assets (excluding cash)	799,260
Property, plant, and equipment	687,890
Other assets	236,417

Liabilities	
Current liabilities (excluding notes payable)	
Accounts payable and accrued liabilities	296,564
Other	100,039
Total current liabilities (excluding notes payable)	396,603
Long-term debt	262,981
Other liabilities	15,484

Additional Information	
Risk-free rate	4.5%
WACC	7.5%
2008 working capital investment	$7,325
2008 dividends	$82,248
Beta	1.10
Investment in fixed capital in 2008	$143,579
Market risk premium	5%
Total equity May 31, 2007	$1,019,869
Principal repayment of long-term debt in 2008	$33,275
Notes payable issued in 2008	$5,866
2008 change in liabilities	$27,409
Tax rate	30%

As part of his analysis, Warner needs to forecast the free cash flow to the firm (FCFF) for 2009. The best information he has points to an increase in sales of 6%. The earnings before interest and tax (EBIT) margin is not expected to change from the rate of 6.4% achieved in 2008. Additional fixed capital spending is expected to be $36,470. Investment in net working capital is expected to be $24,313. Moreover, Warner notes that the only noncash charge is depreciation, which he estimates will be $60,000.

Warner has been asked to analyze the effect each of the following corporate events, if taken during 2009, would have on GDW's free cash flow to equity (FCFE):

- 20% increase in dividends per share.
- Repurchase of 25% of the firm's outstanding shares using cash.
- New common share offering that would increase shares outstanding by 30%.
- New issue of convertible bonds that are not callable for five years and would increase the level of debt by 10%.

19. The 2008 free cash flow to the firm (FCFF) for Global Drug World (GDW) in dollars is *closest* to:
    A. $87,728.
    B. $95,374.
    C. $102,378.

20. By how much (in dollars) does GDW's FCFF exceed its free cash flow to equity (FCFE) in 2008?
    A. $9,567.
    B. $45,251.
    C. $52,897.

21. The cost of equity and the sustainable growth rate (using beginning equity) are *closest* to:

	Cost of equity	Sustainable growth rate
A.	6%	16%
B.	10%	8%
C.	10%	16%

22. The 2009 estimate of FCFF is *closest* to:
    A. $191,646.
    B. $210,329.
    C. $215,329.

23. Warner determines that on a per-share basis, the FCFE for GDW in 2008 is $0.19. Further analysis suggests that FCFE per share will grow by $0.02 in each of the next two years before leveling off to a long-term growth rate of 5%. The current value of one share of GDW's equity is *closest* to:
    A. $4.37.
    B. $7.15.
    C. $13.49.

24. Which corporate event that Warner is analyzing is *likely* to have the largest effect on FCFE in 2009?
    A. Share repurchase.
    B. Share offering.
    C. Convertible bond issue.

Questions 25–30 relate to Lee Nguyen Investments.

Marie LeBlanc, CFA, is an analyst at Lee Nguyen Investments, an international equities investment firm. LeBlanc has been asked to value two European cosmetics companies, Schön AG and Hermosa S.A.

The beauty products industry is a mature industry with few competitors. One segment that is growing is luxury skin care; while the cosmetics industry is expected to grow at a steady rate of 3.5%, the luxury skin care segment is expected to grow at 5.5%.

Schön AG, based in Frankfort, Germany, is the largest company in the luxury skin care segment of the cosmetics industry. Schön is considered a very stable company within the cosmetics industry and the luxury skin care segment. Schön's equity beta is 1.00.

LeBlanc collects selected financial information from Schön's income statement and cash flow statement (for the last fiscal year) and from Schön's balance sheet (for the last 2 fiscal year ends). The information is shown in Exhibit 1. Negative numbers are indicated in parentheses. There is no preferred stock, and no long-term asset sales occurred in 20X9.

Exhibit 1: Selected Schön Financial Information (€ millions except for rates and ratios.)

Income Statement	20X9	Balance Sheet	20X8	20X9
Revenue	4,250	Total current assets	2,408	2,577
EBITDA	1,461	Net PPE	3,794	4,150
Operating income	1,169	Notes payable	600	644
Interest expense	150	Long-term debt	2,020	2,070
Income tax rate	30%	Total liabilities	3,210	3,378
Dividends	357	Total equity	2,992	3,349

Other Information	20X9
CF from operations	1,042
CF from investing	(648)
Risk-free rate	2.50%
After-tax cost of debt	4.50%
Cost of equity	8.50%
Target D/E Ratio	1.00

Hermosa S.A., based in Barcelona, Spain, is the third largest company in the luxury skin care segment of the cosmetics industry. Hermosa is considered a growth company within the cosmetics industry and the luxury skin care segment. Hermosa has not issued bonds and all of Hermosa's debt is considered short and intermediate term. For the fiscal year 20X9, FCFF is €143 million and FCFE is €136.23 million. Hermosa pays no dividends. Hermosa's earnings are expected to grow at 14.0% for three years and then at the expected overall rate of growth in the luxury skin care segment. Hermosa's equity beta is 1.20. The risk-free rate is 2.5%. Hermosa's target weight for debt is 25.0%.

LeBlanc gathers additional information on the various companies in luxury skin care industry as shown in Exhibit 2.

Exhibit 2: Luxury Skin Care Stocks

Company	Price per share	Shares outstanding (in millions)	Earnings (trailing twelve months) (in millions)
Schön	€15.42	1,000	€713
Epiderm	€14.95	500	€345
Hermosa	€22.78	200	€193
Radiance	€18.50	100	€75
Bello	€24.78	50	€24

The trailing price-to-earnings ratio for the luxury skin care segment is 22.9X.

Elizabeth Nguyen, one of the partners at Lee Nguyen Investments, approaches LeBlanc about a client interested in buying Hermosa S.A. Nguyen asks LeBlanc about the different methods LeBlanc used to value Hermosa as a buyout possibility.

LeBlanc states that she used three different approaches in her report:

Approach 1: Dividend discount model.

Approach 2: Free cash flow to the firm model.

Approach 3: Trailing price-to-earnings multiples.

25. The free cash flow to equity for Schön AG for 20X9 is *closest* to:
    A. €439 million.
    B. €488 million.
    C. €499 million.

26. Assuming that the growth rate of Schön earnings is equal to the overall cosmetics industry growth rate, the value of the firm is *closest* to:
    A. €17.2 billion.
    B. €33.6 billion.
    C. €49.9 billion.

27. The estimated value of Hermosa stock using FCFE valuation is *closest* to:
    A. €19.70.
    B. €21.40.
    C. €22.10.

28. If the estimated value of Schön's equity based on free cash flow to equity is €17.1 billion, then based on current market price, Schön's stock is:
    A. overvalued.
    B. undervalued.
    C. fairly valued.

29. Using the luxury skin care P/E ratio as the benchmark, Hermosa is *best described* as:
    A. overvalued.
    B. undervalued.
    C. fairly valued.

30. The best approach to valuing Hermosa for a potential acquirer is *most likely*:
    A. Approach #1—Dividend discount model.
    B. Approach #2—Free cash flow to the firm model.
    C. Approach #3—Trailing price-to-earnings multiples.

Questions 31–36 relate to Amie Lear.

Amie Lear, CFA, is a quantitative analyst employed by a brokerage firm. She has been assigned by her supervisor to cover a number of different equity and debt investments. One of the investments is Taylor, Inc. (Taylor), a manufacturer of a wide range of children's toys. Based on her extensive analysis, she determines that her expected return on the stock, given Taylor's risks, is 10%. In applying the capital asset pricing model (CAPM), the result is a 12% rate of return.

For her analysis of the returns of Devon, Inc. (Devon), a manufacturer of high-end sports apparel, Lear intends to use the Fama-French model (FFM). Devon is a small-cap growth stock that has traded at a low market-to-book value in recent years. Lear's analysis has provided a wealth of quantitative information to consider. The return on a value-weighted market index minus the risk-free rate is 5.5%, the small-cap return premium is 3.1%, the value return premium is 2.2%, and the liquidity premium is 3.3%. The risk-free rate is 3.4%. The market, size, relative value, and liquidity betas for Devon are 0.7, –0.3, 1.4, and 1.2, respectively. In estimating the appropriate equity risk premium, Lear has chosen to use the Gordon growth model.

Lear's assistant, Doug Saunders, presents her with a report on macroeconomic multifactor models that includes the following two statements:

Statement 1: Business cycle risk represents the unexpected change in the difference between the return of risky corporate bonds and government bonds.

Statement 2: Confidence risk represents the unexpected change in the level of real business activity.

Lear is also attempting to determine the most appropriate method for determining the required return for Densmore, Inc. (Densmore), a closely held company that is considering a debt issue within the next year. The company has not previously issued debt securities to the public, relying instead on bank financing. She realizes that there are a number of models to consider, including the CAPM, multifactor models, and build-up models.

31.   Based on Lear's analysis, Taylor's stock is *most likely* to be:
       A. correctly valued.
       B. overvalued.
       C. undervalued.

32. According to the FFM, the estimate of the required return for Devon is *closest* to:
    A. 9.4%.
    B. 11.8%.
    C. 13.4%.

33. Lear's choice of the Gordon growth model is an example of which of the following types of estimates of the equity risk premium?
    A. Historical estimate.
    B. Forward-looking estimate.
    C. Macroeconomic model estimate.

34. Which of the following approaches/methods is *most appropriate* for Lear to consider in determining the required return for Densmore?
    A. Build-up method.
    B. Risk premium approach.
    C. Bond-yield plus risk premium method.

35. Are Saunders's statements regarding the macroeconomic multifactor models correct?
    A. Both statements are incorrect.
    B. Only Statement 1 is correct.
    C. Only Statement 2 is correct.

36. Which of the following statements regarding the models used to estimate the required return is *most accurate*?
    A. A strength of the capital asset pricing model (CAPM) is that it usually has high explanatory power.
    B. A strength of multifactor models is their relative simplicity and ease of calculation.
    C. A weakness of build-up models is that they typically use historical values as estimates that may not be relevant to current market conditions.

Questions 37–42 relate to Ranjit Dhami and Paul Stamper.

Ranjit Dhami has just joined Apex Bank NA as an intern in the bond trading department. Sue Jorgenson, Dhami's immediate supervisor, provides him with the current par rate curve for government bonds shown in Exhibit 1.

Exhibit 1: Selected Par Rates

Maturity	Par Rate
1	1.50%
2	2.00%
3	2.25%

A binomial interest rate tree with a 20% volatility assumption is shown in Exhibit 2.

Exhibit 2: Binomial Interest Rate Tree

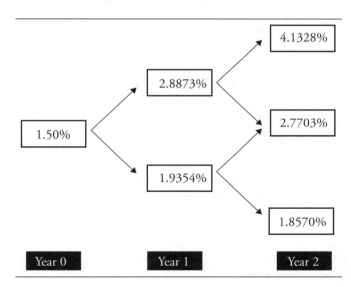

Paul Stamper, one of the bond traders at Apex, shows Dhami information about several trades currently being evaluated. Exhibit 3 shows information on two of the bonds.

Exhibit 3: Selected Information on Potential Trades

Characteristic	Bond A	Bond B
Maturity	3 years	2 years
Option	Callable at par in 1 year	Putable at par in 1 year
Coupon	2%	1.50%
Par Value	$100	$100

Stamper asks Dhami the following questions:

Question 1:   Which bond in Exhibit 3 is most likely to exhibit negative convexity?

Question 2:   For a given decline in interest rate, which bond is most likely to have lower upside potential?

37.   Using the information in Exhibit 1, the three-year spot rate is *closest* to:
A. 2.26%.
B. 2.56%.
C. 2.62%.

38.   Using the information in Exhibit 1, the one-year forward rate two years from now is *closest* to:
A. 2.25%.
B. 2.39%.
C. 2.77%.

39.   If the three-year forward price of a three-year zero-coupon bond is $0.9151 (per $1 par), the price today of a six-year zero-coupon bond should be *closest* to:
A. $0.7899.
B. $0.8431.
C. $0.9311.

40.   The price of bond A in Exhibit 3 is *most accurately* described as being sensitive to shifts in:
A. the one-year par rate only.
B. the three-year par rate only.
C. both the one-year and three-year par rates.

41. The *most accurate* answers to Stamper's questions are:

	Question 1	Question 2
A.	Bond A	Bond A
B.	Bond A	Bond B
C.	Bond B	Bond A

42. Using the rates in Exhibit 2 and the information in Exhibit 3, the value of bond A is *closest* to:
    A. $90.63.
    B. $95.68.
    C. $99.28.

Questions 43–48 relate to Erich Reichmann.

Erich Reichmann, CFA, is a fixed-income portfolio manager with Global Investment Management. A recent increase in interest rate volatility has caused Reichmann and his assistant, Mel O'Shea, to begin investigating methods of hedging interest rate risk in his fixed income portfolio.

Reichmann would like to hedge the interest rate risk of one of his bonds, a floating-rate bond (indexed to LIBOR). O'Shea recommends taking a short position in a Eurodollar futures contract because the Eurodollar contract is a more effective hedging instrument than a Treasury bill futures contract.

Reichmann is also analyzing the possibility of using interest rate caps and floors, as well as interest rate options and options on fixed income securities, to hedge the interest rate risk of his overall portfolio.

Reichmann uses a binomial interest rate model to value 1-year and 2-year 6% floors on 1-year LIBOR, both based on $30 million principal value with annual payments. He values the 1-year floor at $90,000 and the 2-year floor at $285,000.

Reichmann has also heard about using interest rate collars to hedge interest rate risk, but is unsure how to construct a collar.

Finally, Reichmann is interested in using swaptions to hedge certain investments. He evaluates the following comments about swaptions.

- If a firm anticipates floating rate exposure from issuing floating rate bonds at some future date, a payer swaption would *lock in* a fixed rate and provide floating-rate payments for the loan. It would be exercised if the yield curve shifted down.
- Swaptions can be used to speculate on changes in interest rates. The investor would buy a receiver swaption if he expects rates to fall.

43. To *most* effectively hedge his long position in the floating rate bond against declining rates, Reichmann should:
    A. take O'Shea's advice.
    B. go long in a Eurodollar futures contract.
    C. go long in a Treasury bill futures contract.

44. To *most* effectively hedge against an increase in interest rates that would reduce the value of his fixed-income portfolio, what position should Reichmann take?
    A. Long an interest rate cap or long a European call on interest rates.
    B. Short an interest rate cap or short a European call on interest rates.
    C. Long an interest rate cap and short a European call on interest rates.

45.   If LIBOR for Year 2 is 5.8%, the payoff on the 2-year, 6%, $30 million
       interest rate floor at the end of Year 2 is *closest* to:
       A. $56,711.
       B. $60,000.
       C. $30,000.

46.   Based on the results from Reichmann's binomial interest rate model, the
       value of a 2-year, $30 million European put option on LIBOR with a floor
       strike of 6% is *closest* to:
       A. $185,000.
       B. $195,000.
       C. $270,000.

47.   What would be the *most appropriate* way for Reichmann to construct an
       interest rate collar to hedge the fixed-rate portion of the portfolio using the
       2-year 6% floor and a 2-year 12% cap?
       A. Buy the floor and buy the cap.
       B. Buy the floor and sell the cap.
       C. Sell the floor and buy the cap.

48.   Are the comments about swaptions correct?
       A. No, because a payer swaption should be used if the investor anticipates
          a fixed rate exposure at some point in the future.
       B. No, because a payer swaption would be exercised if the yield curve
          shifted up.
       C. No, because an investor would buy a receiver swaption if he expects
          rates to rise.

Questions 49–54 relate to Stan Loper.

Stan Loper is unfamiliar with the Black-Scholes-Merton (BSM) option pricing model and plans to use a two-period binomial model to value some call options. The stock of Arbor Industries pays no dividends and currently trades for $45. The up-move factor for the stock is 1.15, and the risk-free rate is 4%. He is considering buying two-period European style options on Arbor Industries with a strike price of $40. The delta of these options over the first period is 0.83.

Loper is curious about the effect of time on the value of the calls in the binomial model, so he also calculates the value of a one-period European style call option with a strike price of 40.

Loper is also interested in using the BSM model to price European and American call and put options. He is concerned, however, whether the assumptions necessary to derive the model are realistic. The assumptions he is particularly concerned about are:

- The volatility of the option value is known and constant.
- Stock prices are lognormally distributed.
- The continuous risk-free rate is known and constant.

Loper would also like to value options on Rapid Repair, Inc., common stock, but Rapid pays dividends, so Loper is uncertain what the effect will be on the value of the options. Loper uses the two-period model to value long positions in the Rapid Repair call and put options without accounting for the fact that Rapid Repair pays common dividends.

49. The value of a two-period 40 call on Arbor Industries stock is *closest* to:
    A. $6.65.
    B. $8.86.
    C. $9.21.

50. The position in calls necessary to hedge a long position in 1,000 shares of stock over the first period is *closest* to:
    A. short 830 calls.
    B. short 1,150 calls.
    C. short 1,205 calls.

51. The value of the one-period European style call option is *closest* to:
    A. $6.65.
    B. $6.86.
    C. $7.15.

52.   The difference in value between the European 40 calls and otherwise
        identical American 40 calls is *closest* to:
        A. –$1.43.
        B. $0.00.
        C. $1.92.

53.   Are the BSM assumptions listed correctly?
        A. No, because stock prices are assumed to be normally distributed.
        B. No, because the expected return on the stock is assumed to be known
            and constant.
        C. No, because the volatility of the return on the underlying stock is
            assumed to be known and constant.

54.   When Loper failed to account for Rapid Repair dividends, did he *likely*
        overvalue the calls or the puts?
        A. The calls and the puts are overvalued.
        B. Only the calls are overvalued.
        C. Only the puts are overvalued.

Questions 55–60 relate to Sara Robinson and Marvin Gardner.

Sara Robinson and Marvin Gardner are considering an opportunity to start their own money management firm. Their conversation leads them to a discussion on establishing a portfolio management process and investment policy statements. Robinson makes the following statements:

Statement 1: Our only real objective as portfolio managers is to maximize the returns to our clients.

Statement 2: If we are managing only a fraction of a client's total wealth, it is the client's responsibility, not ours, to determine how their investments are allocated among asset classes.

Statement 3: When developing a client's strategic asset allocation, portfolio managers have to consider capital market expectations.

In response, Gardner makes the following statements:

Statement 4: While return maximization is important for a given level of risk, we also need to consider the client's tolerance for risk.

Statement 5: We'll let our clients worry about the tax implications of their investments; our time is better spent on finding undervalued assets.

Statement 6: Since we expect our investor's objectives to be constantly changing, we will need to evaluate their investment policy statements on an annual basis at a minimum.

Robinson wants to focus on younger clientele with the expectation that the new firm will be able to retain the clients for a long time and create long-term profitable relationships. While Gardner felt it was important to develop long-term relationships, he wants to go after older, high-net-worth clients.

55.   Are Statements 1 and 4 consistent with the appropriate method of developing portfolio objectives?
       A. Both statements are correct.
       B. Only Statement 1 is correct.
       C. Only Statement 4 is correct.

56.   Which one of the following factors is the *least likely* to affect the individual investor's ability to accept risk?
       A. Required spending needs.
       B. Financial strength.
       C. Behavioral factors.

57. Are Statements 2 and 3 correct when considering asset allocation?
    A. Both statements are correct.
    B. Only Statement 2 is correct.
    C. Only Statement 3 is correct.

58. Robinson is uncomfortable with Gardner's position on taxes but she can't specifically identify the source of the discomfort. Which of the following statements *least accurately* reflects proper consideration of tax effects on the investment process?
    A. Because investors are ultimately concerned with after-tax returns, it is important that investors consider their own marginal tax rates and the security's tax status when making any investment decision.
    B. Pensions and endowment funds are typically tax-exempt investors and, therefore, are less concerned with tax considerations.
    C. Investors should rely on accountants or other advisors for tax advice; portfolio managers should focus on finding undervalued investments and not be distracted by tax considerations.

59. The *least* important portfolio constraints for individuals are:
    A. legal and regulatory constraints.
    B. investment horizon constraints.
    C. unique needs.

60. In addition to Statement 6, an appropriately developed investment policy statement is *least likely* to address which of the following elements?
    A. Transportability so as to minimize any disruptions if new managers assume responsibility for the portfolio.
    B. Assurances of minimum returns so clients will be better able to ensure their financial goals are met over the long run.
    C. Barriers to short-term strategy shifts driven by panic or overconfidence stemming from portfolio performance or changes in market environments.

End of Morning Session

EXAM 2
AFTERNOON SESSION

Question	Topic	Minutes (Points)
61 to 66	Ethics	18
67 to 72	Quantitative Methods	18
73 to 78	Economics	18
79 to 84	Financial Reporting and Analysis	18
85 to 90	Financial Reporting and Analysis	18
91 to 96	Financial Reporting and Analysis	18
97 to 102	Financial Reporting and Analysis	18
103 to 108	Corporate Finance	18
109 to 114	Alternative Investments	18
115 to 120	Fixed Income	18

61.	(A)	(B)	(C)
62.	(A)	(B)	(C)
63.	(A)	(B)	(C)
64.	(A)	(B)	(C)
65.	(A)	(B)	(C)
66.	(A)	(B)	(C)
67.	(A)	(B)	(C)
68.	(A)	(B)	(C)
69.	(A)	(B)	(C)
70.	(A)	(B)	(C)

71.	(A)	(B)	(C)
72.	(A)	(B)	(C)
73.	(A)	(B)	(C)
74.	(A)	(B)	(C)
75.	(A)	(B)	(C)
76.	(A)	(B)	(C)
77.	(A)	(B)	(C)
78.	(A)	(B)	(C)
79.	(A)	(B)	(C)
80.	(A)	(B)	(C)

81.	(A)	(B)	(C)
82.	(A)	(B)	(C)
83.	(A)	(B)	(C)
84.	(A)	(B)	(C)
85.	(A)	(B)	(C)
86.	(A)	(B)	(C)
87.	(A)	(B)	(C)
88.	(A)	(B)	(C)
89.	(A)	(B)	(C)
90.	(A)	(B)	(C)

91.	(A)	(B)	(C)
92.	(A)	(B)	(C)
93.	(A)	(B)	(C)
94.	(A)	(B)	(C)
95.	(A)	(B)	(C)
96.	(A)	(B)	(C)
97.	(A)	(B)	(C)
98.	(A)	(B)	(C)
99.	(A)	(B)	(C)
100.	(A)	(B)	(C)

101.	(A)	(B)	(C)
102.	(A)	(B)	(C)
103.	(A)	(B)	(C)
104.	(A)	(B)	(C)
105.	(A)	(B)	(C)
106.	(A)	(B)	(C)
107.	(A)	(B)	(C)
108.	(A)	(B)	(C)
109.	(A)	(B)	(C)
110.	(A)	(B)	(C)

111.	(A)	(B)	(C)
112.	(A)	(B)	(C)
113.	(A)	(B)	(C)
114.	(A)	(B)	(C)
115.	(A)	(B)	(C)
116.	(A)	(B)	(C)
117.	(A)	(B)	(C)
118.	(A)	(B)	(C)
119.	(A)	(B)	(C)
120.	(A)	(B)	(C)

Exam 2
Afternoon Session

Questions 61–66 relate to Connor Burton.

Connor Burton, CFA, is the managing partner for United Partners, a small investment advisory firm that employs three investment professionals and currently has approximately $250 million of assets under management. The client base of United Partners is varied, and accounts range in size from small retirement accounts to a $30 million private school endowment. In addition to Burton's administrative responsibilities as the managing partner at United, he also serves as an investment advisor to several clients. Because United Partners is a small firm, the company does not employ any research analysts but instead obtains its investment research products and services from two national brokerage firms, which in turn execute all client trades for United Partners. The arrangement with the two brokers has enabled United to assure its clients that the firm will always seek the best execution for them by having both brokers competitively bid for United's business.

A prospective client, Harold Crossley, has approached Burton about shifting some of his personal assets under management from MoneyCorp to United Partners. Burton provides Crossley with a packet of marketing information that Burton developed himself. The packet contains five years of historical performance data for a value weighted composite of the firm's discretionary accounts. Burton states that the composite's management style and performance results are representative of the management style and returns that United can be expected to achieve for Crossley. Also included in the information packet are brief bios on each of United's three investment professionals. Crossley notices that all three of United's investment professionals are described as "CFA charterholders," but he is not familiar with the designation. In response to Crossley's inquiry, Burton explains the significance of the program by stating that the designation, which is only awarded after passing three rigorous exams and obtaining the requisite years of work experience, represents a commitment to the highest standards of ethical and professional conduct.

As a condition of moving his account to United Partners, Crossley insists that all of his trades be executed through his brother-in-law, a broker for Security Bank. Security Bank is a large, New York-based broker/dealer but is not one of the two brokerage firms with which United currently does business. Burton contacts Crossley's brother-in-law and determines that Security Bank's trade execution is competitive, but Crossley's account alone would not generate enough volume to warrant any soft dollar arrangement for research materials. However, Crossley's brother-in-law does offer for Security Bank to pay a referral fee to Burton for directing any of United's clients to Security Bank's retail banking division. To bring Crossley on as a client, Burton agrees to the arrangement. Going forward, Burton will use Security Bank to execute all of Crossley's trades.

Several months later, Burton is invited to a road show for an initial public offering (IPO) for SolutionWare, a software company. Security Bank is serving as lead underwriter on SolutionWare's IPO. Burton attends the meeting, which is led by two investment bankers and one software industry research analyst from Security Bank who covers SolutionWare. Burton notes that the bankers from Security Bank have included detailed financial statements for SolutionWare in the offering prospectus and also disclosed that Security Bank provides a warehouse line of credit to SolutionWare. After the meeting, Burton calls Crossley to recommend the purchase of SolutionWare equity. Crossley heeds Burton's advice and tells him to purchase 5,000 shares. Before placing Crossley's order, Burton reads the SolutionWare marketing materials and performs a detailed analysis of expected future earnings and other key factors for the investment decision. Burton determines that the offering would be a suitable investment for his own retirement portfolio. United Partners, being a small firm, has no formal written policy regarding trade allocation, employee participation in equity offerings, or established blackout periods for employee trading. Burton adds his order to Crossley's order and places a purchase order for the combined number of shares with Security Bank. Burton is later notified that the offering was oversubscribed, and United Partners was only able to obtain roughly 75% of the desired number of shares. To be fair, Burton allocates the shares on a pro-rata basis between Crossley's account and his own retirement account. When Burton notifies Crossley of the situation, Crossley is nonetheless pleased to have a position, though smaller than requested, in such a "hot" offering.

61. Did the marketing materials presented to Crossley by Burton violate Standard III(D) Performance Presentation or Standard VII(B) Reference to CFA Institute, the CFA Designation, and the CFA Program?
    A. Standard III(D) only.
    B. Standard VII(B) only.
    C. Both Standard III(D) and Standard VII(B) are violated.

62. According to the CFA Institute Standards of Professional Conduct, the trading arrangement between Burton and Security Bank is *most likely*:
    A. a violation because the practice of directed brokerage violates the member's duty of loyalty to the client.
    B. a violation because although Security Bank's execution is competitive, Burton will not be able to always obtain the best execution for his client.
    C. not a violation because the brokerage is the property of the client.

63. According to CFA Institute Standards of Professional Conduct, which of the following statements *best* describes the circumstances under which Burton may enter into the referral agreement with Security Bank? Burton may enter into the agreement:
    A. under no circumstances.
    B. only after receiving written permission from clients.
    C. only after fully disclosing the referral arrangement to clients and prospective clients.

64. With respect to the road show meeting regarding the initial public offering of SolutionWare, did Security Bank comply with the requirements and recommendations of the CFA Institute Research Objectivity Standards?
    A. No, because it publicly revealed that it also provides corporate finance services for SolutionWare.
    B. No, because it failed to provide Burton with adequate information to make an investment decision.
    C. No, because it allowed an analyst to participate in a marketing road show for a company that he covers.

65. According to CFA Institute Standards of Professional Conduct, Burton's recommendation to Crossley that he purchase shares of the SolutionWare initial public offering is *most likely*:
    A. in violation of Standard III(C) Suitability for not determining the appropriateness of the investment for the portfolio and Standard I(B) Independence and Objectivity for not making the investment recommendation to all of his clients at the same time.
    B. in violation of Standard V(A) Diligence and Reasonable Basis for not thoroughly analyzing the investment before making a recommendation and in violation of Standard III(C) Suitability for not determining the appropriateness of the investment for the portfolio.
    C. in violation of Standard V(A) Diligence and Reasonable Basis for not thoroughly analyzing the investment before making a recommendation and in violation of Standard I(B) Independence and Objectivity for not making the investment recommendation to all of his clients at the same time.

66. According to CFA Institute Standards of Professional Conduct, Burton's participation in the SolutionWare offering *most likely*:
    A. is in violation of the Standards because his actions adversely affected the interests of Crossley.
    B. is in violation of the Standards because he did not disclose his participation in the offering to Security Bank.
    C. is not in violation of the Standards since the shares obtained in the IPO were distributed equitably on a pro-rata basis.

Questions 67–72 relate to Ernie Smith.

Ernie Smith and Jamal Sims are analysts with the firm of Madison Consultants. Madison provides statistical modeling and advice to portfolio managers throughout the United States and Canada.

In an effort to estimate future cash flows and value the Canadian stock market, Smith has been examining the country's aggregate retail sales. He runs two autoregressive regression models in an attempt to determine whether there are any patterns in the data, utilizing nine years of unadjusted monthly retail sales data. One model uses a lag one variable and the other adds a lag twelve variable. The results of both regressions are shown in Exhibits 1 and 2.

Exhibit 1: Canadian Autoregressive Model with Lag 1

Multiple R	0.91
R-Square	0.83
Adjusted R-Square	0.83
Standard Error	17,252.76
Observations	108.00

ANOVA

	df	SS	MS	F	Significance F
Regression	1.00	150,813,197,793	150,813,197,793	506.67	0.00
Residual	106.00	31,551,711,544	297,657,656		
Total	107.00	182,364,909,338			

	Coefficients	Standard Error	T-stat	P-value
Intercept	21,750.16	10,379.77	2.10	0.04
Lag 1	0.92	0.04	22.51	0.00

Exhibit 2: Canadian Autoregressive Model with Lag 1 and Lag 12

Regression Statistics for 2nd Regression	
Multiple R	0.96
R-Square	0.93
Adjusted R-Square	0.92
Standard Error	11,336.27
Observations	108.00

ANOVA

	df	SS	MS	F	Significance F
Regression	2.00	168,871,246,751	84,435,623,375	657.03	<0.01
Residual	105.00	13,493,662,586	128,511,072		
Total	107.00	182,364,909,338			

	Coefficients	Standard Error	T-stat	P-value
Intercept	−24,861.28	7,872.56	−3.16	<0.01
Lag 1	0.30	0.06	5.22	<0.01
Lag 12	0.84	0.07	11.85	<0.01

Sims has been assigned the task of valuing the U.S. stock market and uses data similar to the data that Smith uses for Canada. He decides, however, that the data should be transformed. He takes the natural log of the data and uses it in the following model:

$$\Delta \ln \text{sales}_t = b_0 + b_1 \Delta \ln \text{sales}_{t-1}$$

Parameter estimates for the autoregressive model and the actual data for the two most recent months are shown in Exhibit 3.

Exhibit 3: U.S. Autoregressive Model

Intercept	0.052
Lag 1 coefficient	0.684
Actual sales one month ago (−1)	6,270
Actual sales two months ago (−2)	6,184

Smith and Sims are concerned that the data for Canadian retail sales may be more appropriately modeled with an ARCH process. Smith states, that in order to find out, he would take the residuals from the original autoregressive model for Canadian retail sales and then square them.

Sims states that these residuals would then be regressed against the Canadian retail sales data using the following equation: $e_t = b_0 + b_1 X_t$, where e represents the residual terms from the original regression and X represents the Canadian retail sales data. If b_1 is statistically different from zero, then the regression model contains an ARCH process.

Smith also examines the quarterly inflation data for an emerging market over the past nine years. He models the data using an autoregressive model with a lag one independent variable, which he finds is statistically different from zero. He wonders whether he should also include lag two and lag four terms, given the magnitude of the autocorrelations of the residuals shown in Exhibit 4, assuming a 5% significance level. The critical t-values, assuming a 5% significance level and 35 degrees of freedom, are 2.03 for a two-tail test and 1.69 for a one-tail test.

Exhibit 4: Emerging Market Autoregressive Model

Lag	Autocorrelation
1	0.0829
2	0.1293
3	0.0227
4	0.1882

Sims is investigating the performance of 5-year European and British bonds based on the actions of the U.S. Federal Reserve. He uses the U.S. Federal Funds rate. The two regressions he uses are:

$$BY_{E,t} = b_0 + b_1 FF_{US,t}$$

$$BY_{B,t} = b_0 + b_1 FF_{US,t}$$

where: FF is the Federal Funds rate in the United States (US), and BY is the bond yield in the European Union (E) and Great Britain (B).

Before he runs this regression, he investigates the characteristics of the dependent and independent variables. He finds that the Federal Funds rate in the United States and the bond yield in Great Britain have a unit root but that the bond yield in the European Union does not. Furthermore, the Federal Funds rate in the United States and the bond yield in Great Britain are cointegrated, but the Federal Funds rate in the United States and the bond yield in the European Union are not.

67. Which of the following models would be the *best* formulation for the Canadian retail sales data?
    A. $X_t = b_0 + b_1 X_{t-1}$.
    B. $X_t = b_1 X_{t-1} + b_2 X_{t-12}$.
    C. $X_t = b_0 + b_1 X_{t-1} + b_2 X_{t-12}$.

68. The estimate of forecasted sales for the United States this month, using Sims's model, is *closest* to:
    A. $6,329.
    B. $6,453.
    C. $6,667.

69. Are the comments of Smith and Sims on the construction of an ARCH model correct?
    A. Both comments are correct.
    B. Only Smith is correct.
    C. Only Sims is correct.

70. Regarding Smith's emerging market regression, should lag two and lag four terms be included in the regression?
    A. Neither Lag should be included.
    B. Only Lag 2 should be included.
    C. Only Lag 4 should be included.

71. Will Sims's regressions of European and British bond yields on the U.S. Federal Funds rate produce valid results?
    A. Neither Regression is valid.
    B. Only Regression 1 is valid.
    C. Only Regression 2 is valid.

72. Which of the following is the *appropriate* test for cointegration?
    A. Breusch-Pagan.
    B. Durbin-Watson.
    C. Engle-Granger.

Questions 73–78 relate to Frank Hoskins and Paul Lanning.

Frank Hoskins and Paul Lanning are economists for a large U.S. investment advisory firm, Platinum Advisors. Hoskins and Lanning use their independent research on U.S. stocks and international stocks to provide advice for the firm's network of advisors. As the senior economist at Platinum, Hoskins is a partner in the firm and is Lanning's supervisor. Lanning has worked for Platinum for four years. At a lunch meeting, the two economists discuss the usefulness of economic theory, economic data, and the resulting forecasts of the global economic and stock market activity.

Hoskins is investigating the growth prospects of the country of Maldavia. Maldavia is a formerly communist country with a population of 3 million located in Eastern Europe. The Maldavian government had been aggressive in instituting political reform and encouraging the growth of financial markets. However, due to recent increases in stock market volatility, the Maldavian government is considering reigning-in trading volume by imposing a tax on stock market transactions. Hoskins states that this development is not encouraging for future economic growth.

Lanning is examining the country of Petra. Petra is a country of 25 million located in South America and rich with natural resources, including oil. The recently-elected president of Petra, Carlos Basile, has announced that he would like to ensure that the citizens of Petra enjoy the benefits of its natural resources rather than foreign oil companies, and that the government will nationalize these oil companies. Lanning states that these changes would not be beneficial for the future growth of the Petrian economy.

One of the many items they study when examining an economy or stock market is the economic information released by governments and private organizations. Hoskins and Lanning use this information to adjust their economic growth forecasts and to accordingly adjust portfolio allocations to the bond and stock markets. Examining information for Maldavia, Hoskins has learned that the Maldavian private sector has embarked on an ambitious plan to increase labor productivity by purchasing more machinery for its factories. Plotting the productivity curve for Maldavia, Hoskins states that labor productivity should increase because the productivity curve will shift up.

Lanning is examining the historical record of economic growth in Petra. He has gathered the data in Exhibit 1 to determine potential economic growth.

Exhibit 1: Economic Data for Petra from 20X1 to 20X7

Real GDP growth rate	3.9%
Growth rate in capital	1.4%
Growth rate in labor force	1.9%
Labor cost/total factor cost	0.52

Lanning then turns his attention to the countries of Alicia and Felicia. He notes that the GDP growth rate in both countries is comparable. Alicia's capital to labor ratio is USD 5,000 and the output to capital ratio is USD 12,000. Felicia's capital to labor ratio is USD 2,800 while output to capital ratio is USD 10,000. Alicia has a relatively younger labor force and the labor cost represents 35% of total factor cost. Both countries have extensive restrictions on foreign direct investments in their economy.

It has long been Platinum's policy for its economists to use long-term economic growth trends to forecast future economic growth, stock returns, and dividends in a country. Lanning also examines the economy of Tiberia. Tiberia has a population of 11 million and is located in northern Africa. Its economy is diversified, and its main exports are agricultural products and heavy machinery. The country's economy has been growing at an annual rate of 6.2% for the past ten years, in part because of technological advances in the manufacturing of heavy equipment. These advances involve the use of computer-operated welding machines that have made the manufacturing process more efficient. Lanning is worried, however, that the current GDP growth rate may not be sustainable and is considering advising Platinum's portfolio managers to decrease their portfolio allocations to the country. Before doing so, he will consult with Hoskins.

73. Are the statements made by Hoskins and Lanning regarding the future growth of the Maldavian and Petrian economies *most likely* to be correct or incorrect?
    A. Both are correct.
    B. Only Hoskins is correct.
    C. Only Lanning is correct.

74. Hoskins's statement regarding Maldavian labor productivity and its productivity curve is:
    A. incorrect, because labor productivity is not affected in this scenario.
    B. incorrect, because labor productivity will decrease because of the low skill level of the labor force.
    C. incorrect, because although labor productivity will increase, the increase will result from a movement along the productivity curve.

75. Which country will experience a higher growth rate in potential GDP due to capital deepening and due to removal of restrictions on inflow of foreign capital?

	Capital deepening	Removal of restrictions on inflow of capital
A.	Alicia	Felicia
B.	Felicia	Felicia
C.	Felicia	Alicia

76. Petra's GDP growth rate attributable to growth in total factor productivity is *closest* to:
A. 0.6%.
B. 1.6%.
C. 2.24%.

77. The classical growth theory predicts that Tiberia's long-run future GDP per capita is *most likely* to:
A. decline due to diminishing marginal productivity of capital.
B. settle at subsistence level due to adjustments in the population.
C. remain unchanged from the current levels unless the government increases the budget deficit.

78. The endogenous growth theory predicts that the Tiberian GDP growth rate is *most likely* to:
A. settle at a long-run steady state because of diminishing marginal productivity of capital.
B. continue to increase because technological advances will be shared by many sectors of the economy.
C. decline because the current GDP growth rate is not sustainable.

Questions 79–84 relate to Tobin Yoakam.

Tobin Yoakam, CFA, is analyzing the financial performance of Konker Industries, a U.S. company which is publicly traded under the ticker KONK. Yoakam is particularly concerned about the quality of Konker's financial statements and its choices of accounting methodologies.

Below is a summary of Konker's financial statements prepared by Yoakam.

Konker Industries			
Income Statement	**20X8**	**Balance Sheet**	**20X8**
($ in thousands)		*($ in thousands)*	
Gross sales	55,435	Cash and equivalents	457
Sales discounts, returns, and allowances	1,352	Short term marketable securities	927
Net sales	54,083	Accounts receivable (net)	47,740
Cost of goods sold	26,500	Inventories	20,963
SG&A expenses	15,625	PP&E (net of depreciation)	25,371
Depreciation expense	1,082	Total assets	95,458
Earnings before interest and taxes	10,876		
Interest expense	693	Accounts payable	24,994
Earnings before taxes	10,183	Other current liabilities	1,209
Taxes (tax rate 40%)	4,073	Long term debt	21,770
Net income	6,110	Total liabilities	47,973
		Common stock	40,314
Dividends	5,046	Retained earnings	7,171
Net addition to retained earnings	1,064	Total liabilities and shareholders equity	95,458

Konker has an operating lease for several of its large machining tools. The remaining lease term is five years, and the annual lease payments are $2 million. The applicable interest rate on the operating lease is 9%. Yoakam believes that the operating lease should be capitalized and treated as a finance lease. For purposes of adjusting the financial statements, Yoakam believes that the machining tools should be depreciated using straight-line depreciation.

At the beginning of 20X8, Konker formed a qualified special purpose entity (QSPE) and sold a portion of its accounts receivables to the QSPE. Under

U.S. GAAP, QSPE was exempt from consolidation requirements. The total amount of accounts receivables sold to the QSPE was $13.5 million. Yoakam has noted in his research that the Financial Accounting Standards Board (FASB) eliminated qualified special purpose entities.

Konker has three major operating divisions: Konker Industrial, Konker Defense, and Konker Capital. Yoakam has computed the EBIT margin for each division over the last three years, as well as the ratio of the percentage of total capital expenditures to the percentage of total assets for each division.

	EBIT / Assets			CapEx % / Assets %		
	20X8	**20X7**	**20X6**	**20X8**	**20X7**	**20X6**
Konker Industrial	6.2%	7.5%	6.7%	1.5	1.3	1.2
Konker Defense	6.7%	7.2%	6.9%	0.5	0.6	0.7
Konker Capital	10.1%	12.1%	11.1%	0.7	0.6	0.5

Since Yoakam is concerned about the quality of Konker's earnings, he decides to analyze the accrual ratios using the balance sheet approach. The table below contains the last three years of accrual ratios for Konker and the industry average.

Balance Sheet Accrual Ratios	**20X8**	**20X7**	**20X6**
Konker	4.5%	15.0%	7.0%
Industry average	4.8%	4.4%	5.2%

79. With respect to the balance sheet accrual ratio, which of the following, other things equal, would *most likely* lead to an increase in the ratio for a growing company?
   A. Extending the time the firm takes to pay its suppliers.
   B. A significant build-up of cash.
   C. A build-up of inventory.

80. If Yoakam capitalizes Konker's operating lease in his analysis, the Konker's adjusted interest coverage ratio for 20X8 would be *closest* to:
   A. 7.12.
   B. 8.13.
   C. 15.69.

81. When FASB retroactively eliminated the allowance of QSPEs created for the securitization of receivables, the *most likely* impact on Konker's financial statements would have been:
   A. an increase in equity and an increase in interest expense.
   B. no change in assets but an increase in financial leverage ratios.
   C. an increase in financial leverage ratios and a decrease in the interest coverage ratio.

82. An analyst is considering the effects of income reported under the equity method on certain financial ratios. For a firm that reports equity income as non-operating income (not included in EBIT), removing equity income from the financial statements would *most likely* result in:
   A. an increase in the tax burden term in the extended Du Pont decomposition of ROE.
   B. an increase in the asset turnover ratio.
   C. a decrease in the interest coverage ratio.

83. Regarding the three operating divisions of Konker, Yoakam should be *most* concerned that:
   A. Konker is growing the Industrial division over time.
   B. the operating ROA of the Capital division has fallen over the last year.
   C. the ratio of the Capex percent change to the asset percentage is significantly less than one for the Defense division.

84. Based on the balance sheet accruals ratios, Yoakam would *most likely* conclude which of the following regarding the earnings of Konker?
   A. The volatile accruals ratios are indicators that Konker may be manipulating earnings.
   B. Konker's earnings quality was lower than its peer group in 20X8 but higher in 20X6 and 20X7.
   C. Konker's earnings quality worsened from 20X6 to 20X8 but was superior to its peer group over the 3-year period.

Questions 85–90 relate to Galena Petrovich.

Galena Petrovich, CFA, is an analyst in the New York office of TRS Investment Management, Inc. Petrovich is an expert in the industrial electrical equipment sector and is analyzing Fisher Global. Fisher is a global market leader in designing, manufacturing, marketing, and servicing electrical systems and components, including fluid power systems and automotive engine air management systems.

Fisher has generated double-digit growth over the past ten years, primarily as the result of acquisitions, and has reported positive net income in each year. Fisher reports its financial results using International Financial Reporting Standards (IFRS).

Petrovich is particularly interested in a transaction that occurred seven years ago, before the change in accounting standards, in which Fisher used the pooling method to account for a large acquisition of Dartmouth Industries, an industry competitor. She would like to determine the effect of using the purchase method instead of the pooling method on the financial statements of Fisher. Fisher exchanged common stock for all of the outstanding shares of Dartmouth.

Fisher also has a 50% ownership interest in a joint venture with its major distributor, a U.S. company called Hydro Distribution. She determines that Fisher has reported its ownership interest under the equity method, and that the joint venture has been profitable since it was established three years ago. She decides to adjust the financial statements to show how the financial statements would be affected if Fisher had reported its ownership under the acquisition method. Fisher is also considering acquiring 80% to 100% of Brown and Sons Company. Petrovich must consider the effect of such an acquisition on Fisher's financial statements.

Petrovich determines from the financial statement footnotes that Fisher reported an unrealized gain in its most recent income statement related to debt securities that are designated at fair value. Competitor firms following U.S. GAAP classify similar debt securities as available-for-sale.

Finally, Petrovich finds a reference in Fisher's footnotes regarding a special purpose entity (SPE). Fisher has reported its investment in the SPE using the equity method, but Petrovich believes that the consolidation method more accurately reflects Fisher's true financial position, so she makes the appropriate adjustments to the financial statements.

85. Regarding the prior purchase that was accounted for under the pooling of interests method, had Fisher Global reported this purchase under the acquisition method:
   A. the assets and liabilities of the purchased firm would not be included on Fisher's balance sheet.
   B. balance sheet assets and liabilities of the purchased firm would have been reported at fair value.
   C. reported goodwill could be less depending on the fair value of the identifiable assets and liabilities compared to their book values.

86. Had Fisher Global reported its investment in the joint venture under the acquisition method rather than under the equity method, it is *most likely* that:
   A. reported revenue would have been the same.
   B. reported expenses would have been lower.
   C. net income would not have been affected.

87. Regarding any potential goodwill on the acquisition of Brown and Sons being considered by Fisher Global, which of the following statements is *most accurate*? The goodwill will be reported as an asset and:
   A. must be reviewed for impairment at least annually, with different test for impairment under IFRS and U.S. GAAP. Impairment losses can be reversed under U.S. GAAP but not under IFRS.
   B. amortized, and must be reviewed for impairment at least annually, though impairment losses cannot be reversed under either GAAP or IFRS.
   C. must be reviewed for impairment at least annually with different tests for impairment under IFRS and U.S. GAAP. The losses on impairment cannot be reversed under either U.S. GAAP or under IFRS.

88. If Fisher Global decides to purchase only 80% of Brown and Sons, under IFRS they will have the option to:
   A. report the acquisition as either a business combination or as an acquisition.
   B. value the identifiable assets and liabilities of Brown and Sons at their current book values or at fair market value.
   C. report more or less goodwill depending on the accounting method they choose.

89. For comparison purposes, Petrovich decides to reclassify Fisher Global's debt securities as available-for-sale. Ignoring any effect on income taxes, which of the following *best* describes the effects of the necessary adjustments?
   A. Net income is lower and asset turnover is higher.
   B. Return on assets is lower and debt-to-equity is lower.
   C. Return on equity is lower and debt-to-total capital is not affected.

90. What are the *likely* effects on return on assets (ROA) and net profit margin (ignoring any tax effects) of correctly adjusting for Fisher Global's investment in the SPE using the acquisition method?

	ROA	Net profit margin
A.	No change	Decrease
B.	Decrease	No change
C.	Decrease	Decrease

Questions 91–96 relate to Wayward Distributing, Inc.

Jenna Stuart is a financial analyst for Deuce Hardware Company, a U.S. company that reports its results in U.S. dollars. Wayward Distributing, Inc., is a foreign subsidiary of Deuce Hardware, which began operations on January 1, 2007. Wayward is located in a foreign country and reports its results in the local currency called the Rho. Selected balance sheet information for Wayward is shown in the following table.

Selected Balance Sheet Accounts Wayward Distributing Inc. (in Rho)

	12/31/07	12/31/08
Cash and accounts receivable	5,000	5,200
Inventory	3,800	4,900
Net fixed assets	6,200	7,400
Total assets	15,000	17,500
Current liabilities	2,000	2,000
Long-term debt	9,000	9,500
Shareholders' equity	4,000	6,000

Stuart has been asked to analyze how the reported financial results of Wayward will be affected by the choice of the current rate or temporal methods of accounting for foreign operations. She has gathered the following exchange rate information on the $/Rho exchange rate:

- Spot rate on 1/01/08: $0.35 per Rho
- Spot rate on 12/31/08: $0.45 per Rho
- Average spot rate during 2008: $0.42 per Rho

91. Will the current rate method report a translation gain or loss for 2008, and will that gain or loss be reported on Deuce's income statement or the balance sheet?
    A. Gain on the balance sheet.
    B. Gain on the income statement.
    C. Loss on the balance sheet and a gain on the income statement.

92. Will the temporal method report a translation gain or loss for 2008, and will that gain or loss be reported on Deuce's income statement or the balance sheet?
    A. Gain on the balance sheet.
    B. Loss on the income statement.
    C. Gain on the balance sheet and a loss on the income statement.

93. Will total asset turnover (calculated using end-of-period balance sheet figures) *likely* be larger when calculated from the Rho financial statements or the financial statements translated into the reporting currency (U.S.$) using the current rate method?
    A. Larger on US$ statements.
    B. Larger on Rho statements.
    C. No difference.

94. Will fixed asset turnover (calculated using end-of-period balance sheet figures) *likely* be lower when calculated using the current rate method or remeasured using the temporal method?
    A. Lower under the temporal method.
    B. Lower under the current rate method.
    C. The same under either method.

95. Suppose for this question only that Stuart has determined that (1) the operating, financing, and investing decisions related to Wayward's operations are typically made by Wayward's local management located in the foreign country; and (2) some of Wayward's accounts receivable are denominated in a different foreign currency called the Del (Dl). Which method is the *most appropriate* to use to translate the Del receivables into Rho, according to U.S. GAAP?
    A. The current rate method.
    B. The temporal method.
    C. Use the current rate for translation with any gains or losses reflected in the income statement.

96. Suppose for this question only that Stuart decides to use the current rate method to translate Wayward's results into U.S. dollars. Is it *likely* that the quick ratio and the interest coverage ratio will be the same or different in Rho before translation and in U.S. dollars after translation?
    A. Neither the quick ratio nor the interest coverage ratio will change.
    B. Only the interest coverage ratio will change.
    C. Only the quick ratio will change.

Questions 97–102 relate to Monica Garza.

Monica Garza, CFA is a sell-side analyst for Schubert Brokerage Services. Garza is analyzing the financial statements of Project Depot, a home improvement retailer based in the United States that also has operations outside the United States. Garza is particularly concerned with evaluating Project Depot's inventory and long-lived assets.

Project Depot reports under U.S. GAAP and uses the last-in, first-out (LIFO) method to account for inventory. Garza investigates the notes accompanying Project Depot's financial statements. The notes indicate that the prices of new inventory have been steadily rising and that the inventory balance has grown over the last few years.

Garza has collected the following information from Project Depot's financial statements:

Exhibit 1: Selected Financial Information

	($ millions)	
	20X0	*20X1*
Revenues	41,322	45,737
Cost of goods sold	28,687	30,757
Depreciation	1,588	1,614
Interest expense	121	139
Taxes	2,312	2,811
Inventory	8,209	8,249
Gross plant and equipment	30,858	32,268
Accumulated depreciation	8,155	9,769
Working capital	15,132	16,299
LIFO reserve	3,250	5,750

Garza also has been comparing the operating margins of Project Depot to a close competitor, Fine Depot. While analyzing Fine Depot's financial statements, Garza notices that Fine Depot had a major LIFO liquidation in 20X1.

To begin her analysis of Project Depot's long-lived assets, Garza reviews the notes to the financial statements to determine the depreciation method Project Depot uses. The notes indicate that Project Depot currently utilizes a straight-line method of depreciation but is contemplating using the double-declining balance method of depreciation. Garza is concerned about the impact this will have on the financial statements if the change is made.

After determining the depreciation method, Garza wants to analyze the age of the long-lived assets to determine when Project Depot will require major investments.

Continuing her analysis of Project Depot's long-lived assets, Garza reads in a major news publication that Project Depot had assets in Louisiana revalued by a professional appraisal to test for impairment. The fair value of the assets was determined in a professional appraisal to be $350 million. The assets are currently in use and are valued on the balance sheet at $300 million. The current balance sheet value reflects previously recognized impairment losses of $43 million. The original cost of the assets was $525 million.

97. Based on the information collected by Garza, by using last-in, first-out (LIFO) instead of first-in, first-out (FIFO), Project Depot has higher:
   A. cash flows.
   B. net income.
   C. working capital.

98. Based solely on the LIFO liquidation, Fine Depot's financial statements for 20X1 would have reported:
   A. lower earnings.
   B. higher earnings.
   C. an increase in inventory.

99. If Garza adjusts Project Depot's inventory from last-in, first-out (LIFO) to first-in, first-out (FIFO), the COGS for 201X would be ($ millions):
   A. $2,540.
   B. $25,007.
   C. $28,257.

100. If Project Depot switches depreciation methods, which of the following statements is the *most accurate*?
   A. Return on Investment going forward will increase over the life of an asset.
   B. Asset turnover ratio going forward will decrease over the life of an asset.
   C. Current ratio going forward will increase over the life of an asset.

101. Based on the information collected by Garza, the average remaining useful life of Project Depot's plant and equipment is:
   A. 6.05 years.
   B. 13.94 years.
   C. 20.00 years.

102. Based on the new appraised value of the assets in Louisiana, Garza can *most likely* expect:
   A. no change to Project Depot's financial statements.
   B. a $50 million gain in other comprehensive income.
   C. a $43 million gain on the income statement and a $7 million gain in other comprehensive income.

Questions 103–108 relate to Cummings Enterprises, Inc.

Cummings Enterprises, Inc. (CEI), is a U.S. conglomerate that operates in a variety of markets. One of CEI's divisions manufactures small fiberglass products, such as bird baths and outdoor storage lockers. CEI is currently considering the expansion of its fiberglass product line to include booms and buckets for aerial lift trucks (often called cherry pickers), which are used for applications such as high voltage power line maintenance. The addition of this new product line is expected to increase CEI's sales by $750,000 per year.

Cal Holbrook, CEI's manager of fiberglass operations, is deciding whether to purchase a robotic system to produce cherry picker booms and buckets. The price of the robotic system will be $700,000, plus an additional $100,000 for shipping, site preparation, and installation. The new equipment will require a $50,000 increase in inventory and a $20,000 increase in accounts payable. The company uses MACRS to calculate depreciation for tax purposes and the straight-line method for financial reporting. The project has an expected life of four years, at which time the robot is expected to be sold for $75,000. The project will be funded with the debt/equity mix reflected by the company's current capital structure. CEI's pretax cost of new debt is 7%. Assume a WACC of 8%. Some of the relevant end-of-year cash flows for the robotic project are presented in Exhibit 1.

Exhibit 1: Relevant Cash Flows for Robotics Project

	Year 1	Year 2	Year 3	Year 4
Sales	$750,000	$750,000	$750,000	$750,000
Variable costs	$225,000	$225,000	$225,000	$225,000
Fixed expense	$75,000	$75,000	$75,000	$75,000
Depreciation	$264,000	$360,000	$120,000	$56,000
Earnings before tax (EBT)	$186,000	$90,000	$330,000	$394,000
Total after-tax cash flow	**$375,600**	**$414,000**	**$318,000**	?

Holbrook calculates the NPV of the robotic project and presents his findings to his supervisor, Geoffrey Mans. After reviewing the report, Mans makes the following recommendations:

1. "You forgot to include the $100,000 we have spent so far on consultants and project engineers and who knows what else to evaluate the project's feasibility. Rerun the numbers including that amount and get the revised calculations to me this afternoon."

2. "Rerun the analysis assuming straight-line depreciation for tax purposes. The NPV will be higher, and we'll be more likely to get the project funded."

Cummings has two other projects under consideration that would affect the production of storage lockers. Project 1 relates to changing the production process, and Project 2 relates to expanding the distribution facility. Holbrook estimates the NPV of the expected cash flows for Project 1 at negative $7 million. An additional investment of $3 million would allow management to more rapidly adjust to the demand for a certain type of locker. The value of this flexibility is estimated at $9 million. He estimates that the NPV of the expected cash flows for Project 2 at $3 million. An expansion option would require an additional investment of $2 million. At this time, Cummings does not have any capital rationing restrictions.

Holbrook e-mails the lead analyst for the budgeting group and indicates that he cannot make a decision on Project 2 without knowing the value the expansion option will provide.

Holbrook calls a capital budgeting meeting with CEI's production and quality control manager. Holbrook opens the meeting by stating: "I think we should accept this project based solely on the fact that it provides great operating margins. Nevertheless, I think we should conduct net present value (NPV) analysis to confirm my opinion." Holbrook then receives the following comments:

Comment 1:   It is important that interest is included in the discounted cash flows used with NPV analysis because interest is a real and very significant expense.

Comment 2:   If applied correctly, the NPV of this project will be higher if we discount economic profits instead of net after-tax operating cash flows in our analysis. I suggest we calculate economic profit as net operating profit after tax minus the dollar cost of capital.

103.   Which of the following choices is *closest* to the Year 4 total cash flow for the robotics project in Exhibit 1?
  A. $292,400.
  B. $345,400.
  C. $367,400.

104.   Are Mans's recommendations regarding the robotic project correct or incorrect?
  A. Both recommendations are correct.
  B. Only one of the recommendations is correct.
  C. Both recommendations are incorrect.

105. For this question only, assume that the investment in net working capital of $30,000 at the project inception is an inflow and that the amount nets to zero with the outflow that will occur at the end of the project. However, Holbrook does not include a cash flow for net working capital at the beginning or the end of the project. Assuming he correctly analyzes all the other components of the project, has Holbrook correctly estimated the project's net present value?
    A. Yes.
    B. No, he underestimated the project's NPV by approximately $7,950.
    C. No, he underestimated the project's NPV by approximately $2,222.

106. Which of the following choices is *closest* to the overall NPV for Project 1, and is Holbrook correct to wait for more information before deciding on Project 2?
    A. The overall NPV is –$1 million, and Holbrook is correct.
    B. The overall NPV is –$1 million, and Holbrook is incorrect.
    C. The overall NPV is $13 million, and Holbrook is incorrect.

107. The economic income for Year 3 for the robotics project from Exhibit 1 is *closest* to:
    A. $19,400.
    B. $48,700.
    C. $49,400.

108. Are the comments made by the CEI's production and quality assurance manager correct or incorrect?
    A. Both comments are correct.
    B. Only one of the comments is correct.
    C. Both comments are incorrect.

Questions 109–114 relate to Parkway Terrace.

Rita Larson, CFA, is an investment analyst for Siprah Properties, Inc. A group of wealthy investors, Ken Lundy, Chun Park, and Kareem Shabaz, are interested in purchasing Parkway Terrace, a 120-unit luxury apartment complex in Southeastern Florida. The current owners of Parkway Terrace have agreed to sell the property for $40,000,000.

Siprah represents both the existing owners and the potential new owners and are privy to additional information. Exhibits 1 and 2 show the information Larson has collected during her due diligence.

Exhibit 1: Parkway Terrace Specifics

Parkway Terrace	
Projected first year net operating income	$3.3 million
Location/Condition	Prime/Good
NOI growth rate	2.5%
LTV	75.0%
Loan Term	25 years
Loan Interest Rate	4.5%
Monthly Debt Service	$166,750
Square footage	240,000
Expected holding period	10 years
Parkway Terrace	Cost estimates
Effective age of building	10 years
Total economic life	50 years
Estimated value of land	$12,500,000
Replacement cost (p.s.f.)	$175.00
Developer's profit (p.s.f.)	$15.00
Curable deterioration	$5,000,000
Total obsolescence	$4,000,000
Expected selling price in 10 yrs	$60,000,000
Loan balance at end of 10 yrs	$21,797,543

Exhibit 2: Recent Transactions of Luxury Apartment Buildings in Southeastern Florida

Building	Craig Court	Kenton Place	Hester Oasis
Size in square feet	200,000	150,000	300,000
Age in years	7	10	13
Condition	Fair	Good	Good
Location	Prime	Secondary	Secondary
Age of transaction (in months)	9	5	16
Sales price	$32,000,000	$24,000,000	$45,000,000
Projected NOI	$2,560,000	$1,800,000	$3,150,000

Additional information:

- Depreciation is 1.5% per year.
- Condition can be good, fair, or bad. 7.5% is the adjustment needed per classification.
- Location can be prime, secondary, or tertiary. Prime locations are the most sought-after and 7.5% is the adjustment needed per classification.
- Market prices have been increasing at a rate of 0.50% per month.

Lundy states that all returns and ratios must exceed the minimum standards as listed below.

Minimum requirements
Levered required rate of return   20.0%
Debt Service Coverage Ratio   1.50X
Equity Dividend Rate   25.0%

Economic Outlook for Southeast Florida

- Home prices are expected to rise.
- Interest rates are expected to increase.
- Population growth is expected to be higher than in other areas as more wealthy retirees are moving to the region.

The investors make the following statements about how to best approach this investment:

Ken Lundy: "After we buy Parkway Terrace, we should offer shorter leases to take advantage of market conditions."

Chun Park: "I think that after we buy, we should offer long leases to lock-in tenants and maximize profitability."

Kareem Shabaz: "If we buy, we should take advantage of the low interest rates by using as much leverage as possible."

Larson is interested in using a real estate index in her analysis of suitability of real estate as an asset class for several of Siprah's clients. She notes that the firm subscribes to a proprietary index provided by REIQ. The REIQ index is an appraisal-based index that is very popular among real estate professionals. Larson is concerned about appraisal lag in the index and wants to adjust the index to remove this lag.

109. The estimated value of the property using the direct capitalization approach is *closest* to:
    A. $41.3 million.
    B. $42.0 million.
    C. $44.0 million.

110. The estimated value of the property using the sales comparison approach is *closest* to:
    A. $37.6 million.
    B. $42.2 million.
    C. $43.2 million.

111. Based on Lundy's minimum requirements, the Parkway Terrace project is:
    A. not worth pursuing because the equity dividend rate is below the minimum required.
    B. worth pursuing because all three standards are met.
    C. not worth pursuing because the debt service coverage ratio is below the minimum required.

112. The estimated value of the property using the cost approach is *closest* to:
    A. $28.5 million.
    B. $41.0 million.
    C. $45.0 million.

113. Which stated approach is *least likely* to result in an increase in potential returns?
    A. Chun Park's.
    B. Ken Lundy's.
    C. Kareem Shabaz's.

114. To correct for appraisal lag in the REIQ index, which of the following is the *least appropriate* course of action for Larson?
    A. 'Unsmooth' the index.
    B. Use a transaction-based index.
    C. Use more-recent appraisals.

Questions 115–120 relate to Jon Stevenson, CFA.

Jon Stevenson, CFA, is an experienced equity fund manager who has recently taken a position with Lohsi Clearview, a UK-based hedge fund that has combined a wide range of strategies to deliver impressive returns over the last five years. One of the fund's strategies is to invest in high-credit-risk fixed income instruments. The fund has an excellent track record of identifying bonds in this sector that subsequently outperform the market.

Stevenson wishes to familiarize himself with the fund's strategies and has started by looking at some of the techniques used in analyzing fixed income instruments. Exhibit 1 shows the firm's approach to analyzing credit risk.

Exhibit 1: Credit Analysis Tools

Credit Ratings
Before undertaking any level of detailed analysis, the credit rating from the three major agencies should be obtained. Typically an instrument that is investment grade according to all three agencies will not be worthy of further consideration.
Structural Models
An initial analysis using a simple structural model should be undertaken to calculate the present value of the expected loss.
Reduced Form Models
Detailed analysis should be undertaken using the reduced form models used by the fixed income team. This analysis should only be undertaken once the structural model analysis has been completed.

Stevenson is surprised that the fund uses credit ratings to filter out investment grade bonds as not worthy of consideration. In his experience, ratings agencies have often been wrong and he intends to send a note to his supervisor stating the following points arguing that credit ratings should not be relied upon as a filter:

Point 1: Ratings are volatile over time, which reduces their usefulness as an indication of a debt offering's default probability.

Point 2: Ratings do not implicitly depend on the business cycle stage, whereas a debt offering's default probability does.

Stevenson has no experience with structural models and is interested in learning more. He finds an analysis that has been completed for a recent bond issue. The results are shown in Exhibit 2.

Exhibit 2: IMC Bond Issue (ID 062014555612) Structural Model Results

Asset value	A_t	1,200
Expected return on assets	μ	0.04
Risk free rate	r	0.02
Face value	K	850
Time to maturity	T–t	1.5
Return volatility	σ	0.28
d_1		1.26452
d_2		0.92159
$N(-d_1)$		0.1030
$N(-d_2)$		0.1784
e_1		1.35200
e_2		1.00907
$N(-e_1)$		0.0882
$N(-e_2)$		0.1565
Expected loss		22.86
PV expected loss		23.51

115. Which of the credit analysis models shown in Exhibit 1 can only be used under the assumption that the issuing company's assets trade in a frictionless market?
    A. Structural models.
    B. Reduced form models.
    C. Both structural models and reduced form models.

116. When using reduced form models, which of the following statements is *most accurate*?
    A. It must be assumed that the riskless rate of interest is constant over time.
    B. The time T value of the company's assets has a lognormal distribution.
    C. For a given state of the economy, whether a company defaults depends only on company-specific considerations.

117. Which of Stevenson's points regarding the reliability of credit ratings is *most accurate*?
    A. Point 1 only.
    B. Point 2 only.
    C. Neither point is correct.

118. According to the structural model shown in Exhibit 2, the maximum amount an investor holding the bond would pay to a third party to remove the risk of default would be:
    A. $0.65.
    B. $22.86.
    C. $23.51.

119. The results shown in Exhibit 2 indicate that the:
    A. time value of money discount exceeds the risk premium for risk of credit loss.
    B. risk premium for risk of credit loss exceeds the time value of money discount.
    C. risk premium for risk of credit loss is $0.65.

120. If the volatility estimate is changed to 30% in the structural model shown in Exhibit 2, the calculated value of IMC Bond would *most likely:*
    A. remain the same.
    B. decrease.
    C. increase.

End of Afternoon Session

Exam 3
Morning Session

Question	Topic	Minutes (Points)
1 to 6	Ethics	18
7 to 12	Ethics	18
13 to 18	Economics	18
19 to 24	Financial Reporting and Analysis	18
25 to 30	Financial Reporting and Analysis	18
31 to 36	Equity	18
37 to 42	Equity	18
43 to 48	Equity	18
49 to 54	Fixed Income	18
55 to 60	Fixed Income	18

Test Answers

1.	(A)	(B)	(C)		41.	(A)	(B)	(C)
2.	(A)	(B)	(C)		42.	(A)	(B)	(C)
3.	(A)	(B)	(C)		43.	(A)	(B)	(C)
4.	(A)	(B)	(C)		44.	(A)	(B)	(C)
5.	(A)	(B)	(C)		45.	(A)	(B)	(C)
6.	(A)	(B)	(C)		46.	(A)	(B)	(C)
7.	(A)	(B)	(C)		47.	(A)	(B)	(C)
8.	(A)	(B)	(C)		48.	(A)	(B)	(C)
9.	(A)	(B)	(C)		49.	(A)	(B)	(C)
10.	(A)	(B)	(C)		50.	(A)	(B)	(C)
11.	(A)	(B)	(C)		51.	(A)	(B)	(C)
12.	(A)	(B)	(C)		52.	(A)	(B)	(C)
13.	(A)	(B)	(C)		53.	(A)	(B)	(C)
14.	(A)	(B)	(C)		54.	(A)	(B)	(C)
15.	(A)	(B)	(C)		55.	(A)	(B)	(C)
16.	(A)	(B)	(C)		56.	(A)	(B)	(C)
17.	(A)	(B)	(C)		57.	(A)	(B)	(C)
18.	(A)	(B)	(C)		58.	(A)	(B)	(C)
19.	(A)	(B)	(C)		59.	(A)	(B)	(C)
20.	(A)	(B)	(C)		60.	(A)	(B)	(C)
21.	(A)	(B)	(C)					
22.	(A)	(B)	(C)					
23.	(A)	(B)	(C)					
24.	(A)	(B)	(C)					
25.	(A)	(B)	(C)					
26.	(A)	(B)	(C)					
27.	(A)	(B)	(C)					
28.	(A)	(B)	(C)					
29.	(A)	(B)	(C)					
30.	(A)	(B)	(C)					
31.	(A)	(B)	(C)					
32.	(A)	(B)	(C)					
33.	(A)	(B)	(C)					
34.	(A)	(B)	(C)					
35.	(A)	(B)	(C)					
36.	(A)	(B)	(C)					
37.	(A)	(B)	(C)					
38.	(A)	(B)	(C)					
39.	(A)	(B)	(C)					
40.	(A)	(B)	(C)					

Questions 1–6 relate to Glenda Garvey.

Glenda Garvey is interning at Samson Financial in the summer to earn money for her last semester of MBA studies. She took the Level III CFA® exam in June but has not yet received her results. Garvey's work involves preparing research reports on small companies.

Garvey is at lunch with a group of co-workers. She listens to their conversation about various stocks and takes note of a comment from Tony Topel, a veteran analyst. Topel is talking about Vallo Engineering, a small stock he has tried repeatedly to convince the investment director to add to the monitored list. While the investment director does not like Vallo, Topel has faith in the company and has gradually accumulated 5,000 shares for his own account. Another analyst, Mary Kennedy, tells the group about Koral Koatings, a paint and sealant manufacturer. Kennedy has spent most of the last week at the office doing research on Koral. She has concluded that the stock is undervalued and consensus earnings estimates are conservative. However, she has not filed a report for Samson, nor does she intend to. She said she has purchased the stock for herself and advises her colleagues to do the same. After she gets back to the office, Garvey purchases 25 shares of Vallo and 50 shares of Koral for herself.

Samson pays its interns very little, and Garvey works as a waitress at a diner in the financial district to supplement her income. The dinner crowd includes many analysts and brokers who work at nearby businesses. While waiting tables that night, Garvey hears two employees of a major brokerage house discussing Metrona, a nanotechnology company. The restaurant patrons say that the broker's star analyst has issued a report with a buy rating on Metrona that morning. The diners plan to buy the stock the next morning. After Garvey finishes her shift, restaurant manager Mandy Jones, a longtime Samson client, asks to speak with her. Jones commends Garvey for her hard work at the restaurant, praising her punctuality and positive attitude, and offers her two tickets to a Yankees game as a bonus.

The next morning, Garvey buys 40 shares of Metrona for her own account at the market open. Soon afterward, she receives a call from Harold Koons, one of Samson's largest money-management clients. Koons says he got Garvey's name from Bertha Witt, who manages the Koons's account. Koons wanted to reward the analyst who discovered Anvil Hammers, a machine-tool company whose stock soared soon after it was added to his portfolio. Garvey prepared the original report on Anvil Hammers. Koons offers Garvey two free round-trip tickets to the city of her choice. Garvey thanks Koons, then asks her immediate supervisor, Karl May, about the gift from Koons but does not mention the gift from Jones. May approves the Koons' gift.

After talking with May, Garvey starts a research project on Zenith Enterprises, a frozen-juice maker. Garvey's gathers quarterly data on the company's sales and profits over the past two years. Garvey uses a simple linear regression to estimate the relationship between GDP growth and Zenith's sales growth. Next she uses a consensus GDP estimate from a well-known economic data reporting service and her regression model to extrapolate growth rates for the next three years.

Garvey is not working at the diner that night, so she goes home to work on her biography for an online placement service. In it she makes the following two statements:

Statement 1: I'm a Level III CFA candidate, and I expect to receive my charter this fall. The CFA program is a grueling, 3-part, graduate-level course, and passage requires an expertise in a variety of financial instruments, as well as knowledge of the forces that drive our economy and financial markets.

Statement 2: I expect to graduate with my MBA from Braxton College at the end of the fall semester. As both an MBA and a CFA, I'll be in high demand. Hire me now while you still have the chance.

Akshay Nagoree, CFA, is a portfolio manager for several pension funds at Samson. His wife is treasurer and 15% shareholder of Gatedon Electric. The market value of Mrs. Nagoree's Gatedon shares is now $2 million. Samson's research department is recommending the stock to its trust officers and pension fund portfolio managers. Samson has adopted CFA Institute's Research Objectivity Standards.

1. During the lunch conversation, which CFA Institute Standard of Professional Conduct was *most likely* violated?
    A. III(B) Fair Dealing.
    B. IV(A) Loyalty.
    C. V(A) Reasonable Basis.

2. Does Garvey's acceptance of the gifts from Koons and Jones violate Standard I(B) Independence and Objectivity?
    A. Accepting Koons' gift was a violation.
    B. Accepting Jones' gift was a violation.
    C. Neither gift would result in a violation.

3.　Did Garvey violate Standard II(A) Material Nonpublic Information when she purchased Vallo and Metrona?
　　A.　Buying Vallo was a violation.
　　B.　Buying Metrona was a violation.
　　C.　Neither purchase was a violation.

4.　In her estimation of Zenith's future growth rate, what standard did Garvey violate?
　　A.　Standard I(C) Misrepresentation regarding plagiarism.
　　B.　Standard V(A) Diligence and Reasonable Basis.
　　C.　Both I(C) and V(A).

5.　Did the two statements in Garvey's biography violate Standard VII(B) Reference to CFA Institute, the CFA designation, and the CFA program?
　　A.　Statement 1 is a violation.
　　B.　Statement 2 is a violation.
　　C.　Both statements are violations.

6.　Based on the Research Objectivity Standards, which of the following is Nagoree's *most appropriate* course of action for the accounts under his management?
　　A.　Nagoree is permitted to buy Gatedon stock without stipulation because it is his wife, not he, who is a shareholder in Gatedon.
　　B.　Nagoree is permitted to buy the stock after disclosing his wife's ownership to his supervisor and to the trustees of all the pension funds he manages.
　　C.　Nagoree is prohibited from buying the stock because of his inability to render an unbiased and objective investment opinion given his wife's affiliation with the company.

Questions 7–12 relate to Maria Harris.

Maria Harris is a CFA® Level III candidate and portfolio manager for Islandwide Hedge Fund. Harris is commonly involved in complex trading strategies on behalf of Islandwide and maintains a significant relationship with Quadrangle Brokers, which provides portfolio analysis tools to Harris. Recent market volatility has led Islandwide to incur record-high trading volume and commissions with Quadrangle for the quarter. In appreciation of Islandwide's business, Quadrangle offers Harris an all-expenses-paid week of golf at Pebble Beach for her and her husband. Harris discloses the offer to her supervisor and compliance officer and, based on their approval, accepts the trip.

Harris has lunch that day with C. K. Swamy, CFA, her old college roommate and future sister-in-law. While Harris is sitting in the restaurant waiting for Swamy to arrive, Harris overhears a conversation between the president and chief financial officer (CFO) of Progressive Industries. The president informs the CFO that Progressive's board of directors has just approved dropping the company's cash dividend, despite its record of paying dividends for the past 46 quarters. The company plans to announce this information in about a week. Harris owns Progressive's common stock and immediately calls her broker to sell her shares in anticipation of a price decline.

Swamy recently joined Dillon Associates, an investment advisory firm as an equity analyst. Swamy plans to continue serving on the board of directors of Landmark Enterprises, a private company specializing in online gaming owned by her brother-in-law, for which she receives $2,000 annually. Swamy also serves as an unpaid advisor to the local symphony on investing their large endowment and receives four season tickets to the symphony performances.

After lunch, Alice Adams, a client, offers Harris a 1-week cruise as a reward for the great performance of her account over the previous quarter. Bert Baker, also a client, has offered Harris two airplane tickets to Hawaii if his account beats its benchmark by more than 2% over the following year.

Juliann Clark, a CFA candidate, is an analyst at Dillon Associates and a colleague of Swamy's. Clark participates in a conference call for several analysts in which the chief executive officer at Dex says his company's board of directors has just accepted a tender offer from Monolith Chemicals to buy Dex at a 40% premium over the market price. Clark contacts a friend and relates the information about Dex and Monolith. The friend promptly contacts her broker and buys 2,000 shares of Dex's stock.

Ed Michaels, CFA, is director of trading at Quadrangle Brokers. Michaels has recently implemented a buy program for a client. This buy program has driven up the price of a small-cap stock, in which Islandwide owns shares, by approximately 5% because the orders were large in relation to the average daily trading volume of the stock. Michaels's firm is about to bring shares of an OTC firm to market in an

IPO. Michaels has publicly announced that, as a market maker in the shares, his trading desk will create additional liquidity in the stock over its first 90 days of trading by committing to minimum bids and offers of 5,000 shares and to a maximum spread of one-eighth.

Carl Park, CFA, is a retail broker with Quadrangle and has been allocated 5,000 shares of an oversubscribed IPO. One of his clients has been complaining about the execution price of a trade Park made for her last month, but Park knows from researching it that the trade received the best possible execution. In order to calm the client down, Park increases her allocation of shares in the IPO above what it would be if he allocated them to all suitable client accounts based on account size. He allocates a pro-rata portion of the remaining shares to a trust account held at his firm for which his brother-in-law is the primary beneficiary.

7. By accepting the trip from Quadrangle, has Harris complied with the CFA Institute Code and Standards?
    A. Harris may accept the trip because she maintains a significant relationship with Quadrangle that contributes to the performance of client accounts.
    B. Harris may accept the trip because she disclosed the trip to her supervisor and compliance officer and accepted based on their approval.
    C. Harris may not accept the trip because the offer from Quadrangle could impede her ability to make objective investment decisions on behalf of the client.

8. Has either Harris or Clark violated Standard II(A) Integrity of Capital Markets: Material Nonpublic Information?
    A. Harris is in violation.
    B. Clark is in violation.
    C. Both are in violation.

9. According to the Standards of Practice, with respect to the two offers from Adams and Baker, Harris:
    A. may accept both offers if she discloses them to her employer.
    B. may accept both gifts only if she discloses them to her employer and receives permission.
    C. must disclose the offer from Adams to her employer if she accepts it but must receive her employer's permission to accept the offer from Baker.

10. Has Michaels violated Standard II(B) Integrity of Capital Markets: Market Manipulation with respect to any of the following?
    A. The buy program is a violation.
    B. The liquidity activity is a violation.
    C. There is no violation.

11. According to Standard IV Duties to Employers, which of the following is *most likely* required of Swamy? Swamy must:
    A. secure written permission from her employer before performing services for the symphony.
    B. inform her immediate supervisor at Dillon in writing that she (Swamy) must comply with the Code and Standards.
    C. disclose to her employer any additional compensation she receives from Landmark Enterprises and secure written permission to serve on the board.

12. Which action by Park violated Standard III(B) Duties to Clients: Fair Dealing?
    A. Increasing allocation to the problem client.
    B. Decreased allocation to the brother-in-law and other firm clients.
    C. Both actions are violations.

Questions 13–18 relate to Barton Wilson.

Barton Wilson, a junior analyst, is a new hire at a money center bank. He has been assigned to help Juanita Chevas, CFA, in the currency trading department. Together, Wilson and Chevas are working on the development of new trading software designed to detect profitable opportunities in the foreign exchange market. Obviously, they are interested in risk-free arbitrage opportunities. However, they have also been instructed to investigate the possibility of longer-term currency exposures that are not necessarily risk-free. To test the logic of their new software, Wilson gathers the following market data:

- Spot JPY/USD exchange rate = 120.
- Spot EUR/USD exchange rate = 0.7224.
- U.S. risk-free interest rate = 7%.
- Eurozone risk-free rate = 9.08%.
- Japanese risk-free rate = 3.88%.
- Yield curves in all three currencies are flat.

In addition to in-house currency transactions, the new software program is also intended to provide insight into currency exposure and hedging needs for the bank's major customers. These customers typically include large multinational firms. Essentially, the bank wants to provide consulting services to its clients concerning which currency exposures offer the most lucrative opportunities. In this process, the bank will rely on deviations from international parity conditions as an indicator of long-term currency movements. Several bank customers have engaged in a carry trade with Bundovian Bunco (BU) as the investment currency and the USD as the funding currency. The bank will provide risk management advice to customers as it pertains to their FX carry trades.

Wilson obtains the following data from the econometrics department:

- JPY/USD spot rate one year ago = 116.
- EUR/USD spot rate one year ago = 0.7200.
- Anticipated and historical U.S. annual inflation = 3%.
- Anticipated and historical Japanese annual inflation = 0%.
- Anticipated and historical Eurozone annual inflation = 5%.

One of the bank's major customers has significant business interests in Japan and in the Eurozone and has long exposure to both currencies. The customer has traditionally hedged all currency risk. However, the customer's new risk manager has decided to leave some currency exposure unhedged in an attempt to profit from long-term currency exposure.

13.　According to relative purchasing power parity, the expected JPY/EUR spot rate two years from now is *closest* to:
A.　150.67.
B.　158.29.
C.　166.74.

14.　Are the Japanese and Eurozone inflation forecasts provided by the econometrics department consistent with the inflation rates implied by the international Fisher relation, given a U.S. inflation rate of 3%?
A.　Both forecasts are consistent.
B.　Neither forecast is consistent.
C.　One forecast is consistent and the other is not.

15.　According to the uncovered interest rate parity, in 12 months, the JPY/USD exchange rate would *most likely* be:
A.　116.50.
B.　123.74.
C.　117.96.

16.　For this question only, suppose that the Japanese government wants to fix the JPY/USD exchange rate at 100. Under the Mundell-Fleming model, the Japanese government's ability to follow an expansionary monetary policy would be limited by:
A.　its fiscal policy.
B.　the price sensitivity of its exports to the United States.
C.　its USD reserves.

17.　Based on the assumption that international parity conditions will hold in the long run, should the JPY and Euro currency exposures of the bank's major customer be left unhedged?
A.　Both currencies should be left unhedged.
B.　Neither currency should be left unhedged.
C.　One currency should be left unhedged and the other should not.

18.　The *least appropriate* time for advising that the bank's clients close out their carry trade is when:
A.　USD prices of options on BU are high.
B.　BU prices of options on Bundovian equities are high.
C.　the USD is trading above value implied by trends following trading rules.

Questions 19–24 relate to Snowboards and Skateboards, Inc.

Ota L'Abbe, a supervisor at an investment research firm, has asked one of the junior analysts, Andreas Hally, to draft a research report dealing with various accounting issues.

Excerpts from the request are as follows:

- "There's an exciting company that we're starting to follow these days. It's called Snowboards and Skateboards, Inc. They are a multinational company with operations and a head office based in the resort town of Whistler in western Canada. However, they also have a significant subsidiary located in the United States."
- "Look at the subsidiary and deal with some foreign currency issues, including the specific differences between the temporal and current rate methods of translation, as well as the effect on financial ratios."
- "The attached file contains the September 30, 2008, financial statements of the U.S. subsidiary. Translate the financial statements into Canadian dollars in a manner consistent with U.S. GAAP."

The following are statements from the research report subsequently written by Hally:

Statement 1: Subsidiaries whose operations are well-integrated with the parent will use the current rate method of translation.

Statement 2: Self-contained, independent subsidiaries whose operating, investing, and financing activities are primarily located in the local market will use the temporal method of translation.

Snowboards and Skateboards, Inc. (U.S.)	(U.S. dollars)
Balance Sheet as of 9/30/2008	
Cash and accounts receivable	775,000
Inventory	600,000
Property, plant, and equipment (PP&E) – net	730,000
Total assets	2,105,000
Accounts payable	125,000
Long-term debt	400,000
Common stock	535,000
Retained earnings	1,045,000
Total liabilities and shareholders' equity	2,105,000

Income Statement for the Year ended 9/30/2008	
Sales	1,352,000
Cost of goods sold	(1,205,000)
Depreciation	(140,000)
Net income	7,000

Other information to be considered:

- *Exchange rates (CAD/USD)*

Fiscal 2007 (average)	1.44
Fiscal 2008 (average)	1.35
October 1, 2004	1.50
September 30, 2007	1.48
June 30, 2008	1.37
September 30, 2008	1.32

- Beginning inventory for fiscal 2008 had been purchased evenly throughout fiscal 2007. The company uses the FIFO inventory value method.

- Dividends of USD 25,000 were paid to the shareholders on June 30, 2008.

- All of the remaining inventory at the end of fiscal 2008 was purchased evenly throughout fiscal 2008.

- All of the PP&E was purchased, and all of the common equity was issued at the inception of the company on October 1, 2004. No new PP&E has been acquired, and no additional common stock has been issued since then. However, they plan to purchase new PP&E starting in fiscal 2009.

- The beginning retained earnings balance for fiscal 2008 was CAD 1,550,000.

- The accounts payable on the fiscal 2008 balance sheet were all incurred on June 30, 2008.

- The U.S. subsidiary's operations are highly integrated with the main operations in Canada.

- The remeasured inventory for 2008 using the temporal method is CAD 810,000.

- Costs of goods sold under the temporal method in 2008 is CAD 1,667,250.

19. Are Hally's statements regarding foreign currency translation correct?

	Statement 1	Statement 2
A.	Yes	Yes
B.	Yes	No
C.	No	No

20.   Which of the following *best* describes the effect on the parent's fiscal 2008 sales when translated to Canadian dollars? Sales, relative to what it would have been if the CAD/USD exchange rate had not changed, will be:
    A. lower because the U.S. dollar depreciated during fiscal 2008.
    B. higher because the average value of the Canadian dollar depreciated during fiscal 2008.
    C. lower because the U.S. dollar appreciated during fiscal 2008.

21.   As compared to the temporal method, which of the following financial statement elements of the parent are lower under the current rate method?
    A. Cash and accounts receivable.
    B. Depreciation expense and cost of goods sold.
    C. Common stock and dividends paid.

22.   Using the appropriate translation method, which of the following *best* describes the effect of changing exchange rates on the parent's fiscal 2008 financial statements?
    A. An accumulated loss of CAD 242,100 is reported in the shareholders' equity.
    B. A loss of CAD 31,200 is recognized in the income statement.
    C. A gain of CAD 27,400 is recognized in the income statement.

23.   As compared to the temporal method, the parent's fixed asset turnover for fiscal 2008 using the current rate method is:
    A. higher.
    B. lower.
    C. the same.

24.   Suppose the parent uses the current rate method to translate the subsidiary for fiscal 2008. Will return on assets and net profit margin in U.S. dollars before translation be the same as, or different than, the translated Canadian dollar ratios?

	Return on assets	Net profit margin
A.	Same	Different
B.	Different	Different
C.	Different	Same

Questions 25–30 relate to Wayland, Inc., and Optimax.

Kevin Rathbun, CFA, is a financial analyst at a major brokerage firm. His supervisor, Elizabeth Mao, CFA, asks him to analyze the financial position of Wayland, Inc. (Wayland), a manufacturer of components for high quality optic transmission systems. Mao also inquires about the impact of any unconsolidated investments.

On December 31, 2007, Wayland purchased a 35% ownership interest in a strategic new firm called Optimax for $300,000 cash. The pre-acquisition balance sheets of both firms are found in Exhibit 1.

Exhibit 1: Pre-Acquisition Balance Sheets for Wayland and Optimax

Balance sheets as of Dec. 31, 2007 *in thousands*	Wayland	Optimax
Assets		
Cash	$710	$100
Marketable securities	2,550	—
Inventory	2,000	400
Accounts receivable	3,000	500
Property, plant, and equipment	2,450	1,000
Total assets	**$10,710**	**$2,000**
Liabilities		
Accounts payable	$3,310	400
Long-term debt	5,000	1,000
Equity	2,400	600
Total liabilities and equity	**$10,710**	**$2,000**

On the acquisition date, all of Optimax's assets and liabilities were stated on its balance sheet at their fair values except for its property, plant, and equipment (PP&E), which had a fair value of $1.2 million. The remaining useful life of the PP&E is ten years with no salvage value. Both firms use the straight-line depreciation method.

For the year ended 2008, Optimax reported net income of $250,000 and paid dividends of $100,000.

During the first quarter of 2009, Optimax sold goods to Wayland and recognized $15,000 of profit from the sale. At the end of the quarter, half of the goods purchased from Optimax remained in Wayland's inventory.

Wayland currently uses the equity method to account for its investment in Optimax.

Rathbun also notes that Wayland owns shares in Vanry, Inc. (Vanry). Rathbun gathers the data in Exhibit 2 from Wayland's financial statements. The year-end portfolio value is the market value of all Vanry shares held on December 31. All security transactions occurred on July 1, and the transaction price is the price that Wayland actually paid for the shares acquired. Vanry pays a cash dividend of $1 per share at the end of each year. Wayland expects to sell its investment in Vanry in the near term and accounts for it as *held-for-trading*.

Exhibit 2: Share Transaction Data, Vanry, Inc.

Year	Year-End Portfolio Value	Year-End Shares Held	Year-End Share Price	Transaction Price (July 1)
2007	$1,875,000	25,000[a]	$75	$85
2008	$2,280,000	30,000	76	78

[a] Purchased on July 1, 2007.

Wayland owns some publicly traded bonds of the Rotor Corporation that it reports as held-to-maturity securities.

25. The amount of goodwill as a result of Wayland's acquisition of Optimax is *closest* to:
   A. $0.
   B. $20,000.
   C. $50,000.

26. What amount should Wayland report in its balance sheet as a result of its investment in Optimax at the end of 2008?
   A. $352,000.
   B. $345,500.
   C. $380,500.

27. Which of the following *best* describes Wayland's treatment of the intercompany sales transaction for the quarter ended March 31, 2009? Wayland should reduce its equity income by:
   A. $2,625.
   B. $7,500.
   C. $15,000.

28. Which of the following statements is *least accurate* under the new IFRS standards (IFRS 9)?
    A. Equity investments held for trading must be measured at fair value through profit or loss.
    B. Equity investments once measured as fair value through OCI cannot be reclassified to be measured as fair value through profit or loss.
    C. Debt securities that meet the business model test and the cash flow characteristic test must be measured at amortized cost.

29. Regarding the Rotor Corporation bonds, under the current standards, Wayland would have the option to reclassify them as designated at fair value from held-to-maturity under:
    A. U.S. GAAP only.
    B. IFRS only.
    C. both IFRS and U.S. GAAP.

30. As a result of its investment in Vanry, what amount should Wayland recognize in its income statement for the year ended 2008?
    A. $35,000 profit.
    B. $45,000 profit.
    C. $55,000 profit.

Questions 31–36 relate to Lorenz Kummert.

Lorenz Kummert is a junior equity analyst who is following Schubert, Inc. (Schubert), a small publicly traded company in the United States. His supervisor, Markus Alter, CFA, has advised him to use the residual income model to analyze Schubert.

In his preliminary report to Alter, Kummert makes the following statements:

Statement 1: Residual income models are appropriate when expected free cash flows are negative for the foreseeable future.

Statement 2: Residual income models are not applicable when dividends are volatile.

Kummert has determined Schubert's cost of equity, cost of debt, and weighted average cost of capital (WACC) to be 12.8%, 8.4%, and 11.9%, respectively. Book value of long-term debt and equity was $6,200,000 and $3,281,000 respectively on January 1, 2008. The stock price on December 31, 2008, is $36 per share and there are 130,000 shares outstanding. The relevant tax rate is 30%, and return on equity (ROE) is expected to be 14%.

Summarized financial information about Schubert for 2008 is provided in Exhibits 1 and 2.

Exhibit 1: Schubert, Inc., Balance Sheet on December 31, 2008

Cash	$ 125,000	Accounts payable	$ 426,000
Accounts receivable	975,000	Accrued liabilities	774,000
Inventory	1,215,000	Long-term debt	6,211,000
Fixed assets (net)	9,277,000		
		Common shares	2,100,000
		Retained earnings	2,081,000
Total assets	$11,592,000	Total liabilities and equity	$11,592,000

Exhibit 2: Schubert, Inc., Income Statement for the year ended December 31, 2008

Sales	$9,423,000
Cost of sales	4,580,000
Selling, general, and administrative	1,230,000
Depreciation	1,745,000
Interest expense	522,000
Income tax expense	403,800
Net income	$942,200

Based on his analysis of several years of financial statements, Kummert notes that 2008 was an exceptionally profitable year for Schubert, and that its dividend payouts are usually low because the funds are mainly reinvested in the firm to promote growth. Furthermore, there are very few nonrecurring items on the income statement. Upon review of Kummert's preliminary report, Alter concurs with his analysis of the financial statements but reminds him that Schubert's long-term debt is currently trading at 95% of its book value. He also cautions Kummert that violations of the clean surplus relation can bias the results of the residual income model.

The consensus annual EPS estimate for 2009 is $4.50, and the dividend payout ratio for 2009 is estimated at 5%.

31. Are Kummert's statements regarding the residual income model correct?
    A. Both statements are incorrect.
    B. Only Statement 1 is correct.
    C. Only Statement 2 is correct.

32. Assuming that Kummert and Alter are correct with their conclusions regarding Schubert's financial statements, which of the following levels would *best* describe the strength of the persistence factor with respect to Schubert's residual income?
    A. Low persistence factor.
    B. Medium persistence factor.
    C. High persistence factor.

33. Which of the following amounts is *closest* to the forecast of Schubert's book value per share and residual income, respectively, for 2009?

	Book value per share	Residual income
A.	$36.43	$0.38
B.	$38.00	$2.32
C.	$36.40	$2.32

34. Which of the following amounts are *closest* to Schubert's economic value added (EVA) for fiscal year 2008 and market value added (MVA) as of fiscal year-end 2008, respectively?

EVA	MVA
A. $179,361	$188,450
B. $23,455	$369,500
C. ($70,900)	$369,500

35. Which of the following amounts is *closest* to Schubert's implied growth rate in residual income?
    A. 0.34%.
    B. 2.75%.
    C. 12.63%.

36. Regarding Alter's caution about violations of the clean surplus relationship, examples of items that can violate this relationship include:
    A. foreign currency gains and losses under the current rate method.
    B. changes in the market value of debt and equity held as trading securities.
    C. changes in net working capital.

Questions 37–42 relate to Ferguson Department Stores, Inc.

Matthew Emery, CFA, is responsible for analyzing companies in the retail industry. He is currently reviewing the status of Ferguson Department Stores, Inc. (FDS). FDS has recently gone through extensive restructuring in the wake of a slowdown in the economy that has made retailing particularly challenging. As part of his analysis, Emery has gathered information from a number of sources.

Ferguson Department Stores, Inc.

FDS went public in 1969 following a major acquisition, and the Ferguson name quickly became one of the most recognized in retailing. Ferguson had been successful through most of its first 30 years in business and has prided itself on being the one-stop shopping destination for consumers living on the West Coast of the United States. Recently, FDS began to experience both top and bottom line difficulties due to increased competition from specialty retailers who could operate more efficiently and offer a wider range of products in a focused retailing sector. When the company's main bank reduced FDS's line of credit, a serious working capital crisis ensued, and the company was forced to issue additional equity in an effort to overcome the problem. FDS has a cost of capital of 10% and a required rate of return on equity of 12%. Dividends are growing at a rate of 8%, but the growth rate is expected to decline linearly over the next six years to a long-term growth rate of 4%. The company recently paid an annual dividend of $1.

At the end of 2008, FDS announced that it would be expanding its retail operations, moving to a warehouse concept, and opening new stores around the country. FDS also announced it would close some existing stores, write-down assets, and take a large restructuring charge. Upon reviewing the prospects of the firm, Emery issued an earnings-per-share forecast for 2009 of $0.90. He set a 12-month share price target of $22.50. Immediately following the expansion announcement, the share price of FDS jumped from $14 to $18.

Exhibit 1: Summary Income Statement, Ferguson Department Stores, Inc.
(U.S. $ millions, except per share data and shares outstanding)

	2008	2007
Sales	$6,435.9	$6,322.7
Cost of goods sold, operating, administrative, and selling expenses	6,007.9	5,875.9
Depreciation and amortization	148.7	146.6
Interest expense	59.8	59.5
Unusual items—expense	189.1	5.0
Earnings before tax	30.4	235.7
Income taxes—current	49.3	7.5
Income taxes—future	(71.1)	93.5
	(21.8)	101.0
Net earnings for the year	$52.2	$134.7
Earnings per share: Basic	$0.49	$1.26
Fully diluted	$0.49	$1.26
Weighted average shares outstanding	106,530,610	106,530,610

In 2008, FDS also reported an unusual expense of $189.1 million related to restructuring costs and asset write downs.

Exhibit 2: Selected Industry Information for 2008

Estimated earnings growth rate	0.10
Mean trailing price/earnings (P/E) ratio	22.50
Mean price/sales (P/S) ratio	0.50

In response to questions from a colleague, Emery makes the following statements regarding the merits of earnings yield compared to the P/E ratio:

Statement 1: For ranking purposes, earnings yield may be useful whenever earnings are either negative or close to zero.

Statement 2: A high E/P implies the security is overpriced.

37. The value of one share of FDS using the H-model is *closest* to:
  A. $14.50.
  B. $16.50.
  C. $19.33.

38. Given Emery's dividend forecast for FDS, is the H-model the appropriate valuation model to use to value FDS?
    A. Yes.
    B. No, the H-model is appropriate when the dividend growth rate declines at a linear rate for a short period of time during stage one, followed by a 1-year suspension in dividends before the previous dividend is reinstated, and then dividends grow at a long-term constant rate.
    C. No, the H-model is appropriate when the dividend growth rate grows during the first stage followed by a period of stable growth in dividends in stage two, followed by a dividend growth rate that declines linearly in perpetuity.

39. Assuming that the cost of equity for FDS does not change, the present value of growth opportunities in the share price following the announcement that the company would be expanding its retail operations, using Emery's 2009 earnings forecast, is *closest* to:
    A. $9.00.
    B. $10.50.
    C. $12.50.

40. Are Emery's statements regarding the earnings yield and E/P ratio correct?
    A. One statement is correct and the other statement is incorrect.
    B. Both statements are correct.
    C. Both statements are incorrect.

41. Assuming a tax rate of 34%, the underlying earnings per share (EPS) for FDS in 2008 is *closest* to:
    A. $1.26.
    B. $1.36.
    C. $2.27.

42. According to FDS's price-to-sales ratio for 2008, based on the post-expansion announcement stock price, FDS is:
    A. underpriced relative to the industry.
    B. overpriced relative to the industry.
    C. properly priced relative to the industry.

Questions 43–48 relate to Universal Home Supplies, Inc.

Michael Robbins, CFA, is analyzing Universal Home Supplies, Inc. (UHS), which has recently gone through some extensive restructuring.

Universal Home Supplies, Inc.

UHS operates nearly 200 department stores and 78 specialty stores in over 30 states. The company offers a wide range of products, including women's, men's, and children's clothing and accessories, as well as home furnishings, electronics, and other consumer goods. The company is considering cutting back on or eliminating its electronics business entirely. UHS manufactures many of its own apparel products domestically in a large factory located in Kentucky. This central location permits shipping to distribution points around the country at reasonable costs. The company operates primarily in suburban shopping malls and offers mid- to high-end merchandise mainly under its own private label. At present, more than 70% of the company's customers live within a 10-minute drive of one of the company's stores. Web site activity measured in dollar sales volume has increased by over 18% in the past year. Shares of UHS stock are currently priced at $25. Dividends are expected to grow at a rate of 6% over the next eight years and then continue to grow at that same rate indefinitely. The company has a cost of capital of 10.2%, a beta of 0.8, and just paid an annual dividend of $1.25.

UHS has faced serious cash flow problems in recent years as a consequence of its strategy to pursue an upscale clientele in the face of increased competition from several "niche retailers." The firm has been able to issue new debt recently and has also managed to extend its line of credit. The two financing agreements required a pledge of additional assets and a promise to install a super-efficient inventory tracking system in time to meet holiday shopping demand.

Exhibit 1: Summary Income Statement for Universal Home Supplies, Inc.
(U.S. $ millions, except per share data and shares outstanding)

	2008	2007
Sales	$7,400.1	$7,383.8
Cost of goods sold, operating, administrative, and selling expenses	7,081.3	7,028.9
Depreciation and amortization	157.7	155.6
Earnings before interest expense and income taxes	161.1	199.3
Interest expense	42.6	45.4
Earnings before tax	118.5	153.9
Income taxes—current	40.3	52.3
Net earnings for the year	$78.2	$101.6
Earnings per share: Basic	$0.82	$1.40
Fully diluted	$0.82	$1.34
Weighted average shares outstanding	95,366,000	72,572,000

Exhibit 2: Book Value per Share (BVPS in $) and Return on Equity (ROE), Universal Home Supplies, Inc.

Year	2008	2007	2006	2005
BVPS	$25.58	$33.62	$37.54	$32.26
ROE	3.2%	4.0%	4.5%	3.9%

Exhibit 3: 2008 Selected Industry Information

Estimated earnings growth rate	0.10
Mean trailing price/earnings (P/E) ratio	22.50
Mean price/sales (P/S) ratio	0.50

Robbins is asked by his supervisor to carefully consider the advantages and drawbacks of using the price-to-sales ratio (P/S) and to determine the appropriate valuation metrics to use when returns follow patterns of persistence or reversals.

Robbins also estimates a cross-sectional model to predict UHS's P/E:

$$\text{predicted P/E} = 5 - (10 \times \text{beta}) + [3 \times \text{4-year average ROE(\%)}] + [2 \times \text{8-year dividend growth forecast(\%)}]$$

where ROE and growth forecast are in percentages (i.e., 10 instead of 0.10 for 10%).

43. Based on the H-model, the implied expected rate of return for UHS is *closest* to:
    A. 8.8%.
    B. 10.2%.
    C. 11.3%.

44. Robbins should conclude that a key drawback to using the price-to-sales (P/S) ratio in the investment process is that P/S is:
    A. positive even when earnings per share is negative.
    B. not appropriate for valuing the equity of mature companies.
    C. susceptible to manipulation with respect to revenue recognition.

45. Is UHS stock, at the end of 2008, *best* described as overvalued or undervalued according to the:

	Trailing PEG ratio?	P/S ratio?
A.	Undervalued	Undervalued
B.	Overvalued	Undervalued
C.	Undervalued	Overvalued

46. Based on the method of average return on equity (ROE), the normalized EPS for UHS is *closest* to:
    A. $0.94.
    B. $1.00.
    C. $1.26.

47. The predicted P/E for UHS using Robbins's model is *closest* to:
    A. 20.7.
    B. 23.6.
    C. 30.5.

48. Robbins should conclude that patterns of persistence or reversals in returns provide the *most appropriate* rationale for valuation using:
    A. unexpected earnings.
    B. relative-strength indicators.
    C. standardized unexpected earnings.

Questions 49–54 relate to William Rogers.

William Rogers, a fixed-income portfolio manager, needs to eliminate a large cash position in his portfolio. He would like to purchase some corporate bonds. Two bonds that he is evaluating are shown in Exhibit 1. These two bonds are from the same issuer, and the current call price for the callable bond is 100. Assume that the issuer will call if the bond price exceeds the call price.

Rogers is also concerned about increases in interest rates and is considering the purchase of a putable bond. He wants to determine how assumed increases or decreases in interest rate volatility affect the value of the straight bonds and bonds with embedded options. After Rogers performs some analysis, he and his supervisor, Sigourney Walters, discuss the relative price movement between the two bonds in Exhibit 1 when interest rates change significantly.

During the discussions, Rogers makes the following statements:

Statement 1:   If the volatility of interest rates decreases, the value of the callable bond will increase.

Statement 2:   The noncallable bond will not be affected by a change in the volatility or level of interest rates.

Statement 3:   When interest rates decrease, the value of the noncallable bond increases by more than the callable bond.

Statement 4:   If the volatility of interest rates increases, the value of the putable bond will increase.

Walters mentors Rogers on bond concepts and then asks him to consider the pricing of a third bond. The third bond has five years to maturity, a 6% annual coupon, and pays interest semiannually. The bond is both callable and putable at 100 at any time. Walters indicates that the holders of the bond's embedded options will exercise if the option is in-the-money.

Exhibit 1: Bond Descriptions

	Noncallable Bond	Callable Bond
Price	99.77	98.21
Time to maturity (years)	5	5
Time to first call date (years)	n/a	4
Annual coupon	6.00%	6.00%
Interest payment	Semiannual	Semiannual
Yield to maturity	6.0542%	6.4227%

©2015 Kaplan, Inc.

Rogers obtained the prices shown in Exhibit 1 using software that generates an interest rate lattice. He uses his software to generate the interest rate lattice shown in Exhibit 2.

Exhibit 2: Interest Rate Lattice (Annualized Interest Rates)

Years	0.5	1.0	1.5	2.0	2.5	3.0	3.5	4.0	4.5
									15.44%
								14.10%	
							12.69%		12.46%
						11.85%		11.38%	
					9.75%		10.25%		10.05%
				8.95%		9.57%		9.19%	
			7.91%		7.88%		8.28%		8.11%
		7.35%		7.23%		7.74%		7.42%	
	6.62%		6.40%		6.37%		6.69%		6.54%
6.05%		5.95%		5.85%		6.25%		5.99%	
	5.36%		5.17%		5.15%		5.40%		5.28%
		4.81%		4.73%		5.05%		4.83%	
			4.18%		4.16%		4.36%		4.26%
				3.82%		4.08%		3.90%	
					3.37%		3.52%		3.44%
						3.30%		3.15%	
							2.84%		2.77%
								2.54%	
									2.24%

49. Evaluate Rogers's statements 1 and 3.
    A. Only Statement 1 is correct.
    B. Only Statement 3 is correct.
    C. Both statements are correct.

50. Evaluate Rogers's statements 2 and 4.
    A. Only Statement 2 is correct.
    B. Only Statement 4 is correct.
    C. Both statements are correct.

51. The market value of the embedded call option in Exhibit 1 is *closest* to:
    A. 1.56.
    B. 1.65.
    C. 1.79.

52.   For this question only, ignore the information from Exhibit 1 and any other calculations in other questions. Rather, assume that the interest rate lattice provided in Exhibit 2 is constructed to be arbitrage-free. However, when Rogers calculates the price of the callable bond using the interest rates in the lattice, he gets a value higher than the market price of the bond.

Is the price of the third callable and putable bond *likely* to be less than, equal to, or greater than 100%, and is the option-adjusted spread (OAS) on the callable bond *likely* to be zero, positive, or negative?

	Price of third bond	OAS of callable bond
A.	Less than 100%	Zero
B.	Equal to 100%	Positive
C.	Greater than 100%	Negative

53.   Using the information in the question and the following relevant portion of the interest rate and pricing trees, Rogers calculates the value of the noncallable bond at node A.

Corresponding portion of the interest rate tree (given as bond-equivalent yields):

8.95%

7.91%

7.23%

Years	1.5	2.0

Corresponding portion of the binomial price tree:

91.73%

A - - - - ►

96.17%

Years	1.5	2.0

The price of the noncallable bond at node A is *closest* to:
A. 89.84% of par.
B. 93.26% of par.
C. 96.14% of par.

54. Using the information in the question and the following relevant portion of the interest rate and pricing trees, Rogers calculates the value of the callable bond at node B.

Corresponding portion of the interest rate tree (given as bond-equivalent yields):

3.44%

3.15%

2.77%

Years	4.0	4.5

Corresponding portion of the callable bond price tree:

$100.00

B ---->

$100.00

Years	4.0	4.5

The price of the callable bond at node B is *closest* to:
A. 100.0% of par.
B. 101.4% of par.
C. 102.5% of par.

Questions 55–60 relate to Ted Thompson.

Ted Thompson, CIO for Aplius Insurance company, is evaluating the credit risk management models for the company's fixed income portfolio. Thompson meets with Nambi Musa, who is the head of Aplius's credit risk analysis department. Musa assures Thompson that his team has updated the credit risk analysis models over recent years and that these updated models have performed well over the past 12 months. Thompson, however, is not pleased with the losses incurred on Aplius's municipal bond holdings in the last quarter.

Musa mentions that while the credit risk analysis department continues to use credit ratings, they are also evaluating other analytical tools including structural models. He specifically mentions present value of expected loss as one credit risk measure currently being used. Musa makes the following statements:

Statement 1:   "One of the strengths of credit ratings is that they tend to be stable over time and hence reduce the price volatility in debt markets."

Statement 2:   "The present value of expected loss on a bond is the maximum amount an investor would be willing to pay to an insurer to bear the credit risk of that security."

Statement 3:   "One of the assumptions of the structural models of credit analysis is that the default risk changes over a business cycle."

Statement 4:   "In case of an ABS, credit analysis focuses on the probability of loss instead of the probability of default."

Musa further discusses the credit analysis metrics that are newly developed. As an example, he illustrates the valuation conducted on 1-year, 5% Zeta Corp. senior unsecured bonds. Exhibit 1 shows the report.

Exhibit 1: Valuation of 1-year, 5% Zeta Corp. Bond

Time to Cash Flow	Cash Flow	Risk-Free Spot Rate (%)	Credit Spread (%)
0.5	25	0.23	0.8
1	1025	0.25	0.85

Thompson then tells Musa that the credit analysis department should focus on reduced form models. Thompson states that, "reduced form models perform better than structural models as they tend to impose assumptions on the outputs of the structural model. However, reduced form models require a specification of the company's balance sheet composition."

©2015 Kaplan, Inc.

55. Musa's statement 1 is *most likely*:
    A. correct.
    B. incorrect because credit ratings are unstable over time.
    C. incorrect because of the implied relation to price volatility in debt markets.

56. Musa's statement 2 is *most likely*:
    A. correct.
    B. incorrect as the statement only considers credit risk.
    C. incorrect as the statement should refer to expected loss and not to present value of expected loss.

57. Musa's statement 3 is *most likely*:
    A. correct.
    B. incorrect as structural models assume that default risk is constant over a business cycle.
    C. incorrect as structural models assume that default risk is constant over the life of the bond.

58. Musa's statement 4 is *most likely*:
    A. correct.
    B. incorrect as credit analysis of ABS focuses on the probability of default instead of the probability of loss.
    C. incorrect as credit analysis of ABS focuses on probability of tranche default instead of probability of default.

59. Using information in Exhibit 1, the present value of expected loss for the Zeta Corp. bond is *closest* to:
    A. $7.74.
    B. $8.25.
    C. $8.76.

60. Thompson's statement about reduced form models relative to structural model is *most likely*:
    A. correct.
    B. incorrect regarding assumptions imposed.
    C. incorrect regarding specification of balance sheet composition being required.

End of Morning Session

Exam 3
Afternoon Session

Question	Topic	Minutes (Points)
61 to 66	Quantitative Methods	18
67 to 72	Financial Reporting and Analysis	18
73 to 78	Financial Reporting and Analysis	18
79 to 84	Corporate Finance	18
85 to 90	Corporate Finance	18
91 to 96	Equity	18
97 to 102	Alternative Investments	18
103 to 108	Derivatives	18
109 to 114	Derivatives	18
115 to 120	Portfolio Management	18

61.	(A)	(B)	(C)
62.	(A)	(B)	(C)
63.	(A)	(B)	(C)
64.	(A)	(B)	(C)
65.	(A)	(B)	(C)
66.	(A)	(B)	(C)
67.	(A)	(B)	(C)
68.	(A)	(B)	(C)
69.	(A)	(B)	(C)
70.	(A)	(B)	(C)

71.	(A)	(B)	(C)
72.	(A)	(B)	(C)
73.	(A)	(B)	(C)
74.	(A)	(B)	(C)
75.	(A)	(B)	(C)
76.	(A)	(B)	(C)
77.	(A)	(B)	(C)
78.	(A)	(B)	(C)
79.	(A)	(B)	(C)
80.	(A)	(B)	(C)

81.	(A)	(B)	(C)
82.	(A)	(B)	(C)
83.	(A)	(B)	(C)
84.	(A)	(B)	(C)
85.	(A)	(B)	(C)
86.	(A)	(B)	(C)
87.	(A)	(B)	(C)
88.	(A)	(B)	(C)
89.	(A)	(B)	(C)
90.	(A)	(B)	(C)

91.	(A)	(B)	(C)
92.	(A)	(B)	(C)
93.	(A)	(B)	(C)
94.	(A)	(B)	(C)
95.	(A)	(B)	(C)
96.	(A)	(B)	(C)
97.	(A)	(B)	(C)
98.	(A)	(B)	(C)
99.	(A)	(B)	(C)
100.	(A)	(B)	(C)

101.	(A)	(B)	(C)
102.	(A)	(B)	(C)
103.	(A)	(B)	(C)
104.	(A)	(B)	(C)
105.	(A)	(B)	(C)
106.	(A)	(B)	(C)
107.	(A)	(B)	(C)
108.	(A)	(B)	(C)
109.	(A)	(B)	(C)
110.	(A)	(B)	(C)

111.	(A)	(B)	(C)
112.	(A)	(B)	(C)
113.	(A)	(B)	(C)
114.	(A)	(B)	(C)
115.	(A)	(B)	(C)
116.	(A)	(B)	(C)
117.	(A)	(B)	(C)
118.	(A)	(B)	(C)
119.	(A)	(B)	(C)
120.	(A)	(B)	(C)

EXAM 3
AFTERNOON SESSION

Questions 61–66 relate to Joan Fisher and Kim Weatherford.

Joan Fisher and Kim Weatherford are economists responsible for modeling security returns for Quincy Portfolio Managers, which is located in the southwestern United States. Fisher is the firm's chief economist and Weatherford is her assistant.

Fisher has been busy over the past week modeling the macroeconomic data of an emerging market. The data for the past 24 months is shown in Exhibit 1.

Exhibit 1: Time Series of Emerging Markets Data

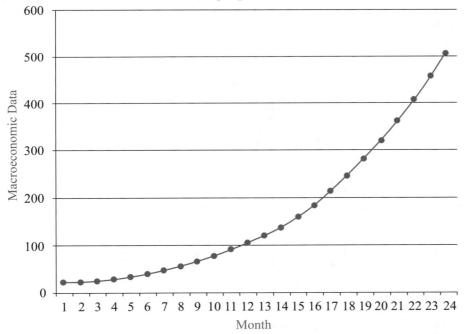

Fisher ponders how she can run a regression that will model the data for this country in the most appropriate way. She decides to regress the macroeconomic values against a time variable. The resulting plot of the residuals is shown in Exhibit 2.

Exhibit 2: Residual Plot from Emerging Markets Data

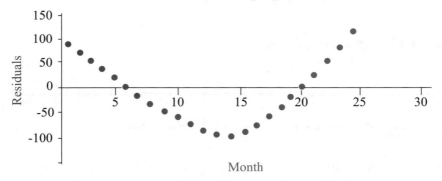

In addition to financial assets, Quincy Portfolio Managers also recommends the use of commodities as a portfolio diversifier. Weatherford has been examining price indices for silver in an attempt to determine whether silver returns are predictable. As an initial step, she uses an autoregressive first-order regression model on daily price data for silver over the past two years. The plot of the raw data and the results of the regression are shown in Exhibits 3 and 4.

Exhibit 3: Time Series of Silver Prices

Exhibit 4: Silver Price Regression Results

Regression Statistics	
Multiple R	0.99
R-Square	0.98
Adjusted R-Square	0.98
Standard Error	123.81
Observations	522.00
Durbin-Watson	2.39

Exhibit 4: Silver Price Regression Results (cont.)

ANOVA

	df	SS	MS	F	Significance F
Regression	1.00	365,730,065	365,730,065	23,859.63	0.00
Residual	520.00	7,970,771	15,328		
Total	521.00	373,700,837			

	Coefficients	Standard Error	t-Stat	P-value
Intercept	21.00	11.56	1.82	0.07
Slope	0.99	0.01	154.47	0.00

Fisher and Weatherford later discuss fluctuations in gold prices. Although the arithmetic and geometric mean returns for gold were negative for much of the 1980s and 1990s, Fisher and Weatherford believe that gold should perform better in the future due to higher expected inflation. After appropriate transformation of the data, they use an autoregressive first-order regression model to examine the characteristics of gold returns, the results of which are shown in Exhibit 5.

Exhibit 5: Gold Price Regression Results

Regression Statistics	
Multiple R	0.09
R-Square	0.01
Adjusted R-Square	0.01
Standard Error	123.95
Observations	520.00

ANOVA

	df	SS	MS	F	Significance F
Regression	1.00	66,742	66,742	4.34	0.04
Residual	518.00	7,958,144	15,363		
Total	519.00	8,024,887			

	Coefficients	Standard Error	t-Stat	P-value
Intercept	2.00	5.44	0.37	0.71
Slope	−0.09	0.04	−2.08	0.04

61.   In order to *best* model the emerging markets data using linear regression, Fisher should use:
        A. an adjustment for multicollinearity.
        B. the natural log of the dependent variable.
        C. White's correction for the standard errors.

62.   The *most likely* problem in Fisher's regression of the emerging market data and the *most appropriate* test for it in the regression are:

Problem	Test
A. Serial correlation	Durbin Watson
B. Serial correlation	Dickey Fuller
C. Cointegrated variables	Engle Granger

63.   Is the use of the Durbin Watson statistic in Weatherford's silver regression appropriate and, if so, how should it be interpreted?
        A. No.
        B. Yes, and it appears that the error terms are positively correlated.
        C. Yes, and it appears that the error terms are negatively correlated.

64.   Which of the following are the *most likely* problem in Weatherford's silver regression and the *most appropriate* test for it?

Problem	Test
A. Multicollinearity	Breusch Pagan
B. Multicollinearity	Dickey Fuller
C. Nonstationary data	Dickey Fuller

65.   In order to *best* model the silver price data using an autoregressive first-order regression model, Weatherford should use:
        A. first differences of the data.
        B. the actual silver price levels.
        C. the predicted silver price levels.

66.   Using the data for the gold regression, what is the mean reverting level and what is the two-step-ahead forecast if the current value of the independent variable is –0.80?

Mean reverting level	Two-step-ahead forecast
A. 1.830	1.75
B. 1.830	1.81
C. 2.072	1.81

Questions 67–72 relate to Iberia Corporation.

Bryan Stephenson is an equity analyst and is developing a research report on Iberia Corporation at the request of his supervisor. Iberia is a conglomerate entity with significant corporate holdings in various industries. Specifically, Stephenson is interested in the effects of Iberia's investments on its financial performance and has decided to focus on two investments: Midland Incorporated and Odessa Company.

Midland Incorporated
On December 31, 2007, Iberia purchased 5 million common shares of Midland Incorporated for €80 million. Midland has a total of 12.5 million common shares outstanding. The market value of Iberia's investment in Midland was €89 million at the end of 2008, and €85 million at the end of 2009. For the year ended 2008, Midland reported net income of €30 million and paid dividends of €10 million. For the year ended 2009, Midland reported a loss of €5 million and paid dividends of €4 million.

During 2010, Midland sold goods to Iberia and reported 20% gross profit from the sale. Iberia sold all of the goods to a third party in 2010.

Odessa Company
On January 2, 2009, Iberia purchased 1 million common shares of Odessa Company as a long-term investment. The purchase price was €20 per share, and on December 31, 2009, the market price of Odessa was €17 per share. The decline in value was considered temporary. For the year ended 2009, Odessa reported net income of €750 million and paid a dividend of €3 per share. Iberia considers its investment in Odessa as an investment in financial assets.

In addition, Iberia has a number of foreign investments, so Stephenson's supervisor has asked him to draft a report on accounting methods and ratio analysis. The following are statements from Stephenson's research report.

Statement 1: Under U.S. GAAP, Iberia cannot account for its investment in associates at fair value as that option is only available to venture capital firms, mutual funds, or similar entities.

Statement 2: In general, if the parent's consolidated net income is positive, the equity method reports a higher net profit margin than the acquisition method.

67. Which of the following is the *most* appropriate classification of Iberia's investment in Odessa Corporation?
    A. Held-to-maturity.
    B. Held-for-trading.
    C. Available-for-sale.

68. What amount should Iberia recognize in its 2009 income statement as a result of its investments in Midland and Odessa?
    A. €1 million profit.
    B. €2 million profit.
    C. €3 million loss.

69. What amount should Iberia report on its balance sheet at the end of 2009 as a result of its investments in Midland and Odessa?
    A. €84.4 million.
    B. €101.4 million.
    C. €102.0 million.

70. What adjustment, if any, must Iberia make to its 2010 income statement as a result of the intercompany transaction with Midland?
    A. Sales and cost of goods sold should be reduced by Iberia's pro-rata ownership interest in the intercompany sale.
    B. Midland's net income should be reduced by 20% of the gross profit from the intercompany sale.
    C. No adjustment is necessary.

71. Is Stephenson's statement 1 correct?
    A. Yes.
    B. No, because under U.S. GAAP, all entities can account for their investment in associates at fair value.
    C. No, because under U.S. GAAP, accounting of investment in associates at fair value is not allowed for any entity.

72. Is Stephenson's statement 2 correct?
    A. Yes.
    B. No. Net profit margin will be lower using the equity method.
    C. No. Net profit margin will be the same using either the equity method or the acquisition method.

Questions 73–78 relate to Andrew Carson and Samilski Enterprises.

Andrew Carson is an equity analyst employed at Lee Vincent and Associates, an investment research firm. Carson is responsible for following Samilski Enterprises (Samilski), a publicly traded firm that produces motorcycles and associated mechanical parts. Samilski reports under U.S. GAAP.

Exhibit 1 shows selected financial data pertaining to Samilski's employee pension plan.

Exhibit 1: Selected Pension Plan Information for FY 20X9

	$ millions
Current service cost	118
Past service cost	36
Beginning PBO	1,022
Ending PBO	1,198
Interest cost	82
Actual return on plan assets	214
Employer contribution	102
Beginning plan assets	896

During fiscal year 20X9, a change in actuarial assumptions regarding employee life expectancy resulted in an actuarial loss of $128 million. Average employee service life is estimated to be 20 years. The discount rate and expected return on plan assets are 8% and 10% respectively. Carson believes that rate of compensation increase will be 5% as opposed to the 4% assumed by the plan.

73. If Samilski's expected rate of return on plan assets was the same as the discount rate used to compute the plan's benefit obligation, the resulting total periodic pension cost and PBO would *most likely* be:

Total periodic pension cost	PBO
A. Higher	Higher
B. Unchanged	Unchanged
C. Higher	Unchanged

74. The amount of benefits paid during the year is *closest* to:
    A. $76 million.
    B. $132 million.
    C. $188 million.

75. The ending fair value of plan assets is *closest* to:
   A. $1,024 million.
   B. $1,128 million.
   C. $1,412 million.

76. The total periodic pension cost is *closest* to:
   A. $62 million.
   B. $76 million.
   C. $150 million.

77. The amount of periodic pension cost reported in P&L if Samilski reported under IFRS would be *closest* to:
   A. $144 million.
   B. $152 million.
   C. $164 million.

78. For this question, assume that Samilski had changed their assumed level of compensation growth rate to the one estimated by Carson. Based on this change only, what will be the *most likely* effects on the next period's current service cost and net interest cost if Samilski reported under IFRS?
   A. Both will increase.
   B. Current service cost will increase while net interest cost will be unaffected.
   C. One will increase and the other will decrease.

Questions 79–84 relate to Kazmaier Foods.

The board members for Kazmaier Foods have gathered for their quarterly board of directors meeting. Presiding at the meeting is the Chairman and CEO for Kazmaier, Phil Hinesman. The other eight members of the board are also present, including Allen Kazmaier, the brother of Kazmaier's founder; Elaine Randall, Executive Vice President for Emerald Bank, which Kazmaier uses to obtain short-term financing; and Bill Schram, Kazmaier's President and Chief Operating Officer. Each of the directors was elected to serve on the board for a 4-year term. They were elected two at a time over the past three years. With the exception of Hinesman, Allen Kazmaier, Randall, and Schram, board members had no ties to Kazmaier prior to joining the board and had no personal relationships with management. In addition to the regular board meetings, the five independent board members get together annually, in a meeting separate from the regular board meetings, to discuss the company's operations.

Item 1 on the board meeting agenda is a discussion about the importance of corporate governance and how Kazmaier can improve its corporate governance system. Hinesman begins the discussion by saying, "A strong system of corporate governance is important to our shareholders. Studies have shown that, on average, companies with strong corporate governance systems have higher measures of profitability than companies with weak corporate governance systems." Randall adds her comment to the discussion: "The lack of an effective corporate governance system increases risk for our investors. If we do not have the appropriate checks and balances in place, our investors may be exposed to the risk that information used to make decisions about our firm is misleading or incomplete, as well as the risk that mergers or acquisitions the firm enters into will benefit management at the expense of shareholders."

After a lengthy discussion, the board agrees on five separate recommendations that will enhance its current system of corporate governance. One of these recommendations is to change the function and structure of the board's audit committee. Currently, the audit committee consists of Matthew Bortz, David Smith, and Ann Williams—three independent directors who each have backgrounds in finance and accounting. The board agrees that one more member should be added to the committee and that the committee should expand its list of responsibilities.

Item 2 on the agenda for the board of directors' meeting is a report from Kazmaier's Chief Financial Officer, Doug Layman. The following information was included in the material that was distributed to each board member before the meeting:

($ Millions)	20X0	20X1[*]
Net income	$98.50	$112.50
Cash flow from operations	$115.00	$132.00
Capital expenditures (FCInv)	$43.00	$150.00
Net borrowing	$22.00	$75.00
Dividends paid	$42.88	$45.00
Stock repurchases	$42.00	$3.00

[*]Estimated

Additional information:

Current share price:	$40.00
Shares outstanding:	56,250,000
Target debt-to-equity ratio:	1 to 1
Cost of equity:	8.0%
Constant growth rate:	5.2%

Layman tells the board that his analysis indicates that, based on a constant-growth dividend discount model, the current stable dividend policy would reduce the cost of equity by 1.2% and increase the value of the firm's stock, assuming that earnings, the cost of debt, and the constant growth rate don't change.

Item 3 on the agenda is the sale of Kazmaier's condiment packaging division to Sautter Packaging and Supply Company. Layman believes the sale will net the company $50 million, payable in cash. After discussing the pros and cons of selling the division, the directors agree that the sale is in the best interests of the company and its shareholders. The directors then move to a vote, and the sale of the condiment packaging division is approved unanimously. The committee then moves on to discuss what to do with the proceeds from the sale. Williams suggests that paying out the $50 million to shareholders as a special dividend would continue to give the firm flexibility in how it uses its excess cash. Smith tells the board that a share repurchase can be thought of as an alternative to a cash dividend, and that if the tax treatment between the two alternatives is the same, investors should be indifferent between the two. After debating the merits of special dividends and stock repurchases, Kazmaier's board authorizes the proceeds from the sale of the condiment packaging division to be used for the purchase of $50 million worth of outstanding shares.

An external agency recently included Kazmaier in a review of corporate governance systems to determine whether the structure of the board of directors was consistent with corporate governance best practices. The agency scored companies based on the following criteria:

Criterion 1: Composition of the board of directors.
Criterion 2: Chairman of the board of directors.
Criterion 3: Method of electing the board.
Criterion 4: Frequency of separate sessions for independent directors.

Each of the four criteria was weighted equally, with the firm receiving a positive mark for being in compliance with corporate governance best practice.

A month after the board meeting, the price of Kazmaier stock is still at $40 per share, and the sale of Kazmaier's condiment packaging division does not go through. In order to finance the approved share repurchase, Kazmaier is forced to borrow funds. Schram states, "I am concerned that the cost of the debt used to repurchase shares may cause a reduction in earnings per share."

Jennifer Nagy, a vice president in Kazmaier's finance division, tells Schram not to be concerned about using debt to finance the share repurchase because the rationale behind the repurchase is sound. Nagy then writes down some of the common rationales for share repurchases and hands them to Schram.

Rationale 1: Repurchasing shares can prevent the EPS dilution that comes from the exercise of employee stock options.

Rationale 2: Management can use a share repurchase to alter the company's capital structure by decreasing the percentage of equity.

Rationale 3: Like a dividend increase, a share repurchase is a way to send a signal to investors that Kazmaier's management believes the outlook for the company's future is strong.

79. Are the comments made by Hinesman and Randall about corporate governance systems correct?
    A. Both comments are correct.
    B. Only Hinesman is correct.
    C. Only Randall is correct.

80. Which of the following pairs of recommendations would be *best* in helping Kazmaier's audit committee comply with corporate governance best practices?
    A. The internal audit staff of the firm should report directly to the audit committee, all of the audit committee members should be independent, and the committee should meet with auditors at least annually without management present.
    B. At least 75% of the audit committee members should be independent, and all of the committee members should have a background in finance and accounting.
    C. All of the audit committee members should be independent and should meet with management at least annually to discuss findings in internal audits.

81. Based on the financial information distributed to the board members, the dividend per share for 20X1 based on a residual dividend approach should be *closest* to:
    A. $0.00.
    B. $0.22.
    C. $0.67.

82. Based on the financial information distributed to the board members, the FCFE coverage ratios for 20X0 and 20X1 are *closest* to:

	20X0	20X1
A.	2.19	1.27
B.	1.11	1.19
C.	1.35	2.75

83. Kazmaier's total score on the corporate governance report is *closest* to:
    A. 25%.
    B. 50%.
    C. 75%.

84. How many of Nagy's rationales for a share repurchase are valid?
    A. One.
    B. Two.
    C. Three.

Questions 85–90 relate to Henke Malfoy.

Henke Malfoy, CFA, is an analyst with a major manufacturing firm. Currently, he is evaluating the replacement of some production equipment. The old machine is still functional and could continue to serve in its current capacity for three more years. If the new equipment is purchased, the old equipment (which is fully depreciated) can be sold for $50,000 now but will be worthless in three years. The new equipment will cost $400,000, including shipping and installation. If the new equipment is purchased, the company's revenues will increase by $175,000 and costs by $25,000 for each year of the equipment's 3-year life. There is no expected change in net working capital.

The new machine will be depreciated using a 3-year MACRS schedule (note: the 3-year MACRS schedule is 33.0% in the first year, 45% in the second year, 15% in the third year, and 7% in the fourth year). At the end of the life of the new equipment (i.e., in three years), Malfoy expects that it can be sold for $10,000. The firm has a marginal tax rate of 40%, and the cost of capital on this project is 20%. In calculation of tax liabilities, Malfoy assumes that the firm is profitable, so any losses on this project can be offset against profits elsewhere in the firm. Malfoy calculates a project NPV of –$62,574.

85. The initial outlay for the project is *closest* to:
    A. $350,000.
    B. $370,000.
    C. $400,000.

86. The after-tax operating cash flow for the first year of operations with the new equipment (excluding the initial outlay) is *closest* to:
    A. $10,800.
    B. $132,000.
    C. $142,800.

87. What is the effect of taxes on the operating cash flow in year 2?
    A. Decrease by $7,200.
    B. Increase by $7,200.
    C. Increase by $12,000.

88. The combined after-tax operating cash flow and terminal year after-tax nonoperating cash flow in year 3 is *closest* to:
    A. $131,200.
    B. $151,200.
    C. $152,200.

89.   Suppose for this question only that Malfoy has forgotten to reflect a decrease in inventory that will result at the beginning of the project. The *most likely* effect on estimated project NPV of this error:
      A. is to overestimate NPV.
      B. is to underestimate NPV.
      C. depends on whether the inventory is assumed to build back up to its previous level at the end of the project or the decrease in inventory is permanent.

90.   What is the IRR based on Malfoy's NPV estimate, and should the project be accepted or rejected in order to maximize shareholder value?

IRR	Project
A. 8.8%	Accept
B. 8.8%	Reject
C. 21.5%	Accept

Questions 91–96 relate to Yi Tang.

Yi Tang updates several economic parameters monthly for use by the analysts and the portfolio managers at her firm. If economic conditions warrant, she will update the parameters even more frequently. As a result of an economic slowdown, she is going through this process now.

The firm has been using an equity risk premium of 5.2%, derived using historical estimates. By comparing the yields on nominal bonds and real bonds, Tang estimates the expected inflation rate to be 2.6%. She expects real domestic growth to be 3.0%. Tang believes that the markets are currently overvalued by 3%. The yield on the market index is 1.7%, and the expected risk-free rate of return is 2.7%.

Elizabeth Trotter, one of the firm's portfolio Managers, asks Tang about the effects of survivorship bias on estimates of the equity risk premium. Trotter asks, "Which method is most susceptible to this bias: historical estimates, Gordon growth model estimates, or survey estimates?"

Tang wishes to estimate the required rate of return for Northeast Electric (NE) using the Capital Asset Pricing Model (CAPM) and the Fama-French model. She uses the following information to accomplish this:

Factor	Risk Premium	Factor Sensitivity
Market	5.2%	0.83 (historical)
Size	3.2%	−0.76
Value	5.4%	−0.04
Liquidity	1.1%	0.20

Trotter has one final question for Tang. Trotter says, "We need to estimate the equity beta for VixPRO, which is a private company that is not publicly traded. We have identified a publicly traded company that has similar operating characteristics to VixPRO, and we have estimated the beta for that company using regression analysis. We used the return on the public company as the dependent variable and the return on the market index as the independent variable. What steps do I need to take to find the beta for VixPRO equity? The companies have different debt/equity ratios. The debt of both companies is very low risk, and I believe I can ignore taxes."

91. The estimate of the equity risk premium using the Ibbotson-Chen model given the estimates determined by Tang is *closest* to:
     A. 1.5%.
     B. 4.2%.
     C. 4.7%.

92. The *best* response to Trotter's question about survivorship bias is:
    A. survey estimates.
    B. Gordon model estimates.
    C. historical estimates.

93. The required rate of return for NE estimated with the CAPM is *closest* to:
    A. 5.7%.
    B. 6.0%.
    C. 7.0%.

94. The required rate of return for NE estimated with the Fama-French model is *closest* to:
    A. 4.4%.
    B. 4.7%.
    C. 9.0%.

95. Using the Blume method, the adjusted beta computed by Tang would be *closest* to:
    A. 0.90.
    B. 0.96.
    C. 1.03.

96. What response should Tang give Trotter about estimating the equity beta for VixPRO?
    A. Estimate the beta for VixPRO by regressing the returns for VixPRO against an index of non-traded equity market securities.
    B. Estimate the VixPRO beta by multiplying the public company beta times the ratio of the equity risk premium of the market to the risk-free rate of return.
    C. Estimate the unlevered beta for the public company based on its debt/equity ratio. Then, use that unlevered beta to estimate the equity beta for VixPRO based on the VixPRO debt/equity ratio.

Questions 97–102 relate to IGS.

The New York-based Irwin Goldreich Schmidt (IGS) is a mid-sized private equity firm with $300 million capital raised from its investors. Amid a turbulent year, the firm has recently dropped its unsuccessful $100 million bid for a Norwegian media company and is now aggressively searching for new venture or buyout investments in the Eurozone. After several months of intense search, IGS believes it identified two potential investments:

1. Sverig, a rapidly expanding Swedish start-up construction company.

2. L'Offre, a struggling French department store in existence since the late 19th Century.

Following several rounds of successful negotiations, IGS makes a $20 million investment in Sverig and a $100 million leveraged buyout investment in L'Offre, committing to an additional $100 million for possible future capital drawdowns. It retains all of Sverig's managers but replaces L'Offre's management team with experienced IGS managers, many of whom are former company senior executives.

IGS also sets up Sverig-L'Offre Private Equity Fund (SLPEF), a fund to manage both firms. The fund manager's compensation is set at 20% of profits net of fees. IGS also specifies that the manager's profits are calculated on the entire portfolio when portfolio value exceeds invested capital by 30%.

Despite the market's recent turbulence, Sverig's original founders are extremely optimistic and believe the firm could be sold for $400 million in six years. To achieve this, they speculate the firm needs another capital infusion of $40 million in four years in addition to the $20 million capital investment today. Given the high risk of the firm, SLPEF's private equity investors decide that a discount rate of 40% for the first four years and 30% for the last two years is appropriate. The founders of Sverig want to hold 5 million shares.

97. If total proceeds net of fees to SLPEF are worth $180 million upon exit in a year, the fund's general partner (GP) under the total return using invested capital method would receive a compensation of:
A. $0.
B. $12 million.
C. $36 million.

98. An appropriate equity valuation technique for Sverig and L'Offre, respectively, would be the:

Sverig	L'Offre
A. Relative value approach	Venture capital method
B. Venture capital method	DCF method
C. DCF method	Relative value approach

99. Common risk factor(s) faced by both IGS investors and the managers of the private equity firm is(are):
   A. market risk but not agency risk.
   B. agency risk but not market risk.
   C. both market and agency risk.

100. SLPEF's general partner's (GP's) share of fund profits, and management's right to sell their equity interest in the event of an acquisition, respectively, are called:

Profits to the GP	Management's right to sell
A. Carried interest	Ratchet
B. Ratchet	Distribution waterfall
C. Carried interest	Tag-along, drag-along clause

101. Sverig's post-money valuation at the first round of financing, using the NPV venture capital method, is *closest* to:
   A. $61.61 million.
   B. $50.08 million.
   C. $51.20 million.

102. The appropriate stock price after the first-round of financing for Sverig's first-round investors is *closest* to:
   A. $6.24.
   B. $8.32.
   C. $6.02.

Questions 103–108 relate to Shirley Nolte.

Shirley Nolte, CFA, is a portfolio manager for McHugh Investments. Her portfolio includes 5,000 shares of Pioneer common stock (ticker symbol PNER), which is currently trading at $40 per share. Pioneer is an energy and petrochemical business that operates or markets its products in the United States, Canada, Mexico, and over 100 other countries around the world. Pioneer's core business is the exploration, production, and transportation of crude oil and natural gas. Pioneer also manufactures and markets petroleum products, basic petrochemicals, and a variety of specialty products.

Nolte would like to fully hedge her exposure to price fluctuations in Pioneer common stock over the next 90 days. She determines that the continuously compounded risk-free rate is 5%. She also gathers some information on exchange-traded options available on Pioneer stock. This data is shown in Exhibit 1.

Exhibit 1: Exchange-Traded Options on Pioneer Stock

Maturity	Exercise Price	Call Option Price	Call Option Delta	Put Option Price
1-month	$40	$2.84	0.54	$2.67
3-month	$40	$5.00	0.58	$4.50
6-month	$40	$7.14	0.61	$6.15
9-month	$40	$8.81	0.63	$7.34

From this data, she determines that the put option deltas are equal to the following:

- 1-month put option delta = –0.46.
- 3-month put option delta = –0.36.
- 6-month put option delta = –0.29.
- 9-month put option delta = –0.17.

She also concludes that the 9-month put option is mispriced relative to the 9-month call option, and an arbitrage opportunity is possible, but that the 3-month put option is correctly priced relative to its comparable call option. She also estimates the gamma of the 3-month call option to be 0.023.

In an unrelated transaction, Nolte is also considering the purchase of a put option on a futures contract with an exercise price of $22. Both the option and the futures contract expire in six months. The call price is $1, and the futures price today is $20.

103. Which of the following positions will *best* delta hedge Nolte's long position in Pioneer?
     A. Short 9,259 1-month call options.
     B. Short 8,197 3-month call options.
     C. Short 7,937 6-month call options.

104. If Nolte hedges the position with the 3-month call options, she:
     A. will have to continuously rebalance the position in order to maintain the delta hedge.
     B. can offset the cost of the hedge and maintain the hedged position by buying an equivalent amount of 3-month put options.
     C. will perfectly hedge the position over the 90-day investment horizon and won't need to rebalance the position only if the stock price of Pioneer remains at $40 for 90 days.

105. The gamma of the 3-month, $40 call option on Pioneer stock is *most likely*:
     A. greater than the gamma of a 3-month $50 call on Pioneer.
     B. less than the gamma of a 3-month $50 call on Pioneer.
     C. less than the gamma of a 3-month $30 call on Pioneer.

106. Is Nolte correct in her analysis of the 1-month and 6-month put option deltas?
     A. Nolte is correct on both options.
     B. Nolte is only correct on the 1-month option.
     C. Nolte is only correct on the 6-month option.

107. Is Nolte correct in her analysis of the relative pricing of the 3-month put option and the 9-month put option?
     A. Nolte is correct on both options.
     B. Nolte is only correct on the 3-month option.
     C. Nolte is only correct on the 9-month option.

108. The value of the put option on the futures contract is *closest* to:
     A. $2.45.
     B. $2.65.
     C. $2.95.

Questions 109–114 relate to Trent Black.

Trent Black is a government fixed-income portfolio manager, and on January 1, he holds $30 million of fixed-rate, semi-annual pay notes. Black is considering entering into a 2-year, $30 million semi-annual pay interest rate swap as the fixed-rate payer. He must first determine the swap rate. Black notes the following term structure:

Days	Annual Rate (%)	Discount Factor
180	3.25	0.9840
360	3.35	0.9676
540	3.60	0.9488
720	3.85	0.9285

Black is also evaluating receiver and payer swaptions on the same $30 million interest rate swap. The swaptions are European-style swaptions that mature in 240 days. Black anticipates a decline in interest rates and would like to use the swaptions to profit from his interest rate forecast.

Black is also concerned about the potential credit risk inherent in both interest rate swaps and swaptions, so he consults Marcus Coleman, a contract specialist in the legal department. Coleman advises Black that:

Statement 1:   The fixed rate payer in any plain vanilla interest rate swap is exposed to potential credit risk at the initiation of the swap, but the floating rate payer is not.

Statement 2:   The long position is exposed to potential credit risk in a payer swaption at initiation, but the short position in a payer swaption is not.

On May 1, after 120 days, Black is asked to determine the value of the 2-year, $30 million swap. The term structure after 120 days is:

Days	Annual Rate (%)	Discount Factor
30	3.21	0.9973
60	3.31	0.9945
180	3.66	0.9820
240	3.69	0.9760
360	4.21	0.9596
420	4.42	0.9510
480	4.69	0.9411
540	4.74	0.9336
600	4.89	0.9246
720	5.00	0.9091

109.   The annualized fixed rate for the $30 million swap on January 1 is *closest* to:
A. 3.73%.
B. 3.80%.
C. 3.91%.

110.   Ignore your answer to Question 115 and assume the annualized fixed rate on the swap is 3.80%. The amount of the first fixed payment due on this swap is *closest* to:
A. $285,000.
B. $570,000.
C. $1,140,000.

111.   One hundred twenty days after issue, the value of a 2-year, semi-annual fixed rate bond and the value of a 2-year, semi-annual floating rate note (based on $1 of notional principal), assuming the annualized fixed rate is 3.80%, are *closest* to:
A. $0.98190 fixed and $0.99970 floating.
B. $0.99000 fixed and $1.01000 floating.
C. $0.99768 fixed and $1.01066 floating.

112.   Ignore your answer to Question 117 for this question. Based on the notional principal, and assuming the value of the fixed-rate bond and floating-rate note are 0.99000 and 1.01000 (per $1 of notional principal), respectively, what is the payment required to terminate the swap, and which party will make the payment?
A. $600,000 paid by the floating-rate payer.
B. $1,200,000 paid by the fixed-rate payer.
C. $600,000 paid by the floating-rate payer, and $1,200,000 paid by the fixed-rate payer.

113.   Which position (long or short) should Black take in the payer and receiver swaptions based on his interest rate forecast?

	Payer swaption	Receiver swaption
A.	Short	Short
B.	Long	Short
C.	Short	Long

114.   Is Coleman correct with respect to the credit risk of swaps and swaptions?
A. Correct on both statements.
B. Only correct on Statement 1.
C. Only correct on Statement 2.

Questions 115–120 relate to Millennium Investments and Richie Shepard.

Millennium Investments (MI), an investment advisory firm, provides asset allocation recommendations for its clients. Richie Shepard, senior analyst at MI, is using a two-factor macroeconomic model to evaluate a portfolio of two stocks: WMB and REL. The two factors in the model are surprises in inflation and in real GDP growth rate (both given in percentages). The portfolio is invested 60% in WMB. Factor sensitivity and other information for the two stocks are shown in Exhibit 1.

Exhibit 1: WMB and REL

Stock	E(R)	Inflation	GDP Growth Rate
WMB	9%	−2.2	+3.0
REL	10.8%	−1.0	+3.3

Another stock (not in the portfolio), PSL, has a factor sensitivity of −0.9 to inflation and +1.2 to GDP growth rate.

Shepard is also looking at evaluating three portfolios using a single-factor model. Information about the three portfolios is shown in Exhibit 2.

Exhibit 2: Portfolio Factor Sensitivity and Expected Return

Portfolio	Expected Return	Factor Sensitivity
X	0.10	1.00
Y	0.12	1.25
Z	0.15	1.50

Shepard is meeting with a client to discuss inclusion of actively managed funds in that client's portfolio. To prepare for the meeting, Shepard prepares a presentation to illustrate the merits and risks of this change. Shepard cannot recall the term that is used to capture the sum of active factor risk and active specific risk.

Shepard feels that the economy is finally out of recession and poised for robust growth over the next three to five years.

115. Using the information in Exhibit 1, the expected return on the portfolio is *closest* to:
    A. 8.4%.
    B. 9.2%.
    C. 9.7%.

116. Using information in Exhibit 1, the portfolio's sensitivity to inflation is *closest* to:
    A. −1.1.
    B. −1.7.
    C. −2.2.

117. Last year, PSL's actual return was 8% (0.5% unexplained by the model). Inflation surprise, as well as GDP growth rate surprise, was +0.5%. PSL's expected return was *closest* to:
    A. 7.35%.
    B. 7.50%.
    C. 8.50%.

118. Using information in Exhibit 2, taking advantage of an arbitrage opportunity would *most likely* require shorting:
    A. portfolio X.
    B. portfolio Y.
    C. portfolio Z.

119. The term that Shepard cannot recall is *most likely*:
    A. active total risk.
    B. active risk squared.
    C. alpha risk.

120. Based on Shepard's economic outlook, it can be *most appropriately* concluded that:
    A. government bonds will outperform corporate bonds.
    B. higher-rated corporate bonds will outperform lower-rated corporate bonds.
    C. lower-rated corporate bonds will outperform higher-rated corporate bonds.

End of Afternoon Session

EXAM 1
MORNING SESSION ANSWERS

To get valuable feedback on how your score compares to those of other Level II candidates, use your Username and Password to gain Online Access at schweser.com and choose the menu item "Practice Exams Vol. 1."

1. A	21. A	41. C
2. A	22. B	42. B
3. B	23. A	43. C
4. C	24. C	44. C
5. C	25. C	45. A
6. B	26. C	46. B
7. A	27. C	47. B
8. B	28. A	48. B
9. B	29. A	49. C
10. B	30. C	50. C
11. B	31. B	51. C
12. B	32. C	52. B
13. B	33. A	53. B
14. B	34. C	54. C
15. A	35. A	55. A
16. A	36. C	56. A
17. A	37. A	57. A
18. A	38. B	58. A
19. A	39. A	59. B
20. A	40. C	60. B

Exam 1
Morning Session Answers

1. **A** Cost of finished jewelry = 11.06 + 2.897 × (cost of gold)
   $2,000 = 11.06 + 2.897× (cost of gold)
   Price of gold = ($2,000 − 11.06) / 2.897 = $686.55

   (Study Session 3, LOS 9.h)

2. **A** Singh is correct that a change in the relationship between gold prices and jewelry costs would be an example of parameter instability.

   Hara is correct to fail to reject the null hypothesis that the value of the slope coefficient is equal to 4.0 at the 5% level of significance.

   The critical t-value for the slope coefficient with 31 − 2 = 29 df at the 5% level for a two-tailed test is 2.045. The test statistic is (2.897 − 4.000)/0.615 = −1.79. The absolute value (1.79) is less than 2.045, and the correct decision is to fail to reject the null hypothesis that the slope coefficient is equal to 4.0. (Study Session 3, LOS 9.g, LOS 11.h)

3. **B** Biscayne is incorrect in the specification of the formula because the appropriate R^2 to use in calculating a Breusch-Pagan chi-square statistic is not the R^2 of the regression of jewelry prices on gold prices but rather the R^2 of the regression of squared residuals from the original regression on the independent variable(s). (Study Session 3, LOS 10.k)

4. **C** Singh is incorrect because a potential result of misspecifying a regression equation is nonstationarity (not stationarity, which is desirable).

   Biscayne is incorrect because the effect of omitting an important variable in a regression is that the regression coefficients are often biased (not unbiased) and/or inconsistent. (Study Session 3, LOS 10.m)

5. **C** While Hara is correct about the remedy for multicollinearity (i.e., remove one or more of the highly correlated dependent variables), he is incorrect about the effect of reducing the number of dependent variables on the coefficient of determination R^2. R^2 never increases when dependent variables are dropped. (Study Session 3, LOS 10.h, l)

6. **B** Biscayne is incorrect because a serial correlation problem can be corrected by using the Hansen method to adjust the coefficient standard errors, not the R^2. (Study Session 3, LOS 10.k)

7. **A** TBBB uses FIFO accounting; hence, GNNY's year-end LIFO reserve will be added to its ending inventory, resulting in an increase in current and total assets. (Study Session 5, LOS 16.b)

8. **B** Net income will decrease by the decrease in the LIFO reserve × (1-t). Revenue would not be affected, and, hence, the net margin will decrease. (Study Session 5, LOS 16.c)

9. **B** Her comment is incorrect. If inventory levels fall under LIFO accounting, the cost of older units flows through cost of sales. If prices are falling, higher-priced (older) items are included in COGS. (Study Session 5, LOS 16.b)

10. **B**   LIFO reserve as of 31 December 2014: $35.0
Tax rate: 28%
Addition to retained earnings: $35 \times 0.72 = 25.2$

Decrease in LIFO reserve in 2015: $7.0
Tax rate: 32%
Addition to retained earnings: $(7.0) \times 0.68 = (4.76)$

Net impact: $25.2 - 4.76 = 20.44$

(Study Session 5, LOS 16.e)

11. **B**   Reported ratio: $980 / 2,890 = 0.34$

IRR finance lease commitments:

10 N   −41.7 PV   5.8 PMT   0 FV
CPT I/Y = 6.5

PV operating commitments:

C01   9.8
F01   3
C02   12.0
F02   12
I   6.5
CPT NPV =   107.0

Adjusted ratio: $980 + 107.0 / 2,890 = 0.38$

(Study Session 5, LOS 17.f)

12. **B**   Under the revaluation method, any increase in market value is taken as a gain directly to equity. There is no impact on the income statement. (Also note that land is not depreciated.) (Study Session 5, LOS 17.c)

13. **B**   The beta of 1.04 is estimated from the slope coefficient on the independent variable (the return on the market) from the regression.

From the CAPM: required return on equity = $0.03 + [1.04 (0.07 - 0.03)] = 0.072 = 7.2\%$. (Study Session 10, LOS 30.c)

14. **B**   The value of the stock in early 2009 is the present value of the future dividends. After 2011, dividends are expected to grow at the rate of 4%. The dividend that begins the constantly growing perpetuity is $2.63 \times 1.04 = \$2.74$. You are given the cost of equity of 10%. Note that for the third cash flow, we add the third dividend ($2.63) to the present value of the constantly growing perpetuity that begins in the fourth year = $\$2.74 / (0.10 - 0.04) = \$45.67$. This is valid since they both occur at the same point in time (i.e., at the end of the third year). Using a financial calculator we can estimate the value of one share of O'Connor stock as follows:

CFO = 0; C01 = $2.13; C02 = $2.36; C03 = $2.63 + $45.67 = $48.30; I = 10;
CPT → NPV = $40.18

(Study Session 11, LOS 34.b)

15. **A** De Jong's estimate of value of $75.00 (based on a high-growth period of three years) is greater than the market's consensus of $70.00, which means the market's consensus high-growth duration must be less than three years, all else equal. (Study Session 11, LOS 34.b)

16. **A** In order for the dividend discount model to produce a reasonable estimate of share price, the investor should have a non-control perspective. For the FCFE model to be appropriate, there should be a link between FCFE and profitability. (Study Session 11, LOS 34.a)

17. **A** $H = 6 / 2 = 3$, $D_0 = 1.92$, $r = 0.095$, $g_s = 0.11$, $g_L = 0.04$

$$P_0 = \frac{D_0(1+g_L)}{(r-g_L)} + \frac{D_0 \times H \times (g_s - g_L)}{(r-g_L)}$$

$$= \frac{1.92(1.04)}{(0.095-0.04)} + \frac{1.92 \times 3 \times 0.07}{(0.095-0.04)} = \$43.64$$

(Study Session 11, LOS 34.l)

18. **A**

$$r = \left[\left(\frac{D_0}{P_0}\right) \times \left[(1+g_L) + [H \times (g_S - g_L)]\right]\right] + g_L$$

$$= \left[\left(\frac{1.92}{48}\right) \times \left[(1.04) + (2.5 \times 0.07)\right]\right] + 0.04 = 0.0914$$

(Study Session 11, LOS 34.m)

19. **A** Increasing invested capital to take advantage of positive NPV projects will increase NOPAT and the dollar cost of capital ($WACC). Because NPV is positive, the increase in NOPAT will be larger than the increase in $WACC, so EVA will increase. (Study Session 8, LOS 25.d and Study Session 12, LOS 37.a)

20. **A** All of the justifications noted by De Jong are appropriate reasons to use the residual income model. (Study Session 12, LOS 37.j)

21. **A** When residual income is expected to persist at its current level forever, the persistence factor is highest. When ROE declines over time to the cost of equity, residual income declines over time to zero, and the persistence factor will have a value between 0 and 1. When residual income falls to zero immediately, the persistence factor has a value of zero. (Study Session 12, LOS 37.h)

22. **B** Residual income = net income − equity charge
Equity charge = equity capital × cost of equity capital
Equity charge = $73,000,000 × 0.08 = $5,840,000
Residual income = $10,035,000 − $5,840,000 = $4,195,000

EVA = NOPAT − (C% × TC)

EVA = $28,517,640 − (0.054 × $324,000,000) = $11,021,640
(Study Session 12, LOS 37.a)

23. **A** We need to solve for *g* in the relationship:

$$V_0 = B_0 + \left(\frac{ROE - r}{r - g}\right)B_0$$

$$\$70.00 = \$4.29 + \left(\frac{0.1184 - 0.08}{0.08 - g}\right)\$4.29$$

Solving for *g*, we get g = 7.75%. (Study Session 12, LOS 37.g)

24. **C** Only Statement 2 is correct. Residual income valuation is related to P/B. When the present value of expected future residual income is negative, the justified P/B based on fundamentals is less than 1. Statement 1 is not correct: residual income models recognize value *earlier* than other valuation models. (Study Session 12, LOS 37.e, i)

25. **C** Private equity funds add value to their portfolio investments in a variety of ways including utilizing optimal financial leverage, incentivizing portfolio company management, and creating operational improvements. Incentivizing the GP is a mechanism to reduce conflict of interest between LP and GP and not a mechanism to add value. (Study Session 13, LOS 41.a)

26. **C** While the other factors do influence the futures price of corn, a consumable asset's value is most influenced by global supply and demand conditions. (Study Session 13, LOS 42.d)

27. **C** The supply shortage would result in an increase in convenience yield, which will in turn lower the futures price relative to the spot price. Note that the spot price would most likely increase, but that is not the question. The question is specifically asking for futures price *relative* to the spot price. (Study Session 13, LOS 42.c)

28. **A** Rebalancing to original fixed weights entails selling contracts that have appreciated in value and purchasing contracts that have lost value. In volatile markets, contracts that have risen in value will be sold and contracts that have lost value will be purchased. This results in a significant positive return in markets that are flat in the long term and volatile in the short term. (Study Session 13, LOS 42.g)

29. **A** The case provides that the pricing in cattle futures market reflects normal contango; futures prices are higher than expected future spot prices. The hedging pressure hypothesis can explain normal contango pricing by suggesting that farmers that wish to hedge their commodity price risk may be outnumbered by commodity consumers reducing their risk by taking long positions in the futures market. The insurance perspective suggests that farmers should dominate the hedging market, which results in normal backwardation and would be least likely to explain a normal contango pricing behavior. The theory of storage relies on the convenience yield to predict the relationship between spot and futures prices; it links storage costs and storability to the convenience yield. Existence of high inventory levels could reduce the convenience yield and hence push futures prices higher, potentially leading to normal contango. (Study Session 13, LOS 42.i)

30. **C** Since futures prices are less than spot prices, the roll return will be positive. Convergence will create identical spot and futures prices at maturity; maturing contracts will be replaced with the next shortest futures contract, which will have a lower price. (Study Session 13, LOS 42.h)

31. **B**   The bond will be called in the lower node if the interest rate (including OAS) is 5.0% because the present value of the remaining cash flows ($100.95) is greater than the call price ($99.50). The bond will not be called if rates increase to 7.5% in the upper node because the value of the bond ($98.60) is less than the call price ($99.50). The value of the callable bond according to the model is 101.01:

$$V_0 = \frac{1}{2} \times \left[\frac{98.60 + 6.00}{1.04} + \frac{99.50 + 6.00}{1.04} \right] = 101.01$$

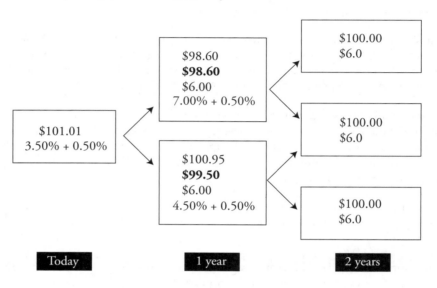

(Study Session 14, LOS 45.f)

32. **C**   The value of a putable bond is equal to the value of an otherwise equivalent option-free bond plus the value of the embedded put option. The value of the embedded put option will decrease if yield volatility decreases. The value of the option-free bond will not be affected by changes in yield volatility, so the value of the putable bond will also decrease. Evermore is incorrect in her analysis of both effects. (Study Session 14, LOS 45.d)

33. **A**   The computed value of a putable bond decreases with a decrease in the assumed level of volatility and therefore the OAS needed to force the model price to be equal to market price will be lower. (Study Session 14, LOS 45.h)

34. **C**   The benchmark securities used to create the tree are Treasury securities, so the OAS for each callable corporate bond reflects additional credit risk and liquidity risk relative to the benchmark. The bonds are overvalued if their OAS are smaller than the required OAS and undervalued if their OAS are larger than the required OAS. The required OAS for both bonds is the *Z*-spread over Treasuries on comparably-rated securities with no embedded options. That required spread is not provided in the vignette.

The BB-rated issue is overvalued because its OAS is less than zero, which means it must be less than the required OAS. Therefore, Evermore is correct in her analysis of the BB-rated issue.

The AA-rated issue has a positive OAS relative to the Treasury benchmark, but we don't know the required OAS on similar bonds, so we can't determine whether or not the AA-rated issue is over or undervalued based on the information given. Therefore, Evermore is incorrect to conclude that the issue is undervalued. (Study Session 14, LOS 45.g)

35. **A**   Davenport has correctly outlined the appropriate methodology for using a binomial model to estimate effective duration and effective convexity. Evermore fails to adjust for the OAS and, instead, simply adds 100 basis points to every rate on the tree rather than shifting the yield curve upward and then recreating the entire tree using the same rate volatility assumption from the first step. Even if both use the same rate volatility assumption and the OAS is equal to zero, the two methodologies will generate significantly different duration and convexity estimates. (Study Session 14, LOS 45.i)

36. **C**   The value of a callable convertible bond is equal to the value of an option-free bond plus the value of the conversion option on the stock minus the value of the call option on the bond.

   A decrease in the volatility of Highfour's common stock returns will decrease the value of the conversion option on the stock. Consequently the value of the convertible bond will also decrease. Evermore was correct in her analysis, and Davenport was incorrect to disagree with her.

   A decrease in the yield volatility will decrease the value of the embedded call option. The issuer has written the call option, so a decrease in the value of the call option will increase the value of the convertible bond. Evermore is incorrect in her analysis, and Davenport was correct to disagree with her. (Study Session 14, LOS 45.n)

37. **A**   Each of the portfolios has an effective duration of five, so a parallel shift in the yield curve will have the same effect on each portfolio, and each will experience the same price performance. (Study Session 14, LOS 43.k)

38. **B**   The exposure of each portfolio to changes in the 5- and 10-year rates are equal to the sum of the 5- and 10-year key rate durations:

   portfolio 1 exposure = 0.20 + 0.15 = 0.35
   portfolio 2 exposure = 0.40 + 4.00 = 4.40

   Portfolio 2 has the largest exposure, and portfolio 1 has the smallest exposure. If the 5- and 10-year key rates increase, portfolio 1 will fall by the smallest amount and will experience the best price performance (i.e., the smallest decrease in value).

   You can confirm this by doing the calculations for a 20 basis point increase:

   % change in portfolio 1 = $(-0.20 \times 0.002 \times 100) + (-0.15 \times 0.002 \times 100)$
   $\qquad\qquad\qquad\qquad = (-0.35 \times 0.002 \times 100) = -0.07\%$

   % change in portfolio 2 = $(-0.40 \times 0.002 \times 100) + (-4.00 \times 0.002 \times 100)$
   $\qquad\qquad\qquad\qquad = (-4.40 \times 0.002 \times 100) = -0.88\%$

   (Study Session 14, LOS 43.k)

39. **A**   Statement 1 is correct. Swap markets tend to have more maturities with which to construct a yield curve as compared to government bond markets. Statement 2 is correct. Retail banks tend to have little exposure to swaps and hence are more likely to use the government spot curve as their benchmark. (Study Session 14, LOS 43.e)

40. **C**   The value of a 3-year bond extendible by one year is equal to an otherwise identical 4-year bond that is putable in three years. Accordingly, the value of bonds B and C should be the same. (Study Session 14, LOS 45.a)

41. **C**   The steps in the process of calculating the effective duration of a callable bond using a binomial tree are as follows:

Step 1: Given assumptions about benchmark interest rates, interest rate volatility, and the call and/or put rule, calculate the OAS for the issue using the binomial model.

Step 2: Impose a small parallel shift in the on-the-run yield curve by an amount equal to $+\Delta y$.

Step 3: Build a new binomial interest rate tree using the new yield curve.

Step 4: Add the OAS to each of the 1-year forward rates in the interest rate tree to get a "modified" tree. (We assume that the OAS does not change when interest rates change.)

Step 5: Compute $BV_{+\Delta y}$ using this modified interest rate tree.

Step 6: Repeat steps 2 through 5 using a parallel rate shift of $-\Delta y$ to estimate a value of $BV_{-\Delta y}$.

There is no restriction on the relationship between the assumed change in the yield (Δy) and the OAS. (Study Session 14, LOS 45.i)

42. **B**   An upward sloping yield curve predicts an increase in short-term rates according to the pure expectations theory but not necessarily the liquidity premium theory.

The liquidity theory says that forward rates are a biased estimate of the market's expectation of future rates because they include a liquidity premium. Therefore, a positive sloping yield curve may indicate either (1) that the market expects future interest rates to rise or (2) that rates are expected to remain constant (or even fall), but the addition of the liquidity premium results in a positive slope. (Study Session 14, LOS 43.i)

43. **C**   The present value of the next coupon payment (per $100 face value) is

$$\frac{2.50}{1.04^{\left(\frac{182}{365}\right)}} = 2.4516.$$

The no-arbitrage forward price is $(98.25 - 2.4516) \times 1.04^{\left(\frac{270}{365}\right)} = 98.62$.

(Study Session 16, LOS 47.c)

44. **C**   PV of the coupon is now $\dfrac{2.50}{1.04^{\left(\frac{122}{365}\right)}} = 2.4674$, and the value of the forward contract to

the long is $98.11 - 2.4674 - \dfrac{98.62}{1.04^{\left(\frac{210}{365}\right)}} = -0.77693$ per $100, or –$77,693.

The value to the short is +$77,693. (Study Session 16, LOS 47.c)

45. **A**   Adams used the 90-day rate (0.0352) and the time period (90/360) in the numerator instead of the 150-day rate (0.0392) and the 150-day time period (150/360). The denominator is correct, so two out of the four terms are used correctly. The correct calculation is:

$$\left[\frac{1+0.0392\left(\frac{150}{360}\right)}{1+0.0332\left(\frac{60}{360}\right)} - 1 \right]\left(\frac{360}{90}\right) = \left[\frac{1.01633}{1.00553} - 1 \right](4) = 4.30\%$$

(Study Session 16, LOS 47.c)

46. **B** $(0.0430 - 0.0414) \times \$10 \text{ million} \times \dfrac{90}{360} = \$4,000$ (expected payoff in 120 days)

PV of payoff is $\dfrac{\$4,000}{1+0.0392\left(\dfrac{120}{360}\right)} = \$3,948$

(Study Session 16, LOS 47.c)

47. **B** $1.1854\left(\dfrac{1.03}{1.04}\right) = \$1.174$ (Study Session 16, LOS 47.c)

48. **B**   If the spot rate for euros at maturity is greater than the forward contract rate at initiation, the long (euros) position value is positive and the short position value is negative. Because the short owes the long, the long has credit risk. (Study Session 16, LOS 47.d)

49. **C**   Current term structure:

LIBOR		Discount Factor
LIBOR_{180}	0.029	0.98571
LIBOR_{360}	0.030	0.97087
LIBOR_{540}	0.032	0.95420

Fixed payments: 0.035 × 180 / 360 = 0.0175
PV fixed payments per $ notional:
   0.0175 × (0.98571 + 0.97087 + 0.9542) + 0.9542 = 1.0051
PV floating payments per $ notional = 1.0000

As the contract is at the settlement date (180 days into the swap), the floating side will be valued at par.

Value to fixed-rate payer: ($1.0000 − $1.0051) × $150,000,000 = −$765,000

(Study Session 17, LOS 50.c)

50. **C** Current term structure:

LIBOR		Discount Factor
LIBOR$_{60}$	0.027	0.99552
LIBOR$_{150}$	0.0285	0.98826
LIBOR$_{240}$	0.0295	0.98071

Fixed-rate payment: $0.037 \times 90 / 360 = 0.00925$
Value to GD (fixed payer) per \$ notional principal:
$(1892.23 / 1926.64) - 0.98071 - 0.00925(0.99552 + 0.98826 + 0.98071) = -0.02599$
Value = $-0.02599 \times \$250,000,000 = -\$6,497,910$

(Study Session 17, LOS 50.e)

51. **C** The original contract was a 90-day FRA on 180-day LIBOR. As 50 days have passed, the equivalent contract is now a 40-day FRA on 180-day LIBOR. Hernandez needs the 40-day rate and the 220-day rate to reprice the FRA and discount the gain or loss back to today. (Study Session 16, LOS 47.c)

52. **B** POPRT is part of the index CDS. GD sold protection of \$350 million over the 125 equally weighted entities, meaning that it has effective exposure of \$350 million / 125 = \$2.8 million.

    On the single-name POPRT CDS, GD purchased protection of \$2.5 million, leaving a net notional exposure of 2.8 − 2.5 = \$0.3 million. (Study Session 17, LOS 52.d)

53. **B** As the credit spread for TRTRS has widened and GD has purchased protection, GD will gain by selling protection at a higher premium. (Study Session 17, LOS 52.c)

54. **C** Typically, an LBO will result in an increase in the probability of default due to the large increase in debt levels. An investor would, therefore, seek to buy protection, as the premium would rise along with the probability of default. Due to the takeover premium that would result from the LBO, Eagen would also benefit by going long TRTRS stock. (Study Session 17, LOS 52.e)

55. **A**

Asset Class (i)	Portfolio Return $E(R_{Pi})$	Benchmark Return $E(R_{Bi})$	Active Weight (Δw_i)	$(\Delta w_i)\,(E(R_{Bi}))$
Equities	13%	12%	10%	1.20%
Bonds	7%	5%	−11%	-0.55%
Cash	3%	3%	1%	0.03%
Total				0.68%

Expected active return from asset allocation = $\Sigma \Delta w_j E(R_{B,j}) = 0.68\%$

(Study Session 18, LOS 54.a)

56. **A**   Both statements are correct. The global optimal risky portfolio is the portfolio with the highest Sharpe ratio. Investors customize their portfolios based on their risk tolerance by combining this optimal risky portfolio and the risk-free asset. A market-neutral long-short equity fund would have beta of zero, and, hence, the appropriate benchmark would be the risk-free asset. The excess return in the numerator is the same for both the information ratio and the Sharpe ratio when the risk-free asset is the benchmark. Additionally, by definition, the active risk will be same as total risk when the benchmark is risk-free (i.e., zero volatility). (Study Session 18, LOS 54.b)

57. **A**   Transfer coefficient can be thought of as a cross-sectional correlation between the forecasted active returns and active weights, adjusted for risk. (Study Session 18, LOS 54.c)

58. **A**   Prime has the highest information ratio and, hence, is most suitable for the investor regardless of the active risk constraint. In this instance, the investor would invest ⅚ or 83.33% in Prime and the remaining 16.67% in the benchmark portfolio to meet the maximum active risk constraint.

Fund	Prime	Redux	Optimus
Expected active return	2.40%	1.25%	1.28%
Active risk	6%	5%	4%
Information ratio	0.40	0.25	0.32

(Study Session 18, LOS 54.d)

59. **B**   Manager B has an information coefficient (IC) of $2(0.55) - 1$ or 0.10.

Given unconstrained optimization for Manager B, TC = 1.0

Manager B information ratio = $IC \times \sqrt{BR} = 0.10 \times \sqrt{12} = 0.35$

Manager A information ratio = $TC \times IC \times \sqrt{BR} = 0.4 \times 0.20 \times \sqrt{BR}$

Setting Manager A information ratio = 0.35, $\sqrt{BR} = 4.375$ and BR = 19.14.

(Study Session 18, LOS 54.e)

60. **B**   Closet index funds are characterized by low active risk and a Sharpe ratio equal to that of the benchmark. The information ratio for closet index funds tends to be zero (or negative after fees). Low information ratio can also occur for (unsuccessful) active funds. (Study Session 18, LOS 54.b)

Exam 1
Afternoon Session Answers

To get valuable feedback on how your score compares to those of other Level II candidates, use your Username and Password to gain Online Access at schweser.com and choose the menu item "Practice Exams Vol. 1."

61. A	81. A	101. A
62. C	82. A	102. C
63. A	83. C	103. C
64. C	84. C	104. B
65. A	85. A	105. C
66. A	86. C	106. A
67. B	87. C	107. A
68. B	88. C	108. A
69. B	89. B	109. A
70. C	90. A	110. A
71. A	91. B	111. C
72. C	92. C	112. B
73. B	93. C	113. C
74. B	94. C	114. C
75. B	95. C	115. B
76. A	96. A	116. A
77. A	97. B	117. C
78. B	98. B	118. B
79. B	99. C	119. A
80. A	100. C	120. C

EXAM 1
AFTERNOON SESSION ANSWERS

61. **A** Item (i) is a likely violation of the Code and Standards. Working as a waitress is not a conflict of interest for an investment analyst, but Cooken's employer can reasonably assume that a 30-hour-a-week side job could be tiring, depriving the company of her skills and ability during her internship, which would violate Standard IV(A) Loyalty (to employer).

Cooken's description of the CFA exam is accurate, and she takes no liberties with a title. Thus she has not violated Standard VII(B) Reference to CFA Institute, the CFA Designation, and the CFA Program.

One conviction as a teenager before working as an investment professional is not a violation of Standard I(D) Misconduct. Standard IV(A) Loyalty (to employer) does not hold when illegal activities are involved, and Cooken's willingness to talk to the FBI would most likely not be considered a violation. The Standards do suggest, however, that the member consult with his employer's compliance personnel or outside counsel before disclosing any confidential client information. (Study Session 1, LOS 2.a)

62. **C** While Cooken's tax avoidance may represent a professional-conduct issue, it has no bearing on her ability to write a report on Mocline. While Clarrison may be an expert on Mocline Tobacco, Cooken does not know enough about the stock to write about it without taking the risk of being in violation of Standard V(A) Diligence and Reasonable Basis. Because of Cooken's relationship to the CFO of Mocline and ownership of Mocline stock, her objectivity might be questioned. (Study Session 1, LOS 2.a)

63. **A** Standard IV(A) Loyalty (to employer) requires that members and candidates act for the benefit of their employer and not deprive the employer of their skills and abilities. In addition, members and candidates must not cause harm to their employers. It's safe to say that a bar does not compete with a stock-analysis company, and a 6-hour-a-week part-time job should not interfere with her ability to perform analysis duties. Standard IV(B) Additional Compensation Arrangements relates to additional compensation related to an employee's services to the employer. The moonlighting is not related to her analysis job and, as such, does not violate the standard. There is nothing inherently unethical about working as a bartender, and moonlighting as a barkeeper does not compromise Cooken's professional reputation, integrity, or competence. Thus, Standard I(D) Misconduct has not been violated. (Study Session 1, LOS 2.a)

64. **C** Request 3 is a likely violation. Potential clients are not entitled to performance data beyond what the company chooses to disclose. Providing data, particularly client-specific data, could be a violation of the clients' confidentiality.

Members and candidates must answer questions asked by CFA Institute's Professional Conduct Program. Members and candidates may report illegal activities (and in some cases may have a legal obligation to report such activities) on the part of clients without fear of violating Standard III(E) Preservation of Confidentiality, so 1 is not likely a violation. And unless the firm's policy requires silence about job openings, answering questions about them is ethical, if not always wise, so 2 is not likely a violation. (Study Session 1, LOS 2.a)

65. **A**   Although Zonding directed the audience to his published report, the ROS also recommends that, during any public appearances, sufficient information be included for investors to assess the appropriateness of the investment for their own personal risk profile. (Study Session 1, LOS 3.b)

66. **A**   Zonding recommended that viewers sell shares on share price increases despite his 12-month buy rating. Firms should not allow analysts to suggest trading actions that differ from the current published rating. (Study Session 1, LOS 3.b)

67. **B**   The CFA Institute Research Objectivity Standards require that research analysts be separated from the investment banking department. The firm must not allow Vrbenic to report to Sheffield, the head of investment banking, in order to avoid compromising the independence of Vrbenic's analysis. (Study Session 1, LOS 3.b)

68. **B**   The requirement is that firms have policies and procedures covering employees' personal investments and trading activities. These policies must prohibit employees and their immediate families from trading contrary to recently published recommendations, except in cases of extreme hardship. Since the analyst needs the money to pay for her father's kidney transplant, Verhallen may sell the securities contrary to the recommendation. (Study Session 1, LOS 3.b)

69. **B**   Research analysts must be prohibited from promising a subject company a favorable report or price target or threatening to change reports, recommendations, or price targets. Sheffield's unique insight may or may not lead to a change in recommendation, but changing the recommendation based on whether the subject company does investment banking business violates the ROS. The ROS require that all conflicts of interest be disclosed but they do not prohibit coverage of companies where such a conflict of interest may be present. (Study Session 1, LOS 3.b)

70. **C**   Firms must establish and implement salary, bonus, and other compensation programs that are tied to the quality of the research and the accuracy of the recommendations over time (not necessarily every quarter). Firms must avoid directly linking analyst compensation to investment banking or corporate finance activity on which the analyst may be collaborating. (Study Session 1, LOS 3.b)

71. **A**   Firms must provide full and fair disclosure of all potential conflicts of interest. Vrbenic's failure to disclose her position in the securities violates the ROS. Vrbenic is not, however, required to provide research to audience members, although the ROS recommends that the firm make the reports available even if they charge for them. The standards recommend—but do not require—that firms disclose availability of subject company research reports and how the audience might acquire such a report, if the firm makes it available to non-clients. This firm does not. (Study Session 1, LOS 3.b)

72. **C**   In order to comply with the CFA Institute Research Objectivity Standards *recommendations*, firms should issue research reports at least quarterly, or whenever material facts about the subject company change if sooner. However, there is no specific frequency of report issuance required by the Research Objectivity Standards. The only *requirement* is that firms issue their research on a regular and timely basis. (Study Session 1, LOS 3.b)

73. **B**   While ability of the self-regulating organizations (SROs) and their enforcement powers are important, the most important element is being properly supervised by formal government authorities. (Study Session 4, LOS 15.b)

74. **B** Given low capital mobility, a restrictive monetary and fiscal policy should lead to domestic currency appreciation under the Mundell-Fleming model. (Study Session 4, LOS 13.l)

75. **B** Under the neoclassical growth theory, capital deepening affects the level of output but not the growth rate in the long run. Once an economy reaches steady-state growth, only further technological progress will increase the growth rate. (Study Session 4, LOS 14.i)

76. **A** GBP/SFr = GBP/USD × USD/SFr.

    We are given USD/GBP, so we convert the provided quotes:

    $$\left(\frac{GBP}{USD}\right)_{bid} = \frac{1}{\left(\frac{USD}{GBP}\right)_{offer}} = \frac{1}{2.0020} = 0.4995$$

    and

    $$\left(\frac{GBP}{USD}\right)_{offer} = \frac{1}{\left(\frac{USD}{GBP}\right)_{bid}} = \frac{1}{2.0010} = 0.4998$$

    Now,

    $$\left(\frac{GBP}{SFr}\right)_{bid} = \left(\frac{GBP}{USD}\right)_{bid} \times \left(\frac{USD}{SFr}\right)_{bid} = 0.4995 \times 0.8550 = 0.4271$$

    and

    $$\left(\frac{GBP}{SFr}\right)_{offer} = \left(\frac{GBP}{USD}\right)_{offer} \times \left(\frac{USD}{SFr}\right)_{offer} = 0.4998 \times 0.8560 = 0.4278$$

    The GBP/SFr quote should be: GBP/SFr = 0.4271 – 78. (Study Session 4, LOS 13.b)

77. **A** The original 60-day forward contract calls for long GBP. So the all-in forward price FP = 2.0085. After 30 days, the contract would still have 30 days remaining to expiration. The new 30-day all-in forward price to sell GBP is 2.0086 +(7.6/10,000) = 2.00936. The relevant 30-day USD interest rate is 4%.

    $$V_t = \frac{(FP_t - FP)(\text{Contract size})}{\left[1 + R\left(\frac{\text{Days}}{360}\right)\right]} = \frac{(2.00936 - 2.0085)(1,000,000)}{\left[1 + 0.04\left(\frac{30}{360}\right)\right]} = \text{USD } 857.14$$

    (Study Session 4, LOS 13.d)

78. **B** Covered interest rate parity requires that $\dfrac{F}{S} = \dfrac{(1 + R_\$)}{(1 + R_{BU})}$

$$\frac{F}{S} = \frac{2.10}{2.00} = 1.05$$

$$\frac{(1 + R_\$)}{(1 + R_{BU})} = \frac{(1 + 0.05)}{(1 + 0.03)} = 1.019$$

The BUN should appreciate by 1.9% per year. However, in the forward market, the BUN is trading at a premium of 5%. Therefore, the appropriate arbitrage strategy is to sell BUN in the forward market as below:

1. Borrow $1,000 at 5%. At the end of one year, Williams will be obligated to repay $1,000(1.05) = $1,050.

2. Convert the $1,000 to BUN at the spot rate, which yields $1,000 / ($2/BUN) = BUN500.

3. Simultaneously enter into a 1-year forward contract to convert BUN to USD at the forward rate of $2.1000/BUN.

4. Invest BUN 500 at 3%. In one year, Williams will receive proceeds of BUN500(1.03) = BUN515.

5. Convert the BUN515 back to USD at the forward rate, which was locked in at the beginning of the year and yields BUN 515($2.1/BUN) = $1,081.50.

6. Arbitrage profits = $1,081.50 – $1,050 = $31.50.

(Study Session 4, LOS 13.e)

79. **B** In Exhibit 1, the cash flow statement shows that payables contributed positively to cash flow for 2013. This means payables increased during the period, suggesting High Plains was *delaying* payments to suppliers to boost CFO. (Study Session 7, LOS 21.i)

80. **A** Revenue should be recognized when earned and payment is assured. High Plains is recognizing revenue as orders are received. Because High Plains has not yet fulfilled its obligation to deliver the goods, revenue is not yet earned. By recognizing revenue too soon, net income is overstated and ending inventory is understated. Understated ending inventory would result in an overstated inventory turnover ratio. (Study Session 7, LOS 21.h)

81. **A**

Net income		$158,177,000
Bill-and-hold revenue	$907,950,000	
EBT margin	5.1%	
Bill-and-hold pre-tax income	$46,305,450	
Tax rate	28%	
Bill-and-hold post-tax income		$33,339,924
		21.08%

(Study Session 7, LOS 21.h)

82. **A**   Discretionary expenses, such as maintenance and repairs, and advertising and marketing expenses, are declining over time even as sales and capital expenditures are increasing. Investment in capital assets is increasing because cash from from income (CFI) is greater than depreciation expense for the period. The change to the straight-line depreciation method is certainly less conservative. However, measuring earnings quality based on conservative earnings is an inferior measure as most accruals will correct over time. Note that using LIFO as an inventory cost flow assumption during periods of stable or rising prices would cause net earnings to reflect economic (real) earnings, thereby leading to a higher quality of earnings. (Study Session 7, LOS 21.f)

83. **C**   A finance (capital) lease is reported on the balance sheet as an asset and as a liability. In the income statement, the leased asset is depreciated and interest expense is recognized on the liability. Thus, capitalizing a lease *enhances* earnings quality. An *operating* lease classification *lowers* earnings quality. The reclassification of inventory will impact the calculation of inventory turnover and inventory days. Reclassifications make trend analysis more difficult and lower financial reporting quality. (Study Session 7, LOS 21.d)

84. **C**   It appears that High Plains manipulated its earnings in 2014 to avoid default under its bond covenants. Extreme earnings (including revenues) tend to revert to normal levels over time (mean reversion). Because of the estimates involved, a *lower* weighting should be assigned to the accrual component of High Plains' earnings. (Study Session 7, LOS 21.g)

85. **A**   In a defined contribution plan, pension expense is equal to the amount contributed by the firm. The plan participants bear the shortfall risk. There is no pension obligation in a defined contribution plan. (Study Session 6, LOS 19.a)

86. **C**   Under U.S. GAAP and under IFRS, Global Oilfield would report the funded status in its balance sheet. (Study Session 6, LOS 19.b)

87. **C**   The assumed discount rate increased from 6.25% in 20X7 to 6.75% in 20X8 (Exhibit 4). There is an inverse relationship between the discount rate and the present value of a future sum. Thus, the increase in the discount rate resulted in an actuarial gain (lower PBO). An increase in life expectancy would result in an actuarial loss. Decrease in expected rate of return would increase reported pension expense but would not affect PBO. (Study Session 6, LOS 19.d)

88. **C**   A decrease in the compensation growth rate will reduce service cost. Lower service cost will result in lower pension expense and, thus, higher net income. Lowering the compensation growth rate will also reduce the PBO. A lower PBO will increase the funded status of the plan (make the plan appear more funded). The compensation growth rate assumption has no effect on the plan assets. (Study Session 6, LOS 19.d)

89. **B**   For the year-ended 20X8, Global Oilfield's reported pension expense was €8,028 (Exhibit 3), and its total periodic pension cost was €3,410. Total periodic pension cost can be calculated as plan contributions minus the change in funded status [€5,000 − (€2,524 funded status for 20X8 − €934 funded status for 20X7)]. (Study Session 6, LOS 19.f)

90. **A** Total periodic pension cost represents the true cost of the pension. If the firm's contributions exceed its true pension expense, the difference can be viewed as a reduction in the overall pension obligation similar to an excess principal payment on a loan. Pension contributions are reported as operating activities in the cash flow statement while principal payments are reported as financing activities. Thus, the adjustment involves increasing operating cash flow by €750 (€5,000 employer contributions – €4,250 total periodic pension cost) and decreasing financing cash flow by the same amount. (Study Session 6, LOS 19.e)

91. **B** Consolidated current assets are equal to $119 million ($96 Valley current assets – $9 cash for investment in Southwest + $32 Southwest current assets). (Study Session 6, LOS 18.a)

92. **C** ROA is calculated as net income / total assets. Both methods result in the same net income, so conclusion 1 is incorrect. However, the acquisition method leads to higher reported total assets. Hence, the ROA is greater under the equity method and lower under the acquisition method (conclusion 2 is correct). (Study Session 6, LOS 18.b)

93. **C** The applicability of equity method and acquisition method is identical under U.S. GAAP and IFRS (convergence project) and hence statement 1 is correct. While equity method reports the same net income as acquisition (statement 2 is correct), due to the inclusion of minority interest in equity under the acquisition method, the amount of equity reported under the acquisition method is higher than the amount of equity reported under the equity method (statement is 3 incorrect). (Study Session 6, LOS 18.b)

94. **C** See following table for 100 and 101. (Study Session 6, LOS 20.d, e)

95. **C** (Study Session 6, LOS 20.d, e)

The following financial statements reflect the use of the current rate method (functional currency is the CHF) since Mountain is a self-contained company and is less dependent on Valley. The solutions to Questions 100 and 101 pertain to the current rate method.

Income Statement (in $ thousands)

Sales	$5,600	= 0.80 × 7,000
Cost of goods sold	$5,440	= 0.80 × 6,800
Depreciation	80	= 0.80 × 100
Net income	$80	

Balance sheet (in $ thousands)

Cash and accounts receivable	$510	= 0.85 × 600
Inventory	425	= 0.85 × 500
Fixed assets	510	= 0.85 × 600
Total assets	$1,445	
Accounts payable	$170	= 0.85 × 200
Long-term debt	85	= 0.85 × 100
Common stock	1,001	= 0.77 × 1,300
Retained earnings	80	= 0 + 80
FC translation adjustment	109	Calculated
Total liabilities and equity	$1,445	

96. **A** Under U.S. GAAP, the nonmonetary assets and liabilities of the foreign subsidiary are not restated for inflation. Under IFRS, the subsidiary's financial statements are adjusted for inflation, and the net purchasing power gain or loss is recognized in the income statement. Then, the subsidiary is translated into U.S. dollars using the current rate method. If Mountain operates in a highly inflationary environment, the appropriate method is the temporal method. Under the temporal method, the functional currency is considered to be the parent's presentation currency. Thus, Mountain's functional currency is the U.S. dollar. (Study Session 6, LOS 20.g)

97. **B** Ozer's memo states that in an acquisition, Alertron would want to maintain the successful Escarigen brand and operational structure. As a result, the most likely form of integration would be a subsidiary merger in which Escarigen would become a subsidiary of Alertron. Most subsidiary mergers occur when the target has a well-known brand that the acquirer wants to maintain, which is the case here. Note that in a statutory merger, the target company would cease to exist as a separate entity. Since both Alertron and Escarigen are involved in the pharmaceutical industry, the type of merger would be best described as horizontal. The merger would not be vertical as Alertron would not be moving up or down the supply chain. (Study Session 9, LOS 28.a)

98. **B** The potential acquisition of Carideo is described as a stock purchase, which means that Carideo's shareholders would be responsible for paying capital gains taxes on the deal and no taxes would be levied against Carideo at the corporate level. The other answers are incorrect. The potential deal with Escarigen is described as a cash offering. In most cash offerings, the acquirer borrows money to raise cash for the deal, which would increase the acquirer's financial leverage. In the potential deal with BriscoePharm, shareholders generally only approve asset purchases when the purchase is substantial (greater than 50% of firm assets). In this case, shareholder approval would not be required. In a proxy battle for Dillon Biotech, Alertron would try to have shareholders approve new members of the board of directors to try to gain control of the company. Trying to purchase shares from shareholders individually is a tender offer. (Study Session 9, LOS 28.e)

99. **C** The only pair combination that correctly identifies a pre-offer and post-offer defense, respectively, is a supermajority voting provision, which is a pre-offer defense requiring shareholder approval in excess of a simple majority; and a leveraged recapitalization, which is a post-offer defense where a target borrows money to repurchase its own shares. Pre-offer defenses suggested include poison puts, fair price amendments, restricted voting rights, poison pills, and staggered board elections. The only other post-offer defense suggested was greenmail, which was incorrectly categorized. (Study Session 9, LOS 28.f)

100. **C** First, calculate the value of the combined firm after the merger:

Post merger value of the combined firm: $V_{AT} = V_A + V_T + S - C$

V_A = $9,000
V_T = $3,120
S = $600
C = $0 because no cash is changing hands

The value of the combined firm is therefore V_{AT} = $9,000 + $3,120 + $600 − 0 = $12,720

Next, to account for the dilution and to find the price per share for the combined firm, P_{AT}, divide the post merger value by the post merger number of shares outstanding. Since we are told that Alertron would exchange 0.75 shares of its stock for each share of Carideo, the number of new shares issued is:

80 million shares × 0.75 = 60 million new shares

So, $P_{AT} = \dfrac{\$12,720}{150 + 60} = \$60.57$

This means the actual value of each share given to Carideo's shareholders is $60.57 and the actual price paid for Carideo is:

P_T = (N × P_{AT}) = (60 × $60.57) = $3,634.20

Carideo's gain in the merger as the target is:

$Gain_T$ = TP = P_T − V_T = $3,634.20 − $3,120 = $514.20

Note that Carideo's gain simply represents the takeover premium in the transaction. (Study Session 9, LOS 28.k)

101. **A** In a cash offer, the acquirer assumes the risk and receives the potential reward from the merger, while the gain to the target shareholders is limited to the takeover premium. In this case, Alertron is comfortable with the estimate of synergies and thinks the estimate may even be conservative. By making a cash offer, the takeover premium realized by Carideo would remain unchanged, with any excess benefit from synergies going to Alertron. Based on its forecasts, Alertron would prefer a cash deal.

However, if the synergies were less than expected, the takeover premium realized by Carideo would still be unchanged with a cash deal, but Alertron's gain may decrease. Since Carideo management believes the estimate of synergies is too high, they would also prefer a cash deal to lock in the gain they realize from the takeover premium. (Study Session 9, LOS 28.l)

102. **C** Pre-merger HHI =
$$(0.20\times100)^2 + (0.18\times100)^2 + (0.15\times100)^2 + (0.12\times100)^2 +$$
$$(0.10\times100)^2 + (0.07\times100)^2 + \left[(0.03\times100)^2\times6\right] = 1,296$$

The post merger market share of the combined firms would be 15% + 10% = 25%.

Post-merger HHI =
$$(0.25\times100)^2 + (0.20\times100)^2 + (0.18\times100)^2 + (0.12\times100)^2 +$$
$$(0.07\times100)^2 + \left[(0.03\times100)^2\times6\right] = 1,596$$

Change in HHI = 1,596 − 1,296 = 300

A post-merger HHI that is between 1,000 and 1,800 indicates a moderately concentrated industry. With a change in an HHI that is greater than 100, there is certainly the potential for an antitrust challenge by regulators. (Study Session 9, LOS 28.g)

103. **C** Benefit 1 is incorrect. Depending on the level of earnings versus positive NPV projects available, the dividend can swing from very high to low (or zero). Positive NPV projects will be financed using earnings, and there will be no dividend if all earnings are used in this way. (Study Session 8, LOS 25.f)

104. **B**

Debt	Short-term	120		
	Long-term	74,953		
	Total		75,073	
Equity	Common stock	200,458		
	APIC	224,909		
	Total		425,367	
Capital structure	Debt	**15.00%**	75,073 / (75,073 + 425,367)	
	Equity	**85.00%**	425,367 / (75,073 + 425,367)	
Capital expenditure	28,000			
Financed by debt	4,200	28,000 × 0.15		
Financed by earnings	23,800	28,000 × 0.85		
Earnings for year	26,034			
Required by capex	23,800			
Residual Dividend	2,234			

(Study Session 8, LOS 25.f)

105. **C**

			Outlay
Proceeds from sale	2,200,000		**2,200,000**
Tax base	0	(full allowance in year 1)	
Taxable gain	2,200,000		
Tax rate	35%		
Tax payable	770,000		**(770,000)**
Cost new machine	3,800,000		**(3,800,000)**
Investment in working capital	200,000		**(200,000)**
Net outlay			**(2,570,000)**

Note that investment in working capital is not tax deductible. Annual tax allowable depreciation on the new machine would be relevant when calculating the tax paid for operating cash flows (at the end of the year).

(Study Session 8, LOS 23.a)

106. **A**

All equity cost	15%						
Cost of debt	8%						
Current D/E	0.18	Debt	75,073	New D/E	0.27	Debt	115,073
Tax Rate	35%	Equity	425,367			Equity	425,367

$$r_e = r_o + [(r_o - r_d) \times (1-t) \times (D/E)]$$
$$= 15\% + [(15\% - 8\%) \times 0.65 \times 0.27]$$
$$= 16.2\%$$

(Study Session 8, LOS 24.a)

107. **A** The costs of financial distress will indeed be lower if the company has tangible, marketable assets, compared to a company with mostly intangible assets.

(Study Session 8, LOS 17.f)

108. **A** The pecking order theory suggests that managers prefer to finance internally as it has the lowest potential information content, followed by debt and finally new equity.

(Study Session 8, LOS 24.b)

109. **A** Based on the APT, the appropriate discount rate for Trailblazer is:

$$E(R_{Trailblazer}) = 3.5\% + (0.81 \times 1.91\%) - (0.45 \times 1.22\%) + (0.24 \times 3.47\%) + (0.74 \times 4.15\%) = 8.4\%$$

Based on the BYPRP method, the required return on Trailblazer's equity = 7.25% + 3% = 10.25%. (Study Session 10, LOS 30.c)

110. **A** Equity risk premium = dividend yield + LT EPS growth rate − LT government bond yield

     = 2.1% + 3.5% − 4.4% = 1.2%

     (Study Session 10, LOS 30.b)

111. **C** All three statements are consistent with the assumptions of the Gordon growth model. Regarding Statement 3, there is nothing to prevent the growth rate from being negative. The model can still be applied in this case. (Study Session 11, LOS 34.d)

112. **B** For a DDM to be appropriate for valuation purposes, dividends must be a reasonably good measure of the cash flow of a firm. Dividends are appropriate for measuring cash flow when a company has a history of dividend payments, when the dividend policy is clear and related to the firm's earnings, and when the perspective is that of a minority shareholder. The two statements relate to the history of dividends and the relationship between dividends and earnings. Statement 4 supports the use of dividends since the history of paying dividends is fairly long and consistent. Statement 5 suggests that the relationship between dividends and earnings is not very strong since the company continues to pay regular dividends regardless of whether losses are incurred or profits are earned. (Study Session 11, LOS 34.a)

113. **C** Statement 6 is correct. Adjusted historical equity risk premium removes any biases in the historical data series. Statement 7 is incorrect. While we adjust peer public company beta for leverage differences, differences in size are not accounted for via adjustment to beta. It is better to account for size differences by additional risk premium for size.

     (Study Session 11, LOS 30.b,d)

114. **C** required return = 3.5% + (1.2 × 4.5%) = 8.9%

     retention ratio = b = ($4.00 − $2.60)/ $4.00 = 0.35

     payout ratio = (1 − b) = 1 − 0.35 = 0.65

     justified leading P/E = $\dfrac{1-b}{r-g} = \dfrac{0.65}{0.089-0.05} = 16.67$

     justified trailing P/E = $\dfrac{(1-b)\times(1+g)}{(r-g)} = \dfrac{0.65\times1.05}{0.089-0.05} = 17.50$

     Notice that the current market price is irrelevant for calculating justified P/E ratios. (Study Session 11, LOS 34.f)

115. **B** Mnoyan is correct. IFRS permits either the partial goodwill or full goodwill method to value goodwill and the noncontrolling interest under the acquisition method. U.S. GAAP requires the full goodwill method. Vadney is incorrect. Both IFRS and U.S. GAAP require equity method accounting for joint ventures. (Study Session 6, LOS 18.b)

116. **A** Switching costs are costs incurred by the buyer in switching from one supplier to another. High switching costs act as a disincentive for buyers to switch products, and decrease the bargaining power of buyers. From the suppliers' perspective, the higher the switching costs, the greater the bargaining power of suppliers. (Study Session 11, LOS 31.a)

117. **C** The neoclassical growth theory relates technological change to increases in labor productivity; however, increases in capital and labor would not increase growth rate in output per worker permanently under neoclassical growth theory.

    The endogenous growth theory holds that technological advances lead to increases in labor productivity. Additionally, capital deepening investments would lead to social benefits and hence lead to further technological advances—increasing growth rate of output per worker.

    Classical growth theory maintains that any increase in per capita GDP above subsistence level is mean reverting. (Study Session 4, LOS 14.i)

118 **B** The value of assets in place is E/r. The difference between this value and the fundamental value is PVGO. (Study Session 11, LOS 34.e)

119. **A** $r = \left[\left(\dfrac{D_0}{P_0}\right) \times \{(1+g_L) + [H \times (g_s - g_L)]\} + g_L\right]$

    Given: dividend yield = 5%, g_s = 12%, g_L = 3% and H = 6 / 2 = 3.

    r = [(0.05) × {(1.03) + 3(0.12 − 0.03)}] + 0.03 = 0.095 or 9.5%

    (Study Session 11, LOS 34.m)

120. **C** Sensitivity to assumptions of growth is a limitation, not a strength. (Study Session 11, LOS 34.h, i)

Exam 2
Morning Session Answers

To get valuable feedback on how your score compares to those of other Level II candidates, use your Username and Password to gain Online Access at schweser.com and choose the menu item "Practice Exams Vol. 1."

1. C	21. B	41. A
2. B	22. A	42. C
3. B	23. A	43. B
4. C	24. C	44. A
5. B	25. B	45. B
6. B	26. A	46. B
7. B	27. B	47. C
8. A	28. B	48. B
9. B	29. A	49. B
10. B	30. B	50. C
11. B	31. B	51. B
12. C	32. A	52. B
13. A	33. B	53. C
14. C	34. A	54. B
15. A	35. A	55. C
16. C	36. C	56. C
17. B	37. A	57. C
18. C	38. C	58. C
19. A	39. B	59. A
20. B	40. C	60. B

Exam 2
Morning Session Answers

1. **C**   The ROS principle of Reasonable and Adequate Basis requires that appropriate due diligence be performed and that recommendations be substantiated. Moreover, the ROS states that supervisory procedures must be in place to ensure compliance with the policy. If the report is released with the supervisor's revision, Blackwell should insist that her name be removed. (Study Session 1, LOS 3.b)

2. **B**   Standard III(A) Loyalty, Prudence, and Care. Unusual proposals, such as hostile takeovers and executive changes, may require more review than routine matters such as renewing stock-repurchase agreements. Money managers should provide a means to review complex proxies. Establishing evaluation criteria and disclosing the firm's proxy voting policies and procedures to clients are basic elements of a proxy-voting policy. Client wishes regarding proxy voting should always be followed. (Study Session 1, LOS 2.a)

3. **B**   Analysts may undertake research related to firms with which they also have an investment banking relationship. The research must remain objective and unbiased to avoid violating the Research Objectivity Standards. Furthermore, the research report must fully disclose the nature of the investment banking relationship and any potential conflict of interest. (Study Session 1, LOS 3.b)

4. **C**   Firms have a fiduciary obligation to their clients to publish adequate and timely information on the companies under coverage. The ROS recommends that firms should publish research reports on covered stocks on a regular basis. At least five months had passed without a published research report from Blanchard regarding a major news story affecting Patel shares. While Baldwin was correct to discuss the reason for dropping coverage, he did not comply with ROS recommendations because he did not publish a timely and/or final report on Patel. It is recommended that firms publish a final research report when dropping coverage discussing the reason and disclosing the analyst's final rating. (Study Session 1, LOS 3.b)

5. **B**   Standard III(B) Fair Dealing requires firms to notify clients of changes in investment advice before executing trades that go counter to that advice. While equal dissemination is usually impossible, it is an admirable goal. Firms should establish dissemination guidelines that are fair to all clients. Trading disclosures and confidentiality regarding investment rating changes are sensible precautions that meet the spirit of the fair dealing Standard. Maintaining client lists that detail client holdings will simplify the process of deciding how to best disseminate a change in investment recommendation. (Study Session 1, LOS 2.a)

6. **B**   Method 2 is the best answer. Quintux should cover the cost of the trading error, and if Borchard is willing to accept investment research in lieu of cash, that's all the better for Quintux. If Quintux compensates Borchard with extra trades, its clients are covering the costs of the error, which may violate Standard III(A) Loyalty, Prudence, and Care if directing future trades to Borchard is not in the clients' best interest. By accepting the CBX shares it did not request and allocating the shares to all client accounts rather than paying for the error, Quintux is violating Standard III(C) Suitability, since the shares are not likely to be appropriate for all of its client accounts and may not be suitable for any

©2015 Kaplan, Inc.

accounts since the shares were obtained as a result of a trading error, not an intentional investment action. Passing on client names is a violation of Standard III(E) Preservation of Confidentiality. (Study Session 1, LOS 2.a)

7.   **B**   Statement 1: Correct, although not all the shares will be offered.
Statement 2: Incorrect because shares are not automatically issued to existing shareholders under a carve-out.
Statement 3: Correct since the results of the business sector will be more easily identifiable once the sector represents a separate company.
Statement 4: Correct for all strategies under consideration.
Statement 5: Incorrect—with a carve-out the "selling" corporation may (usually does) maintain some control of the business that has been split out into a separate company.

(Study Session 9, LOS 28.n)

8.   **A**   Debian s/h gain = $gain_T$ = TP = $P_T - V_T$ = \$90m − \$85m = \$5m

Fedora s/h gain = $gain_A$ = S − TP = 8 − 5 = \$3m.

Synergies are not directly given, but you are given that Fedora's value post merger (after paying the \$5m takeover premium) increases by \$3 million. Synergies must then be \$5m + \$3m = \$8m.

Alternatively, the change in Fedora's value post merger, (\$135m − \$132m) = \$3m, would give the gains to the acquirer in the case of a cash merger.

Note: The total gains = value of combined entity − value of both companies prior to merger

(\$135m + \$90m) − (\$85m + \$132m) = \$8m

Note: The value of the combined entity in a stock merger must include the \$90 million in cash that was paid by Fedora to Debian. For computing the total gains to merger in a cash transaction, we need to add the \$90 million that would be paid out to the seller. (Study Session 9, LOS 28.k)

9.   **B**   Value of Fedora and Ubunta post cash acquisition (given) = \$135 million.

Value of Fedora and Ubunta post stock acquisition = \$135 million + \$90 million cash = \$225 million.

Number of shares outstanding post stock acquisition = 5 + 3 = 8 million.

Value of shares received based on their likely post-acquisition price = [(225m) / 8m] × 3m = \$84,375,000.

Gain to Debian's shareholders is therefore \$84,375,000 − \$85,000,000 = −\$625,000.

(Study Session 9, LOS 28.k)

10.   **B**   New value of their 5m shares = (\$225m / 8m) × 5m   = \$140,625,000
Old value of their 5m shares   = \$132,000,000
Gain   = \$8,625,000

(Study Session 9, LOS 28.k)

11. **B**   Attribute 1: This attribute is incorrect. An effective corporate governance system defines the rights (not the responsibilities) of shareholders and other stakeholders.

Attribute 2: This attribute is correct. An effective corporate governance system provides for fairness and equitable treatment in all dealings between managers, directors, and shareholders.

(Study Session 9, LOS 27.a)

12. **C**   Using comparable company analysis:

Using P/E ratio: 25 × 1.50 =	37.50
Using P/B ratio: 2 ×18 =	36.00
Average	36.75
Add: 30% premium	11.03
Estimated takeover price	$47.78

Using comparable transaction analysis:

Using P/E ratio: 30 × 1.50 =	$45.00
Using P/B ratio: 2.80 × 18 =	50.40
Average	$47.70

Note: No additional premium is applied for comparable transactions.

(Study Session 9, LOS 28.j)

13. **A**   FCFE = NI + depreciation − FCInv − WCInv + net borrowing
$$= 7.0 + 3.5 - 3.2 - 0.4 + (2.4 - 2.0)$$
$$= \text{LC7.3 million, or LC7,300,000}$$
(Study Session 12, LOS 35.d)

14. **C**   FCFF = FCFE + Int(1 − tax rate) − net borrowing = 7.3 + 5.0(1 − 0.34) − (2.4 − 2.0) = LC10.2 million, or LC10,200,000. (Study Session 12, LOS 35.d)

15. **A**   Given the assumptions stated in the problem, this is a simple single stage valuation. Using the firm's modified build-up methodology, the real required rate of return is 8% (= country real rate + industry adjustment + firm adjustment = 3% + 3% + 2%). The real growth rate is $\left[\left(\dfrac{1.12}{1.08738}\right) - 1\right] = 3\%$. FCFE is LC7,3000,000 from an earlier question.

Hence, the value of PCC equity is:

$$V_0 = \frac{\text{FCFE} \times (1+g)}{r-g} = \frac{7,300,000 \times 1.03}{0.08 - 0.03} = \text{LC150,380,000}$$

(Study Session 12, LOS 35.j)

16. **C**   *Dividend policy change*: A change in dividend policy will have no direct impact on future FCFE. Note that dividend payments are a use of equity cash flows, not a reduction in FCFE. It is possible that an increase in dividends could reduce the long-term growth rate of the firm, thus reducing firm value. However, holding all other factors constant, an increase in dividends will not affect FCFE forecasts.

Net change in debt: The increase in debt, LC400,000, will increase future interest expense and decrease future FCFE, but the amount is small, relative to net income of LC7,000,000. (Study Session 12, LOS 35.g)

17. **B** Since the company's capital structure is reasonably stable and FCFE is positive, FCFE is a simpler approach to valuation than FCFF, EVA, or residual income, and is preferred in this case. (Study Session 12, LOS 35.a)

18. **C** Both statements are correct. EBITDA is in fact a poor proxy for FCFF because it does not incorporate the cash taxes paid by the firm. EBITDA also fails to reflect the investment in working capital and the investment in fixed capital. EBITDA is an even worse proxy for FCFE than as a proxy for FCFF. EBITDA does not reflect after-tax interest costs or other cash flows that shareholders care about, such as new borrowing or the repayment of debt. (Study Session 12, LOS 35.h)

19. **A** Free cash flow to the firm can be calculated in various ways. One approach to calculate FCFF is to start with net income:

    FCFF = NI + NCC + Int(1 − tax rate) − FCInv − WCInv
    NI = $164,497   (income statement)
    NCC = Noncash charges = $56,293   (income statement)
    Int = Interest = $20,265 + $5,223 = $25,488   (income statement)
    FCInv = Fixed capital investment = $143,579   (additional information)
    WCInv = Working capital investment = $7,325   (additional information)

    Putting it all together:

    FCFF = $164,497 + $56,293 + $25,488(1 − 0.3) − $143,579 − $7,325 = $87,728
    (Study Session 12, LOS 35.d)

20. **B** FCFE can be expressed in terms of FCFF as follows:

    FCFE = FCFF − Int(1 − tax rate) + net borrowing

    Therefore, the amount by which FCFF exceeds FCFE can be written as:

    FCFF − FCFE = Int(1 − tax rate) − net borrowing

    Int = $25,488

    Net borrowing = $5,866 − $33,275 = −$27,409 (additional information)

    Therefore: FCFF − FCFE = $25,488(1 − 0.3) − (−$27,409) = $45,251
    (Study Session 12, LOS 35.d)

21. **B** The cost of equity can be determined from the capital asset pricing model. We get:

    $r = R_f + \text{beta[market risk premium]} = 4.5\% + 1.10[5\%] = 10\%$.

    The sustainable growth rate can be found from: $g = ROE \times b$

    $$ROE = \frac{\text{net income}}{\text{beginning total equity}} = \frac{\$164,497}{\$1,019,869} = 0.16129$$

    b = retention rate = 1 − ($82,248.50 / $164,497) = 0.5

    $g = 0.16129 \times 0.5 = 0.0806 = 8.06\%$

    (Study Session 11, LOS 34.o)

22. **A**   When depreciation is the only noncash charge, FCFF can be estimated from:

     $$FCFF = EBIT(1 - tax\ rate) + Dep - FCInv - WCInv$$

     $$EBIT_{2009} = \$4,052,173 \times 1.06 \times 0.064 = \$274,899$$

     Therefore: $FCFF_{2009} = \$274,899\,(1 - 0.3) + \$60,000 - \$36,470 - \$24,313 = \$191,646$

     (Study Session 12, LOS 35.d)

23. **A**   This is a two-stage FCFE model. The required return on equity is 10% (from previous problem), and the long-term growth rate after 2 years is 5%.

     $$\text{value of equity} = \frac{\$0.21}{1.1} + \frac{\$0.23}{1.1^2} + \left(\frac{\$0.23 \times 1.05}{0.1 - 0.05} \times \frac{1}{1.1^2} \right)$$

     $$= \frac{\$0.21}{1.1} + \frac{\$0.23}{1.1^2} + \left(\$4.83 \times \frac{1}{1.1^2} \right) = \$4.37$$

     Financial calculators can perform this calculation more quickly and accurately. The appropriate keystrokes are:

     $CFO = 0;\ C01 = \$0.21;\ C02 = \$0.23 + \$4.83 = \$5.06;\ I = 10.0;\ CPT \rightarrow NPV = \$4.37$

     Notice that the second cash flow combines the FCFE for the second year with the present value of the series of constantly growing FCFE terms that begin at the end of the third year. This approach is valid since the timing of these two cash flows is the same (i.e., the end of the second year). (Study Session 12, LOS 35.j)

24. **C**   Dividends, share repurchases, and changes in the number of shares outstanding do not have an effect on either FCFE or FCFF. Therefore, only the new convertible debt offering will have a significant influence on the current level of FCFE because net borrowing changes FCFE. (Study Session 12, LOS 35.i)

25. **B**   FCFE = CFO − FCInv + Net borrowings
     CFO   = 1042 (given), Net borrowings is change in long-term debt and notes payable.
     FCInv = CF from investing = 648
     FCFE = 1042 − 648 + [(2,070 + 644) − (2,020 + 600)] = €488 million.

     Please note that CF from investing activities and FCInv may not be always the same, but in the curriculum (and for this question), they are treated as same. (Study Session 12, LOS 35.d)

26. **A**   FCFF = CFO + Int(1 − Tax rate) − FCInv = 1042 + 150(0.7) − 648 = €499

Overall growth rate for cosmetics industry = 3.5%

	Percentage	Cost
Debt	50%	4.50%
Equity	50%	8.50%
WACC		6.50%
Cosmetics industry growth rate		3.50%

$$\frac{499 \times (1 + 0.035)}{0.065 - 0.035} = 17,216 \text{ million}$$

(Study Session 12, LOS 35.i, j)

27. **B**   To value Hermosa stock, use the following information and apply the two-stage growth model. FCFE for the fiscal year is €136 million. Growth rate for the first 3 years is 14.0%; growth rate after 3 years is 5.5%. For CAPM, expected return on market = 8.5% (since Schön with a beta of 1 should have the same expected rate of return as the market).

Cost of equity (Hermosa) = 0.025 + 1.2 × (0.085 − 0.025) = 9.70%.

	Yr 1	Yr 2	Yr 3
FCFE (in € millions)[1]	155.3	177.0	201.8
Terminal Value			5,069[2]
Total cash flow (in € millions)	155.3	177.0	5,270.8
Cost of Equity		9.70%	

[1]$FCFE_1 = FCFE_0(1 + g) = 136.23(1 + 0.14) = 155.3$

[2]Terminal value $= \dfrac{201.8(1.055)}{(0.097 - 0.055)} = 5069$

For the calculator inputs for NPV function, CF0 = 0, CF1 = 155.3, CF2 = 177.0, CF3 = 5,270.5
I/Y = 9.7

Estimated value is €4,281.26 million. Divide this value by 200 million shares for €21.40 per share. (Study Session 12, LOS 35.j)

28. **B**   Free cash flow to equity values Schön's stock at €17,100,000,000 / 1,000,000,000 or €17.10 per share. This is greater than the market price per share of €15.42; the stock is selling at a price below the implied value which means the stock is undervalued. (Study Session 12, LOS 35.m)

29. **A** The luxury skin care segment's price-to-earnings ratio is 22.9X. The trailing P/E ratio for Hermosa is €22.78 divided by the earnings per share of €193 / 200 or €0.97. Trailing P/E = €22.78 / €0.97 = 23.6X. Hermosa seems to be slightly overvalued relative to the segment. (Study Session 12, LOS 36.a)

30. **B** Approach #2 is the best. The free cash flow to firm approach takes a control perspective in valuation as is appropriate in a buyout. Dividend discount models take a minority perspective, and Hermosa does not pay dividends so Approach #1 is unsuitable. Relative valuation approaches, such as trailing P/E, also focus on market price and hence are based on minority investor perspective. (Study Session 12, LOS 36.d, f)

31. **B** Since the required return (12%) as determined by CAPM is greater than Lear's expected return (10%), then Taylor's stock is overvalued. (Study Session 10, LOS 30.a)

32. **A** Required return under FFM = risk-free rate + market beta (equity risk premium) + size beta (small-cap return premium) + value beta (value-return premium)

    = 3.4% + 0.7(5.5%) + −0.3(3.1%) + 1.4(2.2%) = 9.4%

    Note: The liquidity factor is only applicable to the Pastor-Stambaugh (PS) model. The PS model is otherwise the same as the FFM, save for the addition of the liquidity factor. (Study Session 10, LOS 30.d)

33. **B** The Gordon growth model is a popular method to generate forward-looking estimates using current information and expectations concerning economic and financial variables.

    A historical estimate of the equity risk premium consists of the difference between the historical mean return for a broad-based equity market index and a risk-free rate over a given time period.

    A macroeconomic model estimate of the equity risk premium is based on the relationships between macroeconomic variables and financial variables. (Study Session 10, LOS 30.b, c, d)

34. **A** The build-up method is usually applied to closely held companies (such as Densmore) where betas are not readily obtainable.

    The risk premium approach requires betas for its calculations; betas are generally not readily available for closely held companies.

    The bond-yield plus risk premium method is appropriate only if the company has publicly traded debt. The method simply adds a risk premium to the yield to maturity of the company's long-term debt. (Study Session 10, LOS 30.d)

35. **A** Neither of Saunder's statements is correct. *Confidence risk* represents the unexpected change in the difference between the return of risky corporate bonds and government bonds. *Business cycle risk* represents the unexpected change in the level of real business activity. (Study Session 10, LOS 30.d)

36. **C** A weakness (not strength) of the CAPM is its low explanatory power in some cases. Multifactor models usually have higher explanatory power than the CAPM since they use more than one factor, whereas CAPM uses only one factor.

    A weakness (not strength) of multifactor models is that they are typically more complex to use. (Study Session 10, LOS 30.f)

37. **A** We have to bootstrap the three-year spot rate (S_3) given the par curve.

S_1 = par rate for a one-year bond = 1.50%.

Value of two-year (par) bond = $100 = \dfrac{2}{(1+S_1)} + \dfrac{102}{(1+S_2)^2} = \dfrac{2}{(1.015)} + \dfrac{102}{(1+S_2)^2}$

Hence, $(1 + S_2)^2 = 102 / 98.03 = 1.04$ and $S_2 = 2.005\%$

Value of a three-year (par) bond = 100

$= \dfrac{2.25}{(1+S_1)} + \dfrac{2.25}{(1+S_2)^2} + \dfrac{102.25}{(1+S_3)^3} = \dfrac{2.25}{(1.015)} + \dfrac{2.25}{(1.02005)^2} + \dfrac{102.25}{(1+S_3)^3}$

Hence, $(1+S_3)^3 = 102.25 / 95.62 = 1.0693$ and $S_3 = 2.259\%$

(Study Session 14, LOS 43.c)

38. **C** $[1+f(2,1)]^1 = (1 + S_3)^3 / (1 + S_2)^2$

From the earlier computations, we know that S_2 = 2.005% and S_3 = 2.259%.

$[1+f(2,1)]^1 = (1.02259)^3 / (1.02005)^2 = 1.0277 \rightarrow f(2,1) = 2.77\%$

(Study Session 14, LOS 43.b)

39. **B** $F_{(3,3)}$ = $0.9151 (given)

$P_3 = 1 / (1 + S_3)^3 = 1 / (1.0277)^3 = \$0.9213$

$P_6 = F_{(3,3)} \times P_3 = 0.9151 \times 0.9213 = \$0.8431$

(Study Session 14, LOS 43.b)

40. **C** Bond A is a three-year bond, callable in one year. Callable bonds are sensitive to par rates corresponding to their call date (particularly if their coupon rate is relatively high) and to the par rates corresponding to their maturity date (especially if the coupon rate is relatively low). (Study Session 14, LOS 43.k)

41. **A** Callable bonds exhibit negative convexity due to price compression that occurs when the call option is in the money. Hence, bond A would exhibit negative convexity. Also, the upside potential for a callable bond (that is realized when interest rates fall) is limited due to the embedded short call. (Study Session 14, LOS 43.k,l)

42. **C**

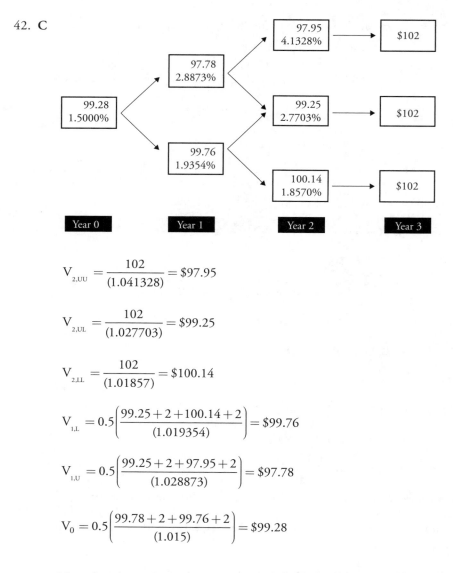

$$V_{2,UU} = \frac{102}{(1.041328)} = \$97.95$$

$$V_{2,UL} = \frac{102}{(1.027703)} = \$99.25$$

$$V_{2,LL} = \frac{102}{(1.01857)} = \$100.14$$

$$V_{1,L} = 0.5\left(\frac{99.25 + 2 + 100.14 + 2}{(1.019354)}\right) = \$99.76$$

$$V_{1,U} = 0.5\left(\frac{99.25 + 2 + 97.95 + 2}{(1.028873)}\right) = \$97.78$$

$$V_0 = 0.5\left(\frac{99.78 + 2 + 99.76 + 2}{(1.015)}\right) = \$99.28$$

Note that the option was never exercised. (Study Session 14, LOS 45.c)

43. **B** The Eurodollar contract is a more effective instrument to hedge LIBOR-based investments because the Eurodollar contract is a LIBOR-based contract. The T-bill contract is based on T-bill rates, which are not perfectly correlated with LIBOR rates, so hedging a LIBOR investment with a T-bill futures contract results in a less effective hedge. Reichmann should take a long position in the Eurodollar contract. If interest rates decrease, his yield on the LIBOR-based security will fall, but the decrease will be offset by gains on a long position in a Eurodollar futures contract. (Study Session 16, LOS 48.g)

44. **A** The interest rate cap pays off when interest rates rise above the cap rate, so a long position in a cap will hedge the risk of an increase in interest rates. A call option on an interest rate also pays off when the index rate at maturity is greater than the strike rate, so a long position in the call option will also hedge the risk of an increase in interest rates. (Study Session 17, LOS 49.a and 51.a)

45. **B** floor payoff = $30,000,000 × (0.060 − 0.058) = $60,000

(Study Session 17, LOS 51.b)

46. **B** The value of the 2-year floor is equal to the value of a comparable 1-year European put option (a 1-year "floorlet") plus the value of a comparable 2-year put option (a 2-year "floorlet"). A 1-year floorlet with an annual payoff is the same as a 1-year put option on annual LIBOR. Therefore the value of the 2-year put option is equal to the value of the 2-year floor less the value of the 1-year put option: $285,000 − $90,000 = $195,000.
(Study Session 17, LOS 51.b)

47. **C** To hedge his fixed income portfolio using an interest rate collar, Reichmann should sell the 6% floor and buy the 12% cap. Reichmann is hedged partially against interest rate increases because when rates rise above 12% and the value of the fixed-income portfolio falls, the cap will pay off. Selling the floor reduces his upside potential if rates fall below 6%, but he can offset some or all of the cost of the cap with the proceeds from the floor.
(Study Session 17, LOS 51.b)

48. **B** The last part of the first comment is incorrect. If a firm anticipates a floating rate exposure at some future date (e.g., it will be issuing bonds or getting a loan), a payer swaption would *lock in* a fixed rate and provide floating-rate payments for the loan. It would be exercised if the yield curve shifted up to give the investor (effectively) a loan at the fixed rate on the swaption. The second comment is correct. Swaptions also can be used to speculate on changes in interest rates. The investor would buy a payer swaption if he expects rates to rise, or buy a receiver swaption if he expects rates to fall.
(Study Session 17, LOS 50.f)

49. **B** For two up-moves, $45(1.15)^2 = \$59.51$. For two down-moves,

$45(1/1.15)^2 = 34.03.$

For two up-moves, the intrinsic call value is $59.51 − $40 = $19.51.

For two down-moves, the call is out-of-the-money, intrinsic value = $0. For an up and a down-move the stock price is unchanged at 45, so the intrinsic value of the calls is $45.00 − $40.00 = $5.

The risk neutral probabilities for the decision tree: $\pi_U = \dfrac{1.04 - 0.87}{1.15 - 0.87} = 0.607$ and $\pi_D = 1 - \pi_U = 0.393$.

The probability weighted present value of the option payoff if there are two up-moves is $\dfrac{0.607^2 (19.51)}{1.04^2} = \$6.65$.

For up-down and down-up (which are equal probabilities), the probability weighted present value of the payoff is $\dfrac{(2)(0.607)(0.393)(\$5.00)}{1.04^2} = \$2.21$.

Sum these to get the option value, $8.86. (Study Session 17, LOS 49.b)

50. **C** To form a delta neutral portfolio Loper needs to write $\dfrac{1,000}{0.83} = 1,204.82$, or 1,205 calls.
(Study Session 17, LOS 49.e)

51. **B** The payoff is zero for a down-move and 11.75 for an up-move. Since the probability of an up-move is 0.607, the present value is $\dfrac{(0.607)11.75}{1.04} = \$6.86$. (Study Session 17, LOS 49.b)

52. **B**   The possibility of early exercise is not valuable for call options on non-dividend paying stocks, so the value of the American call is the same as the value of the European call, and the difference in value is zero. (Study Session 17, LOS 49.b)

53. **C**   The first assumption listed in the vignette should read, "The volatility of the return on the underlying stock is known and constant." The other listed assumptions are correct. (Study Session 17, LOS 49.c)

54. **B**   Dividends on the underlying stock decrease the value of call options and increase the value of put options, all else equal. By ignoring them in his valuation, Loper will likely overvalue a long call option and undervalue a long put. (Study Session 17, LOS 49.g)

55. **C**   The investment process requires consideration of risk and return concurrently. While maximization of returns is always preferable, an investor's risk tolerance must also be determined and included in the investment decision. Recall that risk and return objectives are closely related to one another because of the trade-off between risk and return. Therefore, Statement 1 is incorrect, and Statement 4 is correct. (Study Session 18, LOS 56.e)

56. **C**   Specific factors that determine an investor's ability to accept risk include required spending needs, financial strength, and long-term wealth targets. Behavioral factors affect an individual investor's willingness to accept risk. (Study Session 18, LOS 56.e)

57. **C**   Strategic asset allocation requires investment managers to consider all sources of income and risk. It also requires an analysis of capital market conditions and specific risk and return characteristics of individual assets. Therefore, Statement 2 is incorrect, and Statement 3 is correct. (Study Session 18, LOS 56.d)

58. **C**   Responses A and B are appropriate considerations related to tax considerations. Although investors should rely on accountants and other advisors for tax advice, portfolio managers also need to pay attention to the tax consequences of their investment recommendations and relay those consequences to the investor so proper tax planning can occur. (Study Session 18, LOS 56.e)

59. **A**   The most important portfolio constraints faced by individual investors include liquidity, investment horizon, and unique needs. Legal and regulatory factors are less important for individual investors than they are for institutional investors. (Study Session 18, LOS 56.e)

60. **B**   Investment policy statements should be transportable, foster discipline, and discourage short-term strategy shifts. (Study Session 18, LOS 56.c)

Exam 2
Afternoon Session Answers

To get valuable feedback on how your score compares to those of other Level II candidates, use your Username and Password to gain Online Access at schweser.com and choose the menu item "Practice Exams Vol. 1."

61. A	81. C	101. B
62. C	82. B	102. A
63. C	83. A	103. C
64. C	84. A	104. C
65. B	85. B	105. B
66. A	86. C	106. B
67. C	87. C	107. B
68. C	88. C	108. C
69. B	89. C	109. C
70. A	90. C	110. B
71. C	91. A	111. A
72. C	92. B	112. B
73. A	93. B	113. A
74. C	94. B	114. C
75. B	95. C	115. A
76. C	96. A	116. C
77. B	97. A	117. B
78. B	98. B	118. C
79. C	99. C	119. B
80. B	100. A	120. B

61. **A** By implying that the composite's past performance is representative of future performance, Burton is in violation of Standard III(D) Performance Presentation. A member or candidate should give a fair and complete presentation of performance and not state or imply that clients will obtain a rate of return that was generated in the past.

    Burton's references to the CFA program in his marketing materials were acceptable according Standard VII(B) Reference to CFA Institute, the CFA Designation, and the CFA Program. The Standard states that members and candidates may make references to the rigor of the program and the commitment of members and candidates to ethical and professional standards. However, statements must not exaggerate the meaning or implications of the designation, membership in CFA Institute, or candidacy. (Study Session 1, LOS 2.a)

62. **C** According to CFA Institute Standards of Professional Conduct, client brokerage is the property of the client; client-directed brokerage does not violate the duty of loyalty to clients. Members should disclose to the clients if such arrangements does not result in best execution for the clients (but this stipulation is not applicable in this case). (Study Session 1, LOS 2.a)

63. **C** Standard VI(C) Referral Fees states that members and candidates must disclose to their clients and prospective clients any compensation or benefit received for the recommendation of services. In this case, Burton may accept a referral fee if he discloses it to the client so that the client may evaluate any partiality shown in the recommendation. (Study Session 1, LOS 2.a)

64. **C** According to Requirement 4.0 Investment Banking of the CFA Institute Research Objectivity Standards, firms must prohibit communication between members of the research and investment banking divisions. Recommended compliance procedures for Requirement 4.0 include prohibiting analysts from participating in marketing road shows. Therefore, while Security Bank complies with all of the requirements of the Standards, it does not comply with all of the recommendations.

    Under Requirement 10.0 Disclosure, firms are required to disclose all conflicts of interest to which the firm or its covered employees are subject, including whether the firm engages in any investment banking or other corporate finance activities. Therefore, "publicly revealing" the relationship is not a violation of the client's confidentiality. (Study Session 1, LOS 3.b)

65. **B** Standard V(A) Diligence and Reasonable Basis states that the member or candidate must exercise diligence, independence, and thoroughness before making an investment recommendation. The Standard also requires that members and candidates have a reasonable and adequate basis supported by research and investigation for any investment recommendations or actions. Burton made his purchase recommendation to Crossley purely on the basis of the Security Bank road show and did not perform his own evaluation to determine whether or not the SolutionWare IPO was a good investment opportunity. Burton has therefore violated Standard V(A).

Standard III(C) Suitability was also violated because there is no indication that Burton made any effort to determine if the investment was appropriate for Crossley's portfolio. Burton should have determined that the investment was consistent with Crossley's written objectives and constraints before he recommended the investment. Even though he later determined that the investment was suitable, he did not know this was the case before he told Crossley that he should purchase shares in the IPO. Standard III(B) Fair Dealing (and not I(B) Independence and Objectivity) would also be violated if Burton did not afford all the clients for whom the IPO was suitable to participate in the offering. Standard III(B) Fair Dealing (and not standard I(B)) would also be violated if Burton did not extend IPO participation to all portfolios meeting suitability criteria. (Study Session 1, LOS 2.a)

66. **A**   Standard VI(B) Priority of Transactions clearly states that investment transactions for clients must have priority over members' and candidates' transactions. Members and candidates can profit from personal investments as long as the client is not disadvantaged by the trade. By taking a portion of the IPO shares for his own account, Burton has ensured that Crossley's order will not be completely filled. It does not matter that the trade allocation was done on a pro-rata basis; Burton should have placed his client's transaction ahead of his own. (Study Session 1, LOS 2.a)

67. **C**   The best formulation for Smith's retail sales data would include the intercept, the lag one coefficient, and the lag twelve coefficient. First, note that in the second regression, all of these are statistically significant, with a p-value of less than 1%. Also, the second regression that included the lag twelve term has a higher adjusted R-square at 0.92 compared to 0.83 in the first regression that omits the lag twelve term. Lastly, we should suspect that the lag twelve term is appropriate because this is seasonal, monthly data.

   We could have also looked at the significance of the autocorrelations if they had been provided. If any are significant in either regression, another lag term would be added to the autoregressive model. (Study Session 3, LOS 11.d, l)

68. **C**   To forecast the sales this month, we first calculate the change in the log of sales last month:

   $\Delta \ln \text{sales}_{t-1} = \ln(6{,}270) - \ln(6{,}184) = 8.7435 - 8.7297 = 0.0138$

   Next, use this change in the regression model to obtain the forecasted change for this month:

   $\Delta \ln \text{sales}_t = 0.052 + 0.684(0.0138) = 0.0614$

   Add the forecasted change to last month's log sales to obtain this month's forecasted log sales:

   $\ln \text{sales}_t = 0.0614 + 8.7435 = 8.8049$

   Lastly, convert the forecasted log value to a dollar value by taking its antilog:

   $\text{sales}_t = e^{8.8049} = \$6{,}667$

   (Study Session 3, LOS 11.d)

69. **B** Smith is correct. The first step in testing for an ARCH process is to take the residuals from the original autoregressive model and then square them.

Sims is incorrect. The next step in determining whether an ARCH process exists is to regress the squared residuals from this period against the squared residuals from the previous period as follows:

$$\varepsilon_t^2 = b_0 + b_1\varepsilon_{t-1}^2$$

If b_1 is statistically different from zero, then we conclude that the regression model contains an ARCH process. (Study Session 3, LOS 11.m)

70. **A** Neither the lag two term nor the lag four term should be included. To determine the significance of the autocorrelation of the residuals, we need the standard error, which is calculated as one over the square root of the number of observations. There are 36 quarters of inflation data. One quarter is lost because we have a lag one term, so there are 35 observations in the regression. Therefore, the standard error is $\frac{1}{\sqrt{35}} = 0.1690$.

The t-statistics are the autocorrelations divided by the standard error which results in:

Lag	Autocorrelation	Standard Error	t-Statistic
1	0.0829	0.1690	0.49
2	0.1293	0.1690	0.76
3	0.0227	0.1690	0.13
4	0.1882	0.1690	1.11

The critical t-value is 2.03 for a two-tail test, so none of the t-statistics indicate that the autocorrelations are significantly different from zero. Therefore, we do not need to include additional lag terms. (Study Session 3, LOS 11.d)

71. **C** In the first regression, the Federal Funds rate in the United States has a unit root, but the bond yield in the European Union does not. So the former data series is not covariance stationary, but the latter is. In this case, the regression results will not be valid.

In the second regression, both the Federal Funds rate in the United States and the bond yield in Great Britain have a unit root. So both data series are not covariance stationary. However, because they are cointegrated, the regression results will be valid.

To sum up the possibilities you may face on exam day:
- If neither data series has a unit root, the regression results are valid.
- If only one data series has a unit root, the regression results are invalid.
- If both data series have a unit root and they are cointegrated, the regression results are valid.
- If both data series have a unit root and they are not cointegrated, the regression results are not valid.

(Study Session 3, LOS 11.k, n)

72. **C** To test whether two variables are cointegrated, we regress one data series on the other and examine the residuals for a unit root using the Dickey-Fuller/Engle-Granger test. If we reject the null hypothesis, the error terms of the two data series are covariance stationary and cointegrated. The regression results will be valid. (Study Session 3, LOS 11.n)

73. **A**   Hoskins's statement is likely to be correct. If the Maldavian government is considering taxing stock market transactions, then this will limit future economic growth. Economic growth is dependent in part on markets, because markets facilitate business transactions between buyers and sellers.

Lanning's statement is also likely to be correct. If the president of Petria nationalizes the oil industry, then private property will be seized and property rights will not have been respected. Without property rights, firms and individuals have little incentive to make investments that could lead to future economic growth. (Study Session 4, LOS 14.a)

74. **C**   Hoskins's reasoning is incorrect because although labor productivity will increase, the increase will result from a movement *along* the productivity curve. An upward shift in the productivity curve requires an advancement in technology. (Study Session 4, LOS 15.d)

75. **B**   Felicia has lower capital to labor ratio and would benefit more from capital deepening. Removal of restrictions on the inflow of capital would lead to more investment and hence capital deepening—again benefiting Felicia more. (Study Session 4, LOS 14.d)

76. **C**   GDP growth rate = growth rate in TFP + α (long-term growth rate of capital) + $(1 - \alpha)$ (long-term growth rate of labor).
$(1 - \alpha) = 0.52$ and thus $\alpha = 0.48$
$3.9\% = \Delta\text{TFP} + (0.48)(1.4) + (0.52)(1.9) \rightarrow \Delta\text{TFP} = 2.24\%$
(Study Session 4, LOS 14.e)

77. **B**   Under the classical growth theory, the Tiberian economy will settle at a subsistence level. The high growth in the economy will result in a higher population. The higher population will eventually result in decreased returns to labor and decreased labor productivity. No permanent increase in labor productivity will result and per capita GDP will settle at a subsistence level. (Study Session 4, LOS 14.i)

78. **B**   Under the endogenous growth theory, the Tiberian GDP growth rate can continue to increase because technological advances will be shared by many sectors of the economy. Increasing R&D investment, for example, results in benefits not just to the firm making the investment but also to other firms. As these benefits flow to other firms, the economy becomes more productive and the long-term economic growth rate can continue to increase. (Study Session 4, LOS 14.i)

79. **C**   The balance sheet accrual ratio is the year-over-year increase in net operating assets divided by average net operating assets. An increase in payables (a liability) will tend to decrease (reduce the change in) net operating assets, while an increase in inventory will tend to increase (increase the change in) net operating assets. Cash is not an operating asset and does not affect the ratio. (Study Session 7, LOS 22.e)

80. **B**   The unadjusted interest coverage ratio is calculated as follows:

$$\text{interest coverage} = \frac{\text{EBIT}}{\text{interest expense}} = \frac{10,876.00}{693.00} = 15.69$$

To adjust the interest coverage ratio for the operating lease, we need to take EBIT and add back the lease/rental expense (the lease payment amount) and subtract an estimate of depreciation for the machinery. Then, we need to add the appropriate interest expense for the operating lease to the overall interest expense.

To compute the interest expense and depreciation for the operating lease, we must first calculate the present value of the operating lease as follows:

PMT $= 2,000$
I/Y $= 9$
N $= 5$
FV $= 0$
CPT$\rightarrow$PV $= 7,779.30$

Depreciation and interest expense are then calculated as:

$$\text{depreciation} = \frac{7,779.30}{5} = 1,555.86$$

$$\text{interest expense} = 7,779.30 \times 0.09 = 700.14$$

The adjusted interest coverage ratio is:

$$\text{interest coverage}_{(adjusted)} = \frac{\text{EBIT} + \text{operating lease rent expense} - \text{depreciation}}{\text{interest expense} + \text{interest expense}}$$

$$\text{interest coverage}_{(adjusted)} = \frac{10,876.00 + 2,000.00 - 1,555.86}{693.00 + 700.14} = 8.13$$

(Study Session 7, LOS 22.c)

81. **C** The elimination of the securitization of receivables as an off-balance-sheet item would result in Konker having to report the transaction as securitized borrowing, replacing the receivables on the balance sheet, and reporting a liability equal to the proceeds of the securitization transaction. The impact on Konker's balance sheet would be an increase in assets, and an increase in liabilities. The change in equity from reporting the transaction in this way is likely to be small. Financial leverage would increase, and the consequent increase in interest expense from the liability would decrease the interest coverage ratio. (Study Session 7, LOS 22.d)

82. **B** Removing the effects of the income reported under the equity method involves removing the income and the equity asset reported on the balance sheet. The decrease in total assets will increase the asset turnover ratio. The tax burden term is net income divided by earnings before tax so that the decrease in net income from removing the equity income will decrease the term (an apparently greater reduction in ROE due to taxes). Neither interest expense nor operating earnings (EBIT) are affected by the appropriate adjustments, so the interest coverage ratio is unaffected. (Study Session 7, LOS 22.b)

83. **A** The fact that Konker is growing the Industrial division most rapidly (highest capex percent to asset percent ratio) is a likely cause for concern and further investigation, since this division has the lowest operating return on assets. The decrease in the operating ROA for the Capital division is not particularly troublesome as it mirrors the pattern for the other divisions and likely just reflects year-to-year variation in profitability. The fact that the percent of capex for the Defense division is less than its percent of total assets is not a primary cause for concern since that division has a lower operating ROA, and growth in capital assets likely follows contract awards in the defense industry, rather than drives business. Also, the apparent overinvestment in the Industrial division will decrease the capex percent for other divisions, other things equal. (Study Session 7, LOS 22.b)

84. **A** Volatile accruals ratios are an indicator that a firm may be manipulating earnings. Additionally, increasing accruals ratios may be a sign that a firm may be manipulating earnings. Lower accrual ratios represent higher earnings quality. (Study Session 7, LOS 22.b)

85. **B** The assets and liabilities of the purchased firm are included on the balance sheet of the acquiring firm under either method. Under the pooling method, there is no adjustment of balance sheet asset and liability values to their fair values. Under the acquisition method, assets and liabilities acquired are reported at fair value at the time of the purchase. There is no goodwill reported under the pooling method; the purchase price is not reflected on the balance sheet of the acquiring firm. (Study Session 6, LOS 18.a)

86. **C** Under the acquisition method, the investee firm's revenue and expenses would be reported on Fisher's income statement, increasing both expenses and revenues. Under the equity method, Fisher's revenue and expenses are reported without adjustment, and the proportion of income from the purchased firm is reported separately, so that net income is the same under either method. (Study Session 6, LOS 18.a)

87. **C** Goodwill is not amortized under IFRS or U.S. GAAP. The test for impairment is different under IFRS than under U.S. GAAP. Impairment losses cannot be reversed under U.S. GAAP nor under IFRS. (Study Session 6, LOS 18.b)

88. **C** All business combinations (e.g., merger, purchase, or consolidation) are reported under the acquisition method. Identifiable assets and liabilities must be reported at fair value at the time of the acquisition. Under IFRS, Fisher has the option of calculating the goodwill for the acquisition under either the full goodwill or partial goodwill methods. Goodwill is less under the partial goodwill method. (Study Session 6, LOS 18.b)

89. **C** U.S. GAAP requires that unrealized gains and losses on available-for-sale securities be reported in comprehensive income as part of shareholders' equity. The appropriate adjustment to Fisher's statements is to decrease net income by the amount of the gain. Lower net income will result in lower ROA and ROE (lower numerators). Lower net income results in lower retained earnings. However, the gain increases other comprehensive income; thus, total equity does not change. In summary, assets, liabilities and total equity are not affected by the adjustment; thus, asset turnover, debt-to-equity and debt-to-total capital are not impacted. (Study Session 6, LOS 18.a, b)

90. **C** The acquisition method results in higher assets and higher sales, but the same net income. Therefore, both ROA (net income divided by assets) and net profit margin (net income divided by sales) will decrease. (Study Session 6, LOS 18.c)

91. **A** Exposure under the current rate method is equity. Beginning equity is positive ($4,000) and the change in equity during the year is positive ($6,000 − $4,000 = $2,000). Because the Rho appreciated during the year, the current rate method will report a translation gain for 2008. Under the current rate method, gains and losses are reported as part of the cumulative translation adjustment in the equity section of the balance sheet. (Study Session 6, LOS 20.e, f)

92. **B** Exposure under the temporal method is cash and accounts receivable minus current liabilities and long-term debt. Beginning exposure is negative ($5,000 − $11,000 = −$6,000) and the change in exposure is also negative [−$6,300 − (−$6,000)] = −$300. Because the Rho appreciated during the year, the temporal method will report a translation loss for 2008. Gains and losses are reported on the income statement under the temporal method. (Study Session 6, LOS 20.e, f)

93. **B** If the Rho is appreciating, mixed ratios, like return on assets and total asset turnover (using end-of-period balance sheet figures), calculated from the local currency statements, will be larger than the same ratios calculated from the reporting currency statements that were translated using the current rate method. For example, under the current rate method, net income will be translated at the lower average rate ($0.42) and assets will be translated at the higher ending rate ($0.45). Therefore the original return on assets (net income divided by total assets) from the Rho statements will be higher than the ratio after it is translated into the reporting currency. (Study Session 6, LOS 20.e, f)

94. **B** With the Rho appreciating, fixed asset turnover will be lower under the current rate method. (Study Session 6, LOS 20.e, f)

95. **C** This is an example of transaction exposure for Wayward. The translation of Wayward's Del-denominated receivables to Rho would occur at the current exchange rate (i.e., the exchange rate at balance sheet date) and any gains or losses would be reflected in the income statement. (Study Session 6, LOS 20.b)

96. **A** The quick ratio (cash and receivables divided by current liabilities) is a pure balance sheet ratio, which means both numerator and denominator will be translated at the current exchange rate and the ratio will be the same before and after translation. The result is the same for the interest coverage ratio (EBIT divided by interest expense) because it is a pure income statement ratio; both the numerator and denominator will be translated at the average rate over the reporting period and the ratio will be the same before and after translation. (Study Session 6, LOS 20.e, f)

97. **A** Since inventory prices are rising, COGS is higher under last-in, first-out (LIFO) than under first-in, first-out (FIFO). Therefore, net income and taxes are lower under LIFO. Since taxes are lower under LIFO, cash flows will be higher. Working capital would also be lower under LIFO. (Study Session 5, LOS 16.a)

98. **B** Over an inflationary period, older layers of inventory will have been purchased at lower prices than more recently purchased inventory. Since older layers of inventory that are liquidated were purchased at lower prices, the cost of goods sold will be lower and earnings will be higher. (Study Session 5, LOS 16.b)

99. **C** FIFO COGS is equal to LIFO COGS minus the change in LIFO reserve. Therefore, $30,757 – ($5,750 – 3,250) = $28,257. (Study Session 5, LOS 16.c)

100. **A** Under the double-declining balance method of depreciation, the deductions in assets and net income are greatest in the early years and decline over time. This means that return on investment will increase over time as net income increases. (Study Session 5, LOS 17.b)

101. **B** Remaining useful life = (gross investment – accumulated depreciation) / depreciation expense.

    13.94 = ($32,268 – $9,769) / $1,614

    (Study Session 5, LOS 17.d)

102. **A** Under U.S. GAAP, long-lived assets are reported on the balance sheet at depreciated cost less any impairment losses ($525 million original cost less $182 million accumulated depreciation and less $43 million impairment loss, for a net amount of $300 million). Increases are generally prohibited with the exception of assets held for sale. Since these assets are currently in use, this exception does not apply. Therefore, Project Depot may not revalue the assets upward. (Study Session 5, LOS 17.c)

103. **C** The first step is to determine the tax rate from Exhibit 1.

 net income = (after tax cash flow − depreciation), so net income
   = ($375,600 − $264,000) = $111,600

 net income = EBT − taxes, so taxes = EBT − net income
   = ($186,000 − $111,600) = $74,400

 tax rate = taxes / EBT = ($74,400 / 186,000) = 0.4000 = 40%

 initial investment outlay
  = purchase price + increase in net working capital
   + shipping and installation costs
  = $700,000 + ($50,000 − $20,000) + $100,000 = $830,000

 terminal year after-tax non-operating cash flow (TNOCF)
  $= Sal_T + NWCInv − T(Sal_T − B_T)$
  = 75,000 + 30,000 − 0.4(75,000 − 0)
  = 75,000

 after-tax operating cash flow (Year 4)
  = (S − C)(1 − T) + DT
  = ($750,000 − $225,000 − $75,000)(1 − 0.4) + (0.4)($56,000) = $292,400

The book value at the end of Year 4 is $0 because total depreciation over the four years was $800,000.

total CF (Year 4) = $292,400 + $75,000 = $367,400

(Study Session 8, LOS 23.a)

104. **C** Both recommendations are incorrect. The $100,000 is a sunk cost and is thus not a relevant cash flow. Using straight-line depreciation will reduce the present value of the depreciation tax shield and reduce the NPV. (Study Session 8, LOS 23.a)

105. **B** By ignoring the initial $30,000 cash inflow (recall that you are asked to assume it is an inflow), he has underestimated project NPV by $30,000. By ignoring the terminal cash outflow of $30,000, he has overestimated the project NPV by $\dfrac{\$30,000}{1.08^4} = \$22,050$

The net effect is to underestimate NPV by $30,000 − 22,050 = $7,950.

(Study Session 8, LOS 23.a)

106. **B** The overall NPV of Project 1 = project NPV − option cost + option value

overall NPV = −$7 million − $3 million + $9 million = −$1 million

Without the option, the NPV of the production facility is negative, and the real option does not add enough value to make the overall project profitable.

Holbrook is incorrect that he needs to wait for more information to make the decision on Project 2. If the NPV of the project without the option is positive, the analyst knows that the project with the option must be even more valuable, and determining a specific value for the option is unnecessary. A real option adds value to a project, even if it is difficult to determine the monetary amount of that value. (Study Session 8, LOS 23.f)

107. **B** economic income = cash flow − economic depreciation

economic depreciation = beginning market value − ending market value

market value at time t = present value of all remaining cash flows discounted at the WACC

$$\text{Year 3 beginning market value} = \frac{CF_3}{(1+\text{WACC})^1} + \frac{CF_4}{(1+\text{WACC})^2}$$

$$= \frac{\$318{,}000}{(1.08)^1} + \frac{\$367{,}400}{(1.08)^2} = \$294{,}444 + \$314{,}986 = \$609{,}430$$

$$\text{Year 3 ending market value} = \frac{CF_4}{(1+\text{WACC})^1} = \frac{\$367{,}400}{(1.08)^1} = \$340{,}185$$

Year 3 after-tax operating cash flow (given) = $318,000

Year 3 economic depreciation = $609,430 − $340,185 = $269,245

Year 3 economic income = $318,000 − $269,245 = $48,755

(Study Session 8, LOS 23.h)

108. **C** Comment 1 is incorrect. Interest should not be included in a project's cash flows when conducting NPV analysis because it is a financing cost that is reflected in the discount rate use to compute NPV.

     Comment 2 is incorrect. In theory, when discounted at the WACC, the present value of the economic profits from a project equals the NPV of the project. For a given period, economic profit = NOPAT – $WACC, where NOPAT is net operating profit after taxes and $WACC is the dollar cost of the capital used during the period. Economic profit reflects the income earned by all capital providers. (Study Session 8, LOS 23.a, i)

109. **C** Using direct capitalization:

     Cap rate data:

Office Building	Craig Court	Kenton Place	Hester Oasis
Cap rate	$2.56 / $32.0 = 8.0%	$1.80 / $24.0 = 7.5%	$3.15 / $45.0 = 7.0%

     The average cap rate for the three apartment buildings is 7.5%. The estimated value of Parkway Terrance is calculated as the NOI of $3,300,000 divided by the cap rate of 7.5%, or $44.0 million. (Study Session 13, LOS 39.g)

110. **B** Using the sales comparison approach:

Variable	Craig Court	Kenton Place	Hester Oasis
Sale price	$32,000,000	$24,000,000	$45,000,000
Size	200,000	150,000	300,000
Sale price per sq ft	$160.00	$160.00	$150.00
Age adjustment	-4.5%	0.0%	+4.5%
Condition adjustment	+7.5%	0.0%	0.0%
Location adjustment	0.0%	+7.5%	+7.5%
Date of sale adjustment	+4.5%	+2.5%	+8.0%
Total adjustments	+7.5%	+10.0%	+20.0%
Adjusted sales price psf	$160 × (1 + 0.075) = $172.00	$160 × (1 + 0.100) = $176.00	$150 × (1 + 0.200) = $180.00

     Average sales price per square foot is $176.00. The sales comparison method estimates the value of the property at 240,000 square feet × $176.00 = $42.2 million. (Study Session 13, LOS 39.i)

111. **A**

	Parkway Terrace	*Standards*
NOI	$3,300,000	
Equity[1]	$10,000,000	
Annual Debt Service	$166,750 × 12 = $2,001,000	
Equity Dividend Rate	= ($3,300,000 − $2,001,000) / $10,000,000 = 13.0%	13.0% is less than 25.0%
DSCR	$3,300,000/$2,001,000 = 1.65X	1.65X exceeds 1.50X
Cash flows (PMT)	$3,300,000 − $2,001,000 = $1,299,000	
Equity (PV)	$10,000,000	
Sales Price − Outstanding Loan in 10 Years (FV)	$60,000,000 − $21,797,543 = $38,202,457	
Sales Date (N)	10	
Levered IRR[2]	22.6%	22.6% exceeds 20.0%

1. LTV = 75% (given), Equity = 25% of 40 million.
2. Levered IRR calculation: N = 10; PV = −10,000,000; PMT = 1,299,000; FV = 38,202,457; CPT → I/Y = 22.56%

(Study Session 13, LOS 39.m)

112. **B**

Value of land (given)		$12,500,000	
Replacement cost, including constructor's profit			
Building costs (psf)	$175		
Total area	240,000	$42,000,000	
Developer's profit	$15	$3,600,000	
		$45,600,000	
Reduction for curable deterioration		−$5,000,000	
		$40,600,000	
Reduction for incurable deterioration			
Total economic life	50		
Remaining economic life	40		
Effective age	10		
Ratio of effective to total	20.0%		
Reduction for incurable deterioration		−$8,120,000	
		$32,480,000	
Reduction for total obsolescence		−$4,000,000	
Total building value			$28,480,000
Total Cost Estimate			$40,980,000

(Study Session 13, LOS 39.i)

113. **A** The economic outlook on home prices and population trends indicate favorable conditions going forward. Shorter leases would allow rents to be adjusted upwards as demand for rentals increase, so Lundy's comment is correct. For a buyer of real estate, low interest rates along with a high loan-to-value (LTV) will maximize the potential for high levered returns. Tenants will benefit from longer leases in a high demand environment; this would not benefit the investors so Park's comment is incorrect. (Study Session 13, LOS 39.c, d)

114. **C** Appraisal lag tends to smooth the reported returns of real estate indices, resulting in an artificially low correlation with other asset classes. Appraisal lag can be mitigated by unsmoothing the index or by using a transaction-based index. Using more-recent appraisals still relies on appraisal-based data. (Study Session 13, LOS 39.k)

115. **A** Structural models require that the company's assets trade in a frictionless arbitrage free market. (Study Session 15, LOS 46.f)

116. **C** Reduced form models assume that given the macroeconomic state variables, a company's default represents idiosyncratic risk. Structural models assume a constant (non-stochastic) risk-free rate and that the time T value of the assets is characterized by a lognormal distribution. (Study Session 15, LOS 46.f)

117. **B** Ratings tend to be stable over time, which reduces their correlation to default probabilities; hence, Point 1 is incorrect. (Study Session 15, LOS 46.c)

118. **C** The maximum amount an investor would to pay to remove the credit risk is the present value of the expected loss. (Study Session 15, LOS 46.d)

119. **B** The time value of money discount will always reduce the present value of expected loss. Because the present value of expected loss in this case is higher than the expected loss, the risk premium for risk of credit loss must be larger than the time value of money discount. (Study Session 15, LOS 46.d)

120. **B** Under the option analogy of the structural model, risky debt can be viewed as a portfolio comprising a long position in risk-free debt and a short put option on the company's asset with a strike price equal to the face value of the risky debt. When the asset volatility increases, the value of the put option increases and the value of the portfolio with short exposure to the put option will decrease. Hence the computed value of risky debt will be lower. (Study Session 15, LOS 46.d)

EXAM 3
MORNING SESSION ANSWERS

To get valuable feedback on how your score compares to those of other Level II candidates, use your Username and Password to gain Online Access at schweser.com and choose the menu item "Practice Exams Vol. 1."

1. B	21. B	41. B
2. C	22. B	42. A
3. C	23. A	43. C
4. B	24. C	44. C
5. C	25. B	45. B
6. B	26. B	46. B
7. C	27. A	47. A
8. C	28. C	48. B
9. C	29. A	49. C
10. C	30. B	50. B
11. A	31. B	51. A
12. C	32. C	52. B
13. A	33. A	53. B
14. B	34. A	54. A
15. A	35. B	55. A
16. C	36. A	56. A
17. C	37. A	57. C
18. C	38. A	58. A
19. C	39. B	59. C
20. A	40. A	60. C

EXAM 3
MORNING SESSION ANSWERS

1. **B** Topel recommended the stock to his superiors, but they chose not to buy it. While Topel should not buy the stock in advance of his recommendation, he is not prohibited from purchasing it for himself should the company choose not to act. Kennedy's research may have been thorough, and there is no evidence that she violated the reasonable-basis Standard. However, the loyalty Standard requires that Kennedy put Samson Securities' interest before her own and not deprive her employer of her skills and abilities. Since Kennedy spent five days of company time researching Koral Koatings, the company has a right to benefit from her research. (Study Session 1, LOS 2.a)

2. **C** The Koons's gift does not violate Standard I(B). According to the standard, gifts from clients are different from gifts from other parties because the potential for obtaining influence to the detriment of other clients is not as great. Therefore, according to the standard, Garvey may accept the Koons's gift as long as she discloses it to her employer, which she did.

    The Jones's gift is a bonus from a job that does not compete with Garvey's work for Samson, and as such, does not violate the Standard. The fact that Jones is a Samson client is irrelevant in terms of this gift, as there is no information in the vignette about Garvey providing investment-related services for Jones. (Study Session 1, LOS 2.a)

3. **C** Topel's purchases of Vallo do not violate Standard II(A) because it was not based on material nonpublic information, and he has no duty to keep the information to himself. Therefore, Garvey's purchase of Vallo for her own account is also consistent with Standard II(A).

    The brokers discussing Metrona mentioned that their star analyst came out with a report with a "buy" recommendation that morning, which suggests that the information has already been made public. Therefore, Garvey's purchase of Metrona for her own account is consistent with Standard II(A). (Study Session 1, LOS 2.a)

4. **B** Garvey's idea for a growth estimate is interesting, but a number of factors affect the growth rate of a beverage company, many arguably more so than GDP growth. In addition, it is not sufficient to use two years worth of quarterly data (eight observations) to estimate a regression model and forecast growth over the following three years. The research was not thorough enough to satisfy Standard V(A).

    Standard I(C) as it deals with plagiarism was not violated because the consensus GDP estimates were derived from a recognized reporting service. (Study Session 1, LOS 2.a)

5. **C** In the first statement, Garvey accurately calls herself a Level III CFA candidate, but she is not permitted to project when she will receive the charter, as she must still meet the work and eligibility restrictions and pass the Level III exam. Therefore, the first statement violates Standard VII(B).

    In the second statement, the use of the CFA mark as a noun also violates the Standard VII(B). (Study Session 1, LOS 2.a)

6.   B   Nagoree is obligated to disclose conflicts in any matter that may potentially affect the member's ability to make an unbiased recommendation. The Research Objectivity Policy of the Research Objectivity Standards (ROS) requires that a formal written policy be established on the independence and objectivity of research, and this policy should require disclosure of any conflicts of interest. Additionally, Standard VI(A) Disclosure of Conflicts requires this disclosure to employer, clients, and prospective clients. (Study Session 1, LOS 3.b)

7.   C   Standard I(B) Professionalism: Independence and Objectivity prohibits members and candidates from accepting any gift that reasonably could be expected to compromise their independence and objectivity. The purpose of the gift appears to be to ensure that Islandwide continues to do business with Quadrangle and can be seen, therefore, as a clear attempt to influence her choice of brokers in the future. (Study Session 1, LOS 2.a)

8.   C   Standard II(A) Integrity of Capital Markets: Material Nonpublic Information prohibits members and candidates who possess material nonpublic information to act on or cause others to act on that information. Information disclosed to a select group of analysts is not made "public" by that fact. (Study Session 1, LOS 2.a)

9.   C   Standard I(B) Professionalism: Independence and Objectivity indicates that gifts from clients are seen to less likely affect a member's independence and objectivity, and only disclosure is required. The offer from Baker is based on future performance and is seen to carry greater risk of affecting objectivity because preferential treatment for one client could be detrimental to others. Thus, according to Standard IV(B) Duties to Employer: Additional Compensation Arrangements, Harris must disclose the offer to her employer (in writing) and receive the employer's permission before accepting the offer from Baker. (Study Session 1, LOS 2.a)

10. C   Michaels has not violated Standard II(B) Integrity of Capital Markets: Market Manipulation by either of these actions. In neither case is there the intent to mislead market participants. A large buy program may well increase the price of a stock. The trading desk has informed market participants that they will create additional liquidity for a period of 90 days after the offering and created no expectation that the liquidity of the stock will permanently remain at that level. (Study Session 1, LOS 2.a)

11. A   According to Standard IV Duties to Employers, Swamy must secure written permission before undertaking the investment advisory work for the symphony because this work competes with her employer and could create a conflict of interest, as she is receiving compensation in the form of season tickets. Her service on her brother-in-law's board may be subject to employer rules about outside employment but is not covered by the Standard because there is no likely competition or potential conflict with her employer. The question says *most likely*, so it is important to focus on the key difference between the two outside activities. Both are compensated; the fact that one is cash and the other tickets is irrelevant. The key difference is that for the symphony, Swamy is acting as an investment advisor for a large endowment, which clearly competes with her employer's business. (Study Session 1, LOS 2.a)

12. C   Standard III(B) Fair Dealing requires that shares of an oversubscribed IPO be prorated fairly to all subscribers. Arbitrarily increasing the allocation to the "problem client" is a violation, as is the resulting underallocation to the remainder of the firm's clients. (Study Session 1, LOS 2.a)

13. **A** We must start by calculating the JPY/EUR spot rate. This is a simple algebra problem. We know that the JPY/USD spot rate is 120 and the EUR/USD spot rate is 0.7224. Dividing JPY/USD by EUR/USD leaves us with JPY/EUR. Plugging in the numbers, we get a JPY/EUR spot rate of 166.113 (= 120 / 0.7224). Next, we estimate the JPY/EUR spot rate two years from now using the relative PPP formula (for two years):

$$E(S_1) = S_0 [(1 + i_{JPY})^2 / (1 + i_{EUR})^2] = 166.113 [(1)^2 / (1.05)^2] = 150.67$$

(Study Session 4, LOS 13.g)

14. **B** Using the international Fisher relation, we can solve for the inflation forecasts in Japan and Europe, given interest rate differentials and the U.S. inflation forecast:

$$R\ nominal_A - R\ nominal_B = E(inflation_A) - E(inflation_B)$$

For Japan: $7.00\% - 3.88\% \neq 3\% - 0\%$

For Eurozone: $9.08 - 7.00 \neq 5\% - 3\%$

Both implied inflation rates are inconsistent with the forecasts from the econometrics department. (Study Session 4, LOS 13.e)

15. **A** Uncovered interest rate parity forecast:

120(1.0388) / (1.07) = 116.50

(Study Session 4, LOS 13.g)

16. **C** Under Mundell-Fleming model, an expansionary monetary policy would lead to depreciation of the JPY. Under a fixed exchange rate regime, to counteract the depreciation of the JPY, the Japanese government has to support its currency by purchasing it in the market. This action is limited by its foreign currency reserves. (Study Session 4, LOS 13.k)

17. **C** This question requires you to look at deviations from international parity conditions and then determine whether those deviations will tend to work to the advantage of the customer. In this problem, you are given the necessary information to examine parity conditions using relative purchasing power parity (RPPP). For the JPY, RPPP tells us that, since the spot rate one year ago was 116, the spot rate today should be (JPY is considered the foreign currency):

$$s_{today(assuming\ RPPP\ held)} = s_{last\ year} \left[\frac{1 + i_{JPY}}{1 + i_{USD}} \right] = 116 \left[\frac{1.00}{1.03} \right] = 112.62$$

Since the expected spot rate today, based on RPPP (i.e., 112.62), is not equal to the actual spot rate today (i.e., 120), RPPP did not hold over the past year. Since the actual rate is higher than the rate forecast by RPPP, the long-term trend based on deviations from international parity conditions will be for the rate to fall and the JPY to appreciate. Hence, using deviations from parity conditions as indicators of future currency movements, the bank should recommend that the JPY exposure be left unhedged.

Using the same RPPP process for the EUR exposure, we can calculate an RPPP spot rate today of 0.7340 (given that the rate was 0.72 one year ago).

$$s_{today(assuming\ RPPP\ held)} = s_{last\ year} \left[\frac{1 + i_{EUR}}{1 + i_{USD}} \right] = 0.72 \left[\frac{1.05}{1.03} \right] = 0.7340$$

Again, RPPP did not hold (i.e., the actual rate today, 0.7224, is not equal to the RPPP rate that should exist today given the inflation rates). However, for the EUR case, the RPPP expected spot is higher than the actual spot, indicating that the EUR may be currently overvalued and, thus, more likely to depreciate in the future. EUR exposure should be hedged. (Study Session 4, LOS 13.g)

18. **C**   Bank should advise their clients to close out their FX carry trades when the volatility implied by market prices of options on equities or currency is high. Since option prices are positively related to volatility, higher option prices are correct signals for closing out FX carry trades. Trend following trading rules can also be used for risk management in FX carry trades. We are given that the bank's clients are long BU and hence would be concerned when the BU was trading above its value implied by the trend following trading rule. If USD is trading above its trend following trading rule, the BU would be trading below and therefore it is not a correct indicator for closing out FX carry trades. (Study Session 4, LOS 13.i, p)

19. **C**   Subsidiaries whose operations are well integrated with the parent will use the parent's currency as the functional currency. When the functional currency is the same as the parent's presentation currency (reporting currency), as it is in this case, the temporal method is used. Therefore, Statement 1 is incorrect.

Self-contained, independent subsidiaries whose operating, investing, and financing activities are primarily located in the local market will use the local currency as the functional currency. When the functional currency is not the same as the parent's presentation currency (reporting currency), as in this case, the current rate method is used. Therefore, Statement 2 is incorrect. (Study Session 6, LOS 20.d)

20. **A**   Sales will be lower after translation because of the depreciating U.S. dollar. (Study Session 6, LOS 20.e)

21. **B**   Depreciation expense and COGS are remeasured at the historical rate under the temporal method. Under the current rate method, depreciation and COGS are translated at the average rate. Because the U.S. dollar is depreciating, depreciation expense and COGS are lower under the current rate method. (Study Session 6, LOS 20.e)

22. **B**   Since the subsidiary's operations are highly integrated with the parent, the temporal method is used. Accordingly, a loss of CAD 31,200 is recognized in the parent's income statement (see balance sheet and income statement worksheet below). However, no calculations are actually necessary to answer this question. The parent has a net monetary asset position in the subsidiary (monetary assets > monetary liabilities). Holding net monetary assets when the foreign currency is depreciating will result in a loss. Under the temporal method, the loss is reported in the income statement. Only choice B satisfies this logic. (Study Session 6, LOS 20.e)

The Canadian dollar is the functional currency because the subsidiary is highly integrated with the parent. Therefore, the temporal method applies.

Step 1: Remeasure the balance sheet using the temporal method.

	2008 (USD)	Rate	2008 (CAD)
Cash and account receivables	775,000	1.32	1,023,000
Inventory (given in Item 9)	600,000	Given	810,000
PP&E (net)	730,000	1.50	1,095,000
Total assets	2,105,000		2,928,000
Accounts payable	125,000	1.32	165,000
Long-term debt	400,000	1.32	528,000
Common stock	535,000	1.50	802,500
Retained earnings	1,045,000	(a)	1,432,500
Total liabilities and shareholders' equity	2,105,000		2,928,000

(a) Retained earnings is a plug figure that makes the accounting equation balance CAD 2,928,000 assets – CAD 165,000 accounts payable – CAD 528,000 long-term debt – CAD 802,500 common stock = CAD 1,432,500.

Step 2: Derive net income from the beginning and ending balances of retained earnings and dividends paid as follows:

	CAD	
Beginning retained earnings	1,550,000	Given Item 6
Net income	(83,250)	Calculate
Dividends paid in the year	(34,250)	(25,000 × 1.37 historical rate)
Ending retained earnings	1,432,500	From Step 1

Step 3: Remeasure the income statement using the temporal method.

	2008 (USD)	Rate	2008 (CAD)
Sales	1,352,000	1.35	1,825,200
Cost of goods sold (given Item 11)	(1,205,000)	Given	(1,667,250)
Depreciation expense	(140,000)	1.50	(210,000)
Remeasurement loss		(b)	(31,200)
Net income	7,000	From Step 2	(83,250)

(b) The remeasurement loss is a plug that is equal to the difference in net income of – CAD 83,250 and income before remeasurement of –CAD 52,050 (CAD 1,825,200 sales – CAD 1,667,250 COGS – CAD 210,000 depreciation).

23. **A** The local currency (the USD) is depreciating, so the historical rate will be higher than the current rate. Fixed asset turnover (sales divided by net PP&E) will be higher under the current rate method. Net PP&E will be translated at the lower current rate, and because sales are the same under both methods, the ratio will be higher.

    If you want to do the calculations, net PP&E under the current rate method is USD730,000 × 1.32CAD/USD = CAD 963,600, and fixed asset turnover is CAD 1,825,200/CAD 963,600 = 1.9 times. Fixed asset turnover under the temporal method is CAD 1,825,200/CAD 1,095,000 = 1.7 times. (Study Session 6, LOS 20.e)

24. **C** Return on assets prior to translation will be different than the ratio after translation because the numerator (net income) is translated at the average rate, and the denominator (assets) is translated at the current rate using the current rate method.

    Net profit margin will be the same because both the numerator (net income) and the denominator (sales) are translated at the average rate using the current rate method. (Study Session 6, LOS 20.f)

25. **B** The excess of purchase price over the pro-rata share of the book value of Optimax is allocated to PP&E. The remainder is goodwill.

Purchase price (in thousands)	$300
Less: Pro-rata share of Optimax	210 [$600 Optimax book value × 35%]
Excess of purchase price	90
Less: Excess allocated to PPE	70 [($1,200 fair value − $1,000 book value) × 35%]
Acquisition goodwill	$20

    (Study Session 6, LOS 18.c)

26. **B** Under the equity method, Wayland recognizes its pro-rata share of Optimax's net income less the additional depreciation that resulted from the increase in fair value of Optimax's PP&E.

Pro-rata share of Optimax's net income	$87,500 [$250,000 × 35%]
Less: Additional depreciation from PPE	7,000 [($200,000 / 10 years) × 35%]
Equity income	$80,500

    Wayland's investment account on the balance sheet increased by its equity income and decreased by the dividends received from the investment.

Beginning investment account	$300,000
Equity income from Optimax	80,500
Less: Dividends received	35,000 [$100,000 dividends × 35%]
Ending investment account	$345,500

    (Study Session 6, LOS 18.b)

27. **A** Since all of the profit from the intercompany transaction is included in Optimax's net income, Wayland must reduce its equity income of Optimax by the pro-rata share of the unconfirmed profit. Since half of the goods remain, half of the profit is unconfirmed. Thus, Wayland must reduce its equity income $2,625 [($15,000 total profit × 50% unconfirmed) × 35% ownership interest]. (Study Session 6, LOS 18.b)

28. **C** Under IFRS 9 (new standards), equity investments that are held for trading must be measured at fair value through profit or loss. Other equity investments can be measured at fair value through profit or loss or fair value through OCI and the choice is irrevocable. Debt securities that meet the business model and cash flow characteristic test must be measured at amortized cost *except when such measurement results in accounting mismatch in which case the debt securities can be classified as fair value through profit or loss.* (Study Session 6, LOS 18.a)

29. **A** Under the current standards, IFRS typically does not allow reclassification of investments into and out of fair value through profit or loss category and reclassification of investments out of held-for-trading category. U.S. GAAP does permit securities to be reclassified into or out of held-for-trading or designated at fair value. (Study Session 6, LOS 18.a, b)

30. **B** The change in market value for the period and dividends received from the investment are recognized in the income statement for trading securities. In 2008, there was a $25,000 unrealized gain on the original 25,000 shares [25,000 shares × ($76 − $75)] and a $10,000 unrealized loss on the shares purchased in 2008 [5,000 shares × ($76 − $78)]. Wayland received $30,000 in dividends from Vanry (30,000 shares × $1 per share). For 2008, the income statement impact is a $45,000 profit ($25,000 unrealized gain on original shares − $10,000 unrealized loss on increase in shares + $30,000 dividends received). (Study Session 6, LOS 18.a, b)

31. **B** Residual income models are appropriate when expected free cash flows are negative for the foreseeable future.

    Residual income models are applicable even when dividends are volatile.
    (Study Session 12, LOS 37.j)

32. **C** A high persistence factor will be associated with low dividend payments, which is exactly the case with Schubert.

    A low persistence factor will be associated with significant levels of nonrecurring items. However, Schubert has very few nonrecurring items (which would suggest a high persistence factor). (Study Session 12, LOS 37.h)

33. **A**

Beginning book value (B_{t-1})	$32.16 ($4,181,000 / 130,000)

    Beginning book value = Total Equity
    = Common shares + Retained earnings
    = 2,100,000 + 2,081,000 = $4,181,000

Earnings per share forecast (E_t)	$4.50 (given)
Dividend forecast ($D_t = E_t$ × payout ratio)	$0.23 ($4.50 × 5%)
Forecast book value per share ($B_{t-1} + E_t − D_t$)	$36.43
Equity charge per share ($r \times B_{t-1}$)	$4.12 (0.128 × $32.16)
Per share RI_t [($E_t − (r \times B_{t-1})$)]	$0.38 ($4.50 − $4.12)

    (Study Session 12, LOS 37.c)

34. **A** Economic value added (EVA) is calculated as follows:

$WACC = WACC \times$ total capital (beginning of 2008)

Note that total capital = net working capital + net fixed assets OR
book value of long-term debt + book value of equity

$= 0.119 \times (\$6,200,000 + \$3,281,000) = \$1,128,239$

$$
\begin{aligned}
EVA &= NOPAT - \$WACC \\
&= EBIT(1 - t) - \$WACC \\
&= \$1,868,000(1 - 0.30) - \$1,128,239 \\
&= \$179,361
\end{aligned}
$$

market value of the company (year-end 2008) = market value of the equity + market value of the debt

$= (\$36 \times 130,000) + (0.95 \times 6,211,000)$
$= \$10,580,450$

market value added (MVA) = market value – total capital

$= \$10,580,450 - (\$6,211,000 + \$2,100,000 + \$2,081,000) = \$188,450$

(Study Session 12, LOS 37.a)

35. **B** $$g = r - \frac{\left[B_0 \times (ROE - r)\right]}{V_0 - B_0}$$

$B_0 = [(2,100,000 + 2,081,000)] / 130,000 = \$32.16$

r = cost of equity = 12.8%

$$g = 0.128 - \frac{[32.16 \times (0.14 - 0.128)]}{36 - 32.16}$$

$= 0.0275 = 2.75\%$

(Study Session 12, LOS 37.g)

36. **A** The clean surplus relationship (i.e., ending book value = beginning book value + net income – dividends) may not hold when items bypass the income statement and affect equity directly. Foreign currency gains and losses under the current rate method bypass income statement and are reported under shareholders equity as CTA. Changes in the market value of trading securities are included in net income and do not violate the clean surplus relationship. Changes in working capital do not bypass the income statement. [Usually, changes in working capital do not affect the income statement. When they do (e.g., inventory writeoffs, bad debts, etc.), the income statement will not be bypassed.] (Study Session 12, LOS 37.k)

37. **A** According to the H-model:

$$V_0 = \frac{D_0(1 + g_L)}{r - g_L} + \frac{D_0 H (g_S - g_L)}{r - g_L} = \frac{\$1 \times (1 + 0.04)}{0.12 - 0.04} + \frac{\$1 \times 3 \times (0.08 - 0.04)}{0.12 - 0.04} = \$14.50$$

(Study Session 11, LOS 34.l)

38. **A**   The key assumption underlying the H-model is that the dividend growth rate declines linearly from a high rate in the first stage to a long-term level growth rate. (Study Session 11, LOS 34.i)

39. **B**   The relationship we need to evaluate is $V_0 = \dfrac{E_1}{r} + \text{PVGO}$.

This expression can be rewritten as $\text{PVGO} = V_0 - \dfrac{E_1}{r} = \$18 - \dfrac{\$0.90}{0.12} = \$10.50$.

(Study Session 11, LOS 34.e)

40. **A**   The P/E ratio can become unreliable for ranking purposes when earnings are close to zero. When this happens, the P/E will be unrealistically large and its reciprocal, the earnings yield (E/P), will instead approach zero. Therefore, Statement 1 is correct. A high E/P suggests an underpriced security, and a low (or negative) E/P suggests an overpriced security. Therefore, Statement 2 is incorrect. (Study Session 12, LOS 36.d)

41. **B**   Earnings must be adjusted to reflect the nonrecurring extraordinary item restructuring costs and asset write downs.
Adjusted 2008 earnings before tax = \$30,400,000 + \$189,100,000 = \$219,500,000.
Adjusted 2008 after-tax earnings = \$219,500,000 × (1 − 0.34) = \$144,870,000.
2008 underlying EPS = \$144,870,000 / 106,530,610 = \$1.36

(Study Session 12, LOS 36.c)

42. **A**   FDS has a price-to-sales ratio in 2008 of: $\dfrac{\$18}{\left(\dfrac{\$6,435,900,000}{106,530,610}\right)} = \dfrac{\$18}{\$60.41} = 0.30$.

Because its price-to-sales ratio is less than the industry average of 0.50, FDS is relatively underpriced. (Study Session 12, LOS 36.h, k)

43. **C**   Notice that in this case, $g_S = g_L$ and, accordingly, the H-model simplifies to the Gordon growth model. We can then solve for the unknown rate:

$$r = \frac{D_0\left(1+g_L\right)}{V_0} + g_L = \frac{\$1.25 \times \left(1+0.06\right)}{\$25} + 0.06 = 0.113 = 11.3\%$$

(Study Session 11, LOS 34.m)

44. **C**   Among the choices given, the only drawback to the P/S ratio is that it is susceptible to manipulation if management should choose to act aggressively with respect to the recognition of revenue. (Study Session 12, LOS 36.c)

45. **B**   UHS trailing P/E = $25 / $0.82 = 30.49

         UHS trailing PEG = 30.49 / 6% = 5.08

         Trailing industry P/E = 22.50

         Trailing industry PEG = 22.50 / 10% = 2.25

         The PEG ratio for UHS exceeds that of the industry. This implies that UHS's growth rate is relatively more expensive than is the industry's growth rate. We can therefore conclude that on the basis of the PEG ratio, UHS stock is overvalued.

         UHS P/S = $25 / ($7,400,100,000 / 95,366,000) = 0.32

         Industry P/S = 0.50

         Relative to the industry, the P/S ratio for UHS stock is low, and it would therefore be considered as undervalued.

         Conflicting results between different ratios is common in practice. When this occurs, an analyst must look deeper to arrive at a reliable conclusion. An important consideration in this case is whether or not there has been any manipulation of sales and/or earnings. The estimation of the dividend growth rate is also an important factor. (Study Session 12, LOS 36.h, i)

46. **B**   Average ROE $= \dfrac{0.032 + 0.040 + 0.045 + 0.039}{4} = 0.039$

         $BVPS_{2008} = \$25.58$

         Normalized EPS $= \overline{ROE} \times BVPS_{2008} = 0.039 \times \$25.58 = \$1.00$

         (Study Session 12, LOS 36.e)

47. **A**   Beta = 0.8
         4-year average ROE = 3.9% (Question 34)
         8-year dividend growth forecast = 6%
         Predicted P/E = 5 − (10 × 0.8) + (3 × 3.9%) + (2 × 6%) = 20.7
         (Study Session 12, LOS 36.i)

48. **B**   The belief that there are patterns of persistence or reversals in returns provides the rationale for valuation using relative strength indicators. There has been a considerable amount of empirical research in this area. Research suggests that the investment horizon is also an important determining factor in the appearance of these patterns. (Study Session 12, LOS 36.p)

49. **C**   Statement 1 is correct. If the volatility of interest rates decreases, the call option is less valuable, which increases the value of the callable bond. Recall that $V_{callable} = V_{noncallable} - V_{call}$. Statement 3 is also correct. The value of the noncallable bond increases by more than the callable bond because as yield falls, the value of the call goes up. As the call value increases, the callable value (noncall value − call option value) goes up by less than the noncall value. (Study Session 14, LOS 45.d, e)

50. **B** Statement 2 is incorrect because the noncallable bond value *will be affected* by a change in the *level* of interest rates.

    Statement 4 is correct because higher interest rate volatility will increase the value of the embedded put option and increase the value of the puttable bond. (Study Session 14, LOS 45.d, e)

51. **A** The answer is 1.56 and is found by taking the difference between the value of the callable and the noncallable bonds: Call option value = 99.77 − 98.21 = 1.56. *Note: This is an example of a basic question that you should get right! Don't give up these points or lose time by starting a complicated calculation. The question might be as easy as it seems.* (Study Session 14, LOS 45.b)

52. **B** In this case, the bond is callable and putable at the same price (100). Because Walters states that the embedded options (the issuer's call option and the holder's put option) will be exercised if the option has value (i.e., is in-the-money), the value of the bond must be 100 (plus the interest) at all times. Why? If rates fall and the computed value goes above 100, the company will call the issue at 100. Conversely, if rates increase and the computed value goes below 100, the bondholder will "put" the bond back to the issuer for 100.

    The OAS is a constant spread added to every interest rate in the tree so that the model price of the bond is equal to the market price of the bond. In this case, using the interest rate lattice, the model price of the callable bond is greater than the market price. Hence, a positive spread must be added to every interest rate in the lattice. When a constant spread is added to all the rates such that the model price is equal to the market price, you have found the OAS. The OAS will be positive for the callable bond. (Study Session 14, LOS 45.f, g)

53. **B** The answer is 93.26. This value of the non-callable bond at node A is computed as follows:

$$\text{value} = \frac{\left[0.5 \times \left(V_{up} + \frac{\text{coupon}}{2}\right)\right] + \left[0.5 \times \left(V_{down} + \frac{\text{coupon}}{2}\right)\right]}{\left(1 + \frac{\text{interest rate}}{2}\right)}$$

$$= \frac{\left[0.5 \times \left(91.73 + \frac{6}{2}\right)\right] + \left[0.5 \times \left(96.17 + \frac{6}{2}\right)\right]}{\left(1 + \frac{0.0791}{2}\right)} = 93.26$$

    (Study Session 14, LOS 44.d)

54. **A** The correct value is 100.00. The computed value of the callable bond at node A is obtained as follows:

$$\text{value} = \frac{\left[0.5 \times \left(100 + \frac{6}{2}\right)\right] + \left[0.5 \times \left(100 + \frac{6}{2}\right)\right]}{\left(1 + \frac{0.0315}{2}\right)} = 101.4$$

However, when working with a callable bond, you have to remember that the value of the bond at any node is the lesser of (1) the bonds computed value or (2) the call price. So, we have:

$$\text{value} = \text{Min}\left[100, \frac{\left[0.5 \times \left(100 + \frac{6}{2}\right)\right] + \left[0.5 \times \left(100 + \frac{6}{2}\right)\right]}{\left(1 + \frac{0.0315}{2}\right)}\right] = 100$$

In this case, since the computed value (101.4) is greater than the call price (100), the nodal value is $100. (Study Session 15, LOS 45.f)

55. **A** Statement 1 is correct. Credit ratings tend to be stable over time and across business cycles, which has the effect of reducing price volatility in the debt market. (Study Session 15, LOS 46.c)

56. **A** Statement 2 is correct. (Study Session 15, LOS 46.a)

57. **C** One of the assumptions of structural models is that default risk is constant during the life of the bond and hence does not change over business cycles or in response to changing economic variables. (Study Session 15, LOS 46.f)

58. **A** Statement 4 is correct. Probability of default does not apply to asset-backed securities because ABS do not default when an underlying collateral defaults. For this reason, probability of loss is used in place of probability of default for ABS. (Study Session 15, LOS 46.i)

59. **C**

Time to Cash Flow	Cash Flow	Risk-Free Spot Rate	Credit Spread (%)	Total Yield (%)	PV (Risk-Free Rate)	PV (Total Yield)
0.5	25	0.23%	0.80%	1.03%	24.97	24.87
1	1,025	0.25%	0.85%	1.10%	1,022.44	1,013.79
				Total	$ 1,047.41	$ 1,038.66

PV(risky $1,025) = 1,025/e^{(1*0.011)} = $1,013.787
Present value of expected loss = PV(risk-free rate) − PV(total yield)
= 1,047.41 − 1,038.66 = $8.75

(Study Session 15, LOS 46.h)

60. **C** While Thompson's statement about reduced form models imposing assumptions on the output of structural models is correct, Thompson is incorrect about balance sheet composition being required; reduced form models do not require a specification of the company's balance sheet structure. (Study Session 15, LOS 46.f)

©2015 Kaplan, Inc.

Exam 3
Afternoon Session Answers

To get valuable feedback on how your score compares to those of other Level II candidates, use your Username and Password to gain Online Access at schweser.com and choose the menu item "Practice Exams Vol. 1."

61. B	81. C	101. C
62. A	82. B	102. A
63. A	83. A	103. A
64. C	84. C	104. A
65. A	85. B	105. A
66. B	86. C	106. B
67. C	87. C	107. B
68. A	88. A	108. C
69. B	89. B	109. A
70. C	90. B	110. B
71. B	91. A	111. C
72. A	92. C	112. A
73. B	93. C	113. C
74. C	94. A	114. C
75. A	95. A	115. C
76. C	96. C	116. B
77. C	97. B	117. A
78. A	98. B	118. B
79. A	99. C	119. B
80. A	100. C	120. C

Exam 3
Afternoon Session Answers

61. **B** Fisher should take the natural log of the dependent variable so that the data in Exhibit 1 are transformed and can be better modeled using a linear regression. From the plot, it appears that the data follow a log-linear trend. If the natural log is taken of the dependent variable, the data will be more linear so that it is readily modeled in a regression. The transformed data will plot as follows:

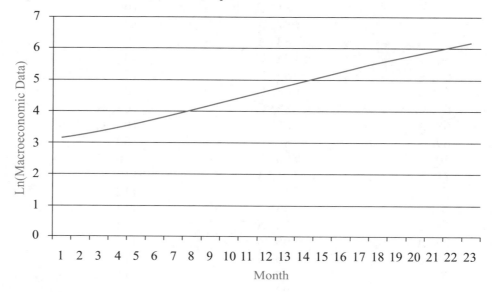

(Study Session 3, LOS 10.k, l and 11.a)

62. **A** The most likely problem in Fisher's regression of the emerging market data is that the error terms appear to be positively correlated in Exhibit 2. The first few error terms are positive, then negative, and then positive. This indicates serial correlation, which is common in trend models. As Fisher regresses the macroeconomic data against a time variable, she is using a trend model. In a trend model, the Durbin Watson statistic can be used to detect serial correlation. (Study Session 3, LOS 10.k)

63. **A** The use of the Durbin Watson statistic is inappropriate in an autoregressive regression, which is what Weatherford is using. The Durbin Watson statistic is appropriate for trend models but not autoregressive models. To determine whether the errors terms are serially correlated in an autoregressive model, the significance of the autocorrelations should be tested using the t-statistic. (Study Session 3, LOS 11.d)

64. **C** Weatherford is using an autoregressive first-order regression model in which this period's silver price is regressed on the previous period's price. The regression is of the form:

$$X_t = b_0 + b_1 X_{t-1}$$

The most likely problem in this regression is that the data is not covariance stationary. In the plot of the data, the mean of the data does not appear to be constant (it is much higher in the middle period.) The estimate of the lag one slope coefficient is close to 1.0, which also suggests that the data is nonstationary.

To definitively test this, the Dickey Fuller test should be used, where the null hypothesis is that $b_1 - 1$ is equal to zero. If the null hypothesis is not rejected, we say that the data has a unit root and is nonstationary. (Study Session 3, LOS 10.l and 11.f, k, n)

65. **A** Weatherford should use the first differences of the data in the regression. That is, instead of using the actual price levels, she should use the change in the data rather than levels:

$$Y_t = X_t - X_{t-1}$$

Then the appropriate regression will be:

$$Y_t = b_0 + b_1 Y_{t-1}$$

The transformed time series data will have a mean reverting level and be covariance stationary. (Study Session 3, LOS 11.j)

66. **B** To determine the mean reverting level, we divide the intercept by one minus the slope coefficient:

$$\text{mean-reverting level} = \frac{b_0}{1 - b_1} = \frac{2.00}{1 - (-0.09)} = 1.83$$

The one-step-ahead predicted value is calculated by substituting the current value into the regression equation:

$$\hat{y}_{t+1} = b_0 + b_1 (y_t) = 2.00 + (-0.09)(-0.80) = 2.072$$

The two-step-ahead predicted value is then calculated by substituting the one-step-ahead predicted value into the regression equation:

$$\hat{y}_{t+2} = b_0 + b_1 (\hat{y}_{t+1}) = 2.00 + (-0.09)(2.072) = 1.81$$

(Study Session 3, LOS 11.d, e)

67. **C** Investments in financial assets are classified as held-to-maturity, held-for-trading, designated at fair value, and available-for-sale. Held-to-maturity applies to debt securities only. Held-for-trading securities are debt or equity securities that are expected to be sold in the near term. Since the investment in Odessa is long-term, the securities are classified as available-for-sale. (Study Session 6, LOS 18.a)

68. **A**   Since Iberia owns 40% of Midland (5 million shares owned / 12.5 million total shares outstanding), the equity method is used. Under the equity method, Iberia reports its pro-rata share of Midland's net income (€5 million loss × 40% = €2 million loss). Changes in market value are ignored under the equity method.

   Iberia's investment in Odessa is classified as available-for-sale since the investment is considered long-term. Dividend income from available-for-sale securities is recognized in the income statement (€3 dividend × 1 million shares = €3 million). The changes in market value are reported in shareholders' equity.

   Investment income from Midland and Odessa is €1 million (€3 million dividend income from Odessa – €2 million pro-rata loss from Midland). (Study Session 6, LOS 18.a)

69. **B**   Under the equity method, the balance sheet carrying value is increased by the pro-rata earnings of the investee and decreased by the dividends received from the investee. The balance sheet value at the end of 2008 is €88 million [€80 million + (€30 million Midland 2008 net income × 40%) – (€10 million dividend × 40%)]. The balance sheet value at the end of 2009 is €84.4 million [€88 million – (€5 million loss × 40%) – (€4 million dividend × 40%)].

   Available-for-sale securities are reported on the balance sheet at fair value. Thus, the fair value of Odessa is €17 million (€17 × 1 million shares).

   As a result of its investment in Midland and Odessa, Iberia will report investment assets of €101.4 million (€84.4 million book value of Midland + €17 million fair value Odessa). (Study Session 6, LOS 18.a)

70. **C**   Profit from intercompany transactions must be deferred until the profit is confirmed through use or sale to a third party. Since all of the goods purchased from Midland have been sold to third parties, all of the profit from the intercompany sale has been confirmed. Thus, no adjustment is needed. (Study Session 6, LOS 18.a)

71. **B**   Under U.S. GAAP, all entities can account for their equity method investments at fair value. Under IFRS, the fair value option is only available for venture capital firms/mutual funds and similar entities. (Study Session 6, LOS 18.b)

72. **A**   In a profitable year, net profit margin (net income/sales) will be higher under the equity method because sales are lower under the equity method. Acquisition includes the sales figures for both the parent and subsidiary, while the equity method only includes the sales figure for the parent company. Net income is the same under both methods. Therefore, the statement is correct. (Study Session 6, LOS 18.c)

73. **B**   Lower expected rate of return on plan assets (i.e., 8% instead of 10%) would not affect the PBO or the total periodic pension cost. PBO is the present value of benefits earned to date and is unaffected by changes in expected return on plan assets (but is sensitive to changes in discount rate). Total periodic pension cost is affected by *actual* return on plan assets and not the *expected* return on plan assets. (Study Session 6, LOS 19.d)

74. **C** Benefits paid can be determined by reconciling ending PBO to beginning PBO:

Beginning PBO	1,022
+ Current service cost	118
+ Past service cost	36
+ Interest cost	82
+ Acturial Loss	128
(–) benefit paid	188
(=) Ending PBO	1,198

(Study Session 6, LOS 19.b)

75. **A** ending fair value of plan assets

= beginning fair value + contributions + actual return – benefits paid

= 896 + 102 + 214 – 188 = 1,024 million

(Study Session 6, LOS 19.b)

76. **C** Total periodic pension cost = employer contributions – change in funded status

= 102 – [ending funded status – beginning funded status]

= 102 – [(1,024 – 1,198) – (896-1,022)] = $150 million

or

total periodic pension cost = current service cost + past service cost + interest cost + actuarial loss – actual return on plan assets = 118 + 36 + 82 + 128 – 214 = $150 million.

(Study Session 6, LOS 19.c)

77. **C** Under IFRS, periodic pension cost reported in P&L would consist of current and past service cost plus/minus net interest expense/income. Net interest income is computed as the discount rate multiplied by beginning funded status.

periodic pension cost in P&L = 118 + 36 – 0.08[896 – 1,022] = 164.08

Note that since the beginning funded status is negative, there is a net interest cost.

(Study Session 6, LOS 19.c)

78. **A** PBO will increase with a higher rate of compensation growth. A higher rate of compensation growth will also increase the total periodic pension cost as well as the periodic pension cost in P&L by increasing both the service and interest costs. Under IFRS, the net interest cost is computed as the discount rate multiplied by beginning funded status. The beginning PBO for the next period would be higher due to the higher compensation growth assumption and hence the net interest cost will be higher. (Study Session 6, LOS 19.d)

79. **A**   Hinesman's comment is correct. Studies have shown, that on average, companies with strong corporate governance systems have higher measures of profitability and generate higher returns for shareholders.

Randall's comment is also correct. The lack of an effective corporate governance system increases risk to an investor. Four main risks of not having an effective corporate governance system include asset risk and liability risk, as well as the two risks described by Randall: financial disclosure risk and strategic policy risk. (Study Session 9, LOS 27.a, h)

80. **A**   According to corporate governance best practice, the audit committee should consist only of independent directors; it should have expertise in financial and accounting matters (for purposes of the exam, at least two members of the committee should have relevant accounting and auditing experience); the internal audit staff for the firm should report directly to the audit committee; and the committee should meet with external auditors at least once annually without management present. (Study Session 9, LOS 27.e)

81. **C**   Using a target debt-to-equity ratio of 1:1, the $150 million in capital spending for 20X1 will be financed with $75 million in internal equity and $75 million in debt. The total dividend is the remaining internal equity of $112.5 − $75 = $37.5 million, or $37.5 / 56.25 = $0.67 per share. (Study Session 8, LOS 25.j)

82. **B**   FCFE = cash flow from operations − FcInv + net borrowings

20X0: FCFE = 115 − 43 + 22 = 94

20X1: FCFE = 132 − 150 + 75 = 57

FCFE coverage ratio = FCFE / (dividends + share repurchases)

20X0: 94 / (42.88 + 42) = 1.11

20X1: 57 / (45 + 3) = 1.19

(Study Session 8, LOS 25.i)

83. **A**   Kazmaier received a score of 25% because it was in compliance with global best practice with respect to only one of the four criteria.

Criterion 1:   Global best practice recommends that three-quarters (75%) of the board members be independent. Of the nine total board members, only five are independent. Kazmaier fails this criterion.

Criterion 2:   Global best practice recommends that the Chairman of the Board be independent. Since Kazmaier's Chairman is also the CEO, Kazmaier fails this criterion.

Criterion 3:   Global best practice recommends that the entire board of directors stand for reelection annually. Since it appears that Kazmaier has staggered board elections, Kazmaier fails this criterion.

Criterion 4:   Global best practice requires independent board members to meet in separate sessions at least annually. Although quarterly meetings between independent directors are preferable, the fact that they happen annually means Kazmaier passes this criterion.

(Study Session 9, LOS 27.e)

84. **C**   Nagy's three rationales all correctly describe common advantages of share repurchases. (Study Session 8, LOS 25.g)

The complete solution to Questions 85 to 90 is as follows (in thousands):

		Years		
Cost Item	0	1	2	3
Cost	(400)			
Sale of old*	30			
Revenue		175.0	175.0	175.0
Less: operating cost		25.0	25.0	25.0
Less: depreciation (400,000 × MACRS%)		132.0	180.0	60.0
EBT		18.0	(30.0)	90.0
− Tax (40%)		7.2	(12.0)	36.0
NI		10.8	(18.0)	54.0
+ Depreciation		132.0	180.0	60.0
+ Sale				10.0
+ Sale tax shield**				7.2
= CF		142.8	162.0	131.2

NPV (@ 20%) = −62,574

IRR = 8.796%

Therefore, REJECT, because the NPV < 0, IRR < 20%.

Using the calculator: CF0 = −370, C01 = 142.8, C02 = 162, C03 = 131.2, I = 20, CPT → NPV = −62,574, CPT → IRR = 8.796.

** Sale tax shield		*Sale of old
BV =	28 (= 400 × 0.07)	BV = 0
−sale	−10	Sale = 50
Loss	18	Gain = 50
Tax shield = loss × tax rate = 18 × 0.4 = 7.2		Tax (40%) = 20
Net impact of sale = $10 sale proceeds + $7.2 tax shield = 17.2		Net proceeds = 30

85. **B**   See solution above. Alternatively, initial outlay = $FCInv + WCInv - Sal_0 + T(Sal_T - B_0)$ = $400 + 0 - 50 + 0.4(50 - 0) = 400 - 50 + 20 = \$370$. (Study Session 8, LOS 23.a)

86. **C**   See solution above. Alternatively, $CF_1 = (S - C)(1 - T) + DT = (175 - 25)(0.6) + (0.4)(0.33)(400) = 90 + 52.8 = \$142.8$. (Study Session 8, LOS 23.a)

87. **C**   See solution above. Alternatively, CF = $-(175 - 25)(0.4) + 400(0.45)(0.4) = -60 + 72 = +\$12$. (Study Session 8, LOS 23.a)

88. **A**   See solution above. Alternatively, $CF_3 = (175 - 25)(0.6) + (400)(0.15)(0.4) = 90 + 24 = \$114$. TNOCF = $Sal_T + WCInv - T(Sal_T - B_T) = 10 + 0 - 0.4(10 - 28) = 10 + 7.2 = \$17.2$. CF_3 + TNOCF = $\$114 + \$17.2 = \$131.2$ (Study Session 8, LOS 23.a)

89. **B**   NPV will be underestimated because the reduction in inventory should reflect a cash inflow at the beginning of the project. Even if the inventory builds back up to its previous level at the end of the project (resulting in a cash outflow), the cash inflow will be larger than the present value of the cash outflow. (Study Session 8, LOS 23.a)

90. **B**   If the NPV is less than zero, the IRR must be less than the discount rate of 20% (so 8.8% is the only possible answer), and the project should be rejected. The actual calculations of NPV and IRR are shown in the solution, but these calculations are not necessary to answer the question. (Study Session 8, LOS 23.a)

91. **A**   The equity risk premium is estimated as:

$$ERP = [1 + i] \times [1 + REg] \times [1 + PEg] - 1 + Y - RF$$

where:
i	= the expected inflation rate = 2.6%
REg	= expected real growth in GDP = 3.0%
PEg	= relative value changed due to changes in P/E ratio = −0.03
Y	= yield on the market index = 1.7%
RF	= risk-free rate of return = 2.7%
ERP	= (1.026) × (1.030) × (0.97) − 1 + 0.017 − 0.027 = 0.015 = 1.50%

Note: We do not add the risk-free rate because we are computing the equity risk premium and not the required rate of return. Conversely, we can compute the required rate of return and then subtract the risk-free rate to obtain the equity risk premium.

(Study Session 10, LOS 30.b)

92. **C**   Historical estimates are subject to survivorship bias. If the data are not adjusted for the effects of non-survivors, returns (based only on survivors) will be biased upwards. (Study Session 10, LOS 30.b)

93. **C**   Using CAPM, the required return is:

required rate of return = risk-free rate + (beta × equity risk premium)

required return for NE = 2.7% + (0.83 × 5.2%) = 7.02%

(Study Session 10, LOS 30.c)

94. **A**   With the Fama-French model, the required return is:

required rate of return = risk-free rate + β_{MKT} (market risk premium) + β_{size} (size risk premium) + β_{value} (value premium)

required rate of return for NE = 2.7% + 0.83(5.2%) + (−0.76)(3.2%) + (−0.04)(5.4%) = 4.37%

(Study Session 10, LOS 30.c)

95. **A**   adjusted beta = (2/3)(0.83) + (1/3)(1.0) = 0.89. (Study Session 10, LOS 30.c)

96. **C**   The recommended method for estimating the beta of a nonpublic company from the beta of a public company is as follows: (1) Unlever the beta for the public company, using the public company's debt/equity ratio. (2) Relever (adjust upward) this beta using VixPRO's debt/equity ratio to get the estimated equity beta for VixPRO. (Study Session 10, LOS 30.d)

97. **B** Invested capital in the fund was $20 million + $100 million = $120 million. Committed capital was $120 million + $100 million = $220 million. Since the fund was sold for $180 million, the fund earned a profit of $180 million − $120 million = $60 million.

Under the total return using invested capital method, carried interest is paid to the GP only after the portfolio value exceeds invested capital (by 30% as specified by IGS). Since the $180 million exceeds ($120 million)(1.3) = $156 million, the GP is entitled to carried interest. Carried interest is calculated as:

$180 million − $120 million = $60 million. 20% of $60 million is $12 million.

(Study Session 13, LOS 39.h, i)

98. **B** The DCF method and relative value approach would be less appropriate for Sverig. Given that Sverig is a startup venture capital firm, it would be difficult to assess its future cash flows and there are likely few comparables to benchmark against. Given that L'Offre has been in existence for over a century, it likely has relatively stable and predictable cash flows. Several comparables would also likely exist in the same industry. This would make either the DCF method or relative value approach an appropriate valuation technique. (Study Session 13, LOS 41.i)

99. **C** Market risk is the uncertainty in long-term macroeconomic factors, such as changes in interest rates and foreign exchange rates. If these changes adversely affect the private equity fund firms, both the fund's investors (limited partners) and the firms' managers could see their equity stake and investment declining. Agency risk refers to the possibility that the managers of the portfolio (investee) companies may place their personal interests ahead of the interests of the firm and of private equity investors. (Study Session 13, LOS 41.g)

100. **C** The GP's share in profits is referred to as carried interest and is generally set at 20% of net profits after fees. A tag-along, drag-along clause would give management the right to buy an equity stake upon sale by the private equity owners.

Ratchet specifies the equity allocation between the limited partners (LPs) and management. Distribution waterfall specifies how profits will flow to the LPs and also the conditions under which the GP may receive carried interest. (Study Session 13, LOS 41.b)

101. **C** First, the $400 million terminal value must be discounted two years at 30% to the second round of financing:

$$POST_2 = \frac{\$400 \text{ million}}{(1.3)^2} = \$236.686 \text{ million}$$

The second-round pre-money valuation (PRE_2) is calculated by netting the $40 million second-round investment from the $POST_2$ calculation:

$$PRE_2 = POST_2 - INV_2 = \$236.686 \text{ million} - \$40 \text{ million} = \$196.686 \text{ million}.$$

Finally, the PRE_2 valuation must be discounted back 4 years at 40% to arrive at the $POST_1$ valuation:

$$POST_1 = \frac{\$196.686 \text{ million}}{(1.4)^4} = \$51.199 \text{ million}$$

(Study Session 13, LOS 41.j)

102. **A** Calculating the number shares for Sverig's first-round investors requires a three-step approach where:

- f_1 is the fractional ownership for first-round investors.
- INV_1 is the initial investment in Sverig by the private equity partners.
- S_e is the number of shares owned by Sverig's founders.
- S_{pe} is the number of shares owned by the private equity LPs.

Step 1: Determine the fractional ownership for first-round investors (f_1):

$$f_1 = \frac{INV}{POST_1} = \frac{\$20 \text{ million}}{\$51.199 \text{ million}} = 39.06\%$$

First-round investors thus own approximately 39.06% of the firm.

Step 2: Determine the number of shares first-round investors need to receive their fractional ownership:

$$S_{pe1} = S_e\left(\frac{f_1}{1-f_1}\right) = 5,000,000\left(\frac{0.3906}{1-0.3906}\right) = 3,204,792$$

To obtain a 39.06% stake in Sverig, first-round investors would have to receive 3,204,792 shares.

Step 3: Determine the stock price after the first round of financing (P_1):

$$P_1 = \frac{INV_1}{S_{pe1}} = \frac{\$20 \text{ million}}{3,204,792} = \$6.24$$

(Study Session 13, LOS 41.j)

103. **A** Nolte is long in the underlying stock, so she should short call options, and she can use any of the options to delta hedge. The hedge ratio (the number of calls per share) is (1 / delta), so any of these four short call positions will hedge her long position in the stock:

$$\frac{1}{0.54} \times 5,000 = 9,259 \text{ 1-month call options}$$

$$\frac{1}{0.58} \times 5,000 = 8,621 \text{ 3-month call options}$$

$$\frac{1}{0.61} \times 5,000 = 8,197 \text{ 6-month call options}$$

$$\frac{1}{0.63} \times 5,000 = 7,937 \text{ 9-month call options}$$

(Study Session 17, LOS 49.e)

104. **A** The hedge must be continually rebalanced, even in the un' price doesn't change, because the option's delta changes ' approaches maturity. If she simultaneously buys an eq' the overall position (including the calls, the puts, an. longer be delta hedged. (Study Session 17, LOS 49.e)

105. **A**   The $40 call option is at-the-money, and gamma is largest for at-the-money options. Therefore, the gamma on the $40 call is greater than a $20 call, a $30 call, and a $50 call. (Study Session 17, LOS 49.f)

106. **B**   The delta of a put option is equal to the delta of the comparable call option minus one:

1-month put delta = $0.54 - 1 = -0.46$

6-month put delta = $0.61 - 1 = -0.39$

Therefore her estimate of the 1-month put delta is correct, but her estimate of the 6-month put delta is incorrect. (Study Session 17, LOS 49.e)

107. **B**   Both the 3-month and the 9-month put options are correctly priced according to put-call parity. Note that you are given the continuously compounded risk-free rate, so you have to use the continuous version of put-call parity.

$$P_0 = C_0 - S_0 + \frac{X}{e^{R_f^c \times T}}$$

$$P(3\text{-month}) = \$5 + \frac{\$40}{e^{0.05 \times 0.25}} - \$40 = \$4.50$$

$$P(9\text{-month}) = \$8.81 + \frac{\$40}{e^{0.05 \times 0.75}} - \$40 = \$7.34$$

Therefore, she's correct that the 3-month put is not mispriced, but incorrect in her conclusion that the 9-month put is mispriced. (Study Session 17, LOS 49.a)

108. **C**   Put-call parity for futures options is:

$$P_0 = C_0 + \frac{X - F_T}{e^{r \times T}} = \$1 + \frac{\$22 - \$20}{e^{0.05 \times 0.5}} = \$2.95$$

(Study Session 17, LOS 49.i)

109. **A**   The semi-annual fixed payment is calculated as

$$\frac{1 - 0.9285}{0.9840 + 0.9676 + 0.9488 + 0.9285} = 0.01867 \text{, which, when annualized, is 3.73\%.}$$

(Study Session 17, LOS 50.c)

110. **B**   The amount owed by the fixed payer of the swap would be (0.038 / 2) × $30,000,000 = $570,000. (Study Session 17, LOS 50.c)

111. **C**   The value of the fixed rate bond for $1 of notional principal is calculated as:

($0.038 / 2) × (0.9945 + 0.9760 + 0.9510 + 0.9246) + [$1 × (0.9246)] = $0.99768

The value of the floating rate note for $1 of notional principal is calculated by looking at the floating rate when the swap was created. $R_{180\text{-day}} = 3.25\%$ and the 60-day discount factor as of today is 0.9945; therefore, the calculation is:
{$1 + [$0.0325 × (180 / 360)]} × 0.9945 = $1.01066.

(Study Session 17, LOS 50.c)

112. **A**   The value of the swap to the floating rate payer would be (0.99000 − 1.01000) × $30,000,000 = −$600,000. In this case, the floating rate payer would need to pay $600,000 to terminate the swap, based on the value of the swap to the fixed rate payer. (Study Session 17, LOS 50.c)

113. **C** A long position in a payer swaption decreases in value as rates decrease, and a short position increases. A long position in a receiver swaption increases in value as rates decrease, and a short position decreases.

Therefore, to exploit the anticipated drop in rates, Black should go short in the payer swaption or long in the receiver swaption. (Study Session 17, LOS 50.f)

114. **C** Statement 1 is not correct. At the initiation of an interest rate swap, both parties are exposed to some potential credit risk, although the exposure is relatively low.

Statement 2 is correct. The long position in a payer swaption (and, indeed, in any option) is exposed to potential credit risk because of the likelihood that the counterparty will default if the swaption expires in-the-money. The short position, however, is not exposed to credit risk because they will not receive a payment at maturity no matter if the swaption expires in or out-of-the-money. (Study Session 17, LOS 50.i)

115. **C** $E(R_p) = 0.6E(R_{WMB}) + 0.4E(R_{REL}) = 0.6(9\%) + 0.4(10.8\%) = 9.72\%$

(Study Session 18, LOS 53.d)

116. **B** $\beta_{P,INF} = 0.6\beta_{WMB,INF} + 0.4\beta_{REL,INF} = 0.6(-2.2) + 0.4(-1.0) = -1.72$

(Study Session 18, LOS 53.d)

117. **A** $8 = E(R) + (-0.9 \times 0.5) + (1.2 \times 0.5) + (0.5)$

$E(R) = 7.35\%$

(Study Session 18, LOS 53.d)

118. **B** Consider portfolio A comprising 50% portfolio X and 50% portfolio Z. Portfolio A will have an expected return of 12.5% and a factor sensitivity of 1.25. A long position in portfolio A and short position in portfolio Y will have an expected return of 0.5% with zero factor sensitivity.

(Study Session 18, LOS 53.b)

119. **B** Active risk squared = active factor risk + active specific risk

(Study Session 18, LOS 53.e)

120. **C** Credit spreads tighten during times of economic expansions. During such times, lower-rated bonds outperform higher-rated bonds. (Study Session 18, LOS 55.f)

Notes

Notes

Notes

Notes

Notes